MADNESS AND THE CRIMINAL LAW

MADNESS AND

NORVAL MORRIS

THE CRIMINAL LAW

The University of Chicago Press
Chicago and London

Norval Morris is the Julius Kreeger Professor of Law and
Criminology at the University of Chicago.

The University of Chicago Press, Chicago 60637
The University of Chicago Press, Ltd., London

Chapter 1, "The Brothel Boy," appeared as number 18 of *Occasional
Papers,* published by the Law School of the University of Chicago
(1982). Chapter 3, "The Planter's Dream," appeared in the *University
of Chicago Law Review,* volume 49, number 3 (Summer, 1982). Chapters
1 and 3 © 1982 by Norval Morris.

Library of Congress Cataloging in Publication Data

Morris, Norval.
    Madness and the criminal law.

    (Studies in crime and justice)
    Includes bibliographical references and index.
    1. Insanity—Jurisprudence. 2. Criminal liability.
3. Competency to stand trial. I. Title. II. Series.
K5077.M67   1983   345'.04   82-13435
ISBN 0-226-53907-5   342.54

TO MY WIFE, ELAINE

Contents

Acknowledgments

The errors in this book are mine, any insights of value are largely plagiarized—and so they should be since that is how knowledge grows, if it grows at all. Particular burdens of responsibility are born by the Edna McConnell Clark Foundation, who gave me released time to write this book; by the University of Chicago and its Law School for the most hospitable and supportive scholarly environment the world has to offer; by Michael Tonry, Gordon Hawkins, and Franklin Zimring for struggling with my successive drafts; by Richard Friedman, Mark Jenkins, Robert Monk, and Jeffrey Peck for their ready and efficient research assistance; and by Helen Flint and Barrik Van Winkle for their generous assistance with this book as with my everyday work. And, in less committed vein, my thanks go to the National Rifle Association, without whose intervention this book would not have been written.

Introduction

Why "madness" as part of the title of this book?
Is it not peculiarly imprecise? It is, indeed, but that
very imprecision justifies its usage here. I am anxious to avoid any particular view of mental illness
as part of the argument and analytic structure of
this book. I wish to include all reasonable percep-
tions of mental illness flowing from, at one extreme,
Thomas Szasz's almost total rejection of the concept
of mental illness (unless there be organic brain dam-
age or physiological symptoms correlated to behavioral disorders), to the all-embracing views of
psychiatrists like Karl Menninger who see all of us
as more or less mentally ill at different times of our
lives. It is clear to me that there are genetic, physiological, and sometimes determining sociological
influences on the normal patterns of cognitive processes and volitional controls of the human animal;
that there are endogenous aberrations within the
cranium influencing behavior. Nobody can go to an
institution for the retarded without recognizing
pathology and sometimes pain; no one of any sensitivity can go to a state mental hospital without
recognizing the existence of mental illness and its
concomitant, deep suffering.

1

I am not in this book pretending to any expert knowledge of mental illness, however it be defined; I am considering something quite different, namely, the ways in which mental illness and retardation, no matter how defined, relate to the criminal-law power of the state. It is thus a deliberate choice to select the word "madness" and put aside any pretense to the precision claimed, for example, by the *Diagnostic Statistical Manual III* or any other nosology of mental illness and retardation.

This book is a jurisprudential study in this sense: it deals with the relationship between individual autonomy and the power of the state as exercised under both the mental health power and the criminal-law power. In particular, my concern is with situations where these two powers overlap. And in even closer concentration, the book deals largely with the overlapping of the two powers in situations where the citizen is incarcerated, it being alleged that he is both a criminal and mentally ill.

Here is the structure of the book:

Chapter 1, "The Brothel Boy," deals with the relationship between moral guilt and criminal guilt. Its underlying theme is that there is a cleavage between the two and that governmental capacities to fashion structures of punishment must recognize their relative incompetence in the assessment of moral worth. This is an impressionistic argument, presented in fictional form.

Chapter 2, "The Criminal Responsibility of the Mentally Ill," deals with the proper limits of trying and convicting the mentally ill for criminal conduct. It presents the central thesis that there is an advantage in pursuing questions of criminal guilt of the mentally ill and in not finessing those issues by mechanisms which confuse the mental health power with the criminal-law power of the state. A lengthy chapter, it brings together two considerably canvassed areas of criminal responsibility of the mentally ill: their fitness to plead and the special defense of insanity. Underlying much of the argument in this chapter is the view that too many of the problems of overlap between these two powers have been considered as questions of fitness to stand trial or questions of the application of the defense of insanity and that too few have been handled (as they should be) as questions of sentencing. There is, however, one relationship between mental illness and criminal guilt that is not considered in this chapter or in the concluding chapters on sentencing: the situation where mental illness does indeed prevent perception of reality and thus should lead both to an acquittal under the criminal law and, in some circumstances, to the accused's not being subject to civil commitment. Chapter 3 is intended to fill this gap.

Chapter 3, "The Planter's Dream," deals with the problem of involuntary conduct—conduct in fugue states—for which it seems clear that there should be no criminal liability unless the danger that such involuntary conduct might create was known beforehand to the accused. This, like the subject of chapter 1, is an impressionistic theme, for which fiction seems the best method of presentation.

The setting of the stories in chapters 1 and 3 in Burma in the mid-1920s, and their focus on imagined events in the life of Eric Blair (later George Orwell) merits comment. Eric Blair was then in Burma as a police officer and magistrate in the Indian Imperial Police; later, of course, he became a celebrated novelist and a superb political polemicist. His life in Burma and some of his later writings combine to provide a fine frame of reference for presentation of moral problems in the criminal law related to mental illness. The form of chapters 1 and 3, discovered "lost" manuscripts, is an ancient literary device which set me free to advance ideas I would otherwise have been hesitant to offer.

Chapter 4, "Sentencing the Mentally Ill," addresses important and largely neglected themes. There is widespread agreement that mental illness is relevant to sentencing convicted criminals, but the analysis rarely proceeds far beyond that proposition. This chapter attempts to state some principles both of aggravation and of mitigation of punishment by reason of mental illness, to state the guiding principles for reconciling that apparent contradiction, and to relate the whole to emerging reforms in sentencing practice.

Chapter 5, the concluding chapter, "Anisonomy, or Treating Like Cases Unlike," deals with an important aspect omitted from the preceding chapter. A precept of justice frequently suggested, particularly in relation to sentencing convicted criminals, is that like cases should be treated alike and that unlike cases should not be treated alike. In this chapter I seek to controvert those propositions. To a degree the argument harks back to the relationship between moral guilt and criminal guilt illustrated in chapter 1, but an effort is made to develop a defensible position of limited retributivism in relation to punishment under which the clear disadvantages of a rigid adherence to equality in punishment can be avoided.

ONE

The Brothel Boy
A fragment of a manuscript

The piece is handwritten, in Eric Blair's characteristic, cramped, meticulous script. There are frequent
crossings out and emendations. There are occasional
spelling inversions, such as "gaurd" for "guard,"
which are surprising, considering the obvious overall attention the document apparently received.

As an essay it is uneven. Parts reveal Blair-
Orwell at his most masterful—phrases and sentences that he will use again in his later writings;
parts are verbose and pretentious, like the early
efforts of one ambitious to be a writer but insecure
in the craft, struggling too hard for effect.

The document also foreshadows many of the
ideas its author later developed in depth and subtlety, themes that later supported novels and essays.
That alone would assure its lasting importance. It
is a major find.

I bought it for the equivalent of $185 while
on a holiday pilgrimage retracing Blair's travels during his period in Burma. The vendor was a Parsee;
at least he was either a Parsee or a half-caste Anglo-
Indian, but I think probably a Parsee since he did
not affect an English accent. He had bought the
manuscript, he said, from some Dacoits who had

boasted to him of their courage in breaking into a government bungalow. He confessed to having purchased the few sticks of furniture and the few personal effects they had stolen, and he had quickly got rid of everything other than these papers, which he now held in a crumpled, yellow, paper bag. All this was many years ago; he had turned to legitimate business long since of course— on that I could rely. He had heard of my interest in Eric Blair and thought I might like to see these papers.

It is true that Blair once wrote to his mother about a burglary of his quarters—"who should guard this guardian if he can't guard himself"—though he had not, possibly for reasons of embarrassment, reported it to his superiors in Mandalay; but he had made no mention to either of the loss of a manuscript, which is surprising.

So much for my find. The amount I paid for it, annas to the value of $185, still puzzles me; the sum is a tribute either to the vendor's ignorance or to the purchaser's gullibility.

Here it is, gaps and all.

Moulmein
Upper Burma
1927

I wonder does any other Old Etonian roll his own cigarettes? And I'm not sure why I do. They are cheaper, of course, but the taste is not very different and bits and pieces of tobacco do drift into one's mouth and require picking off the tongue or lips, which seems to disturb some who observe it. In the Club they make no secret of their disapproval—"A frightfully low-bred habit."

"Blair, *do* take one of mine, it's so much easier."

"No thanks, I prefer these," and I watch their foreheads wrinkle in revulsion.

I had carefully rolled a cigarette and was about to moisten the paper, my tongue protruding, mouth agape, when a native boy burst into my office shouting, "Come, Come Sir. Hurry please. They are killing the brothel boy."

I knew, of course, of the local brothel, but not of any "brothel boy." A homosexual prostitute seemed most unlikely in Burma, quite out of character with local values and prevailing behaviour—but I had mistaken his role. At all events, I hurried to where I was led to find several village men standing over the unconscious youth but desisting now from further violence. They were, it seemed immediately obvious, the remainder of a mob of assailants, though how I knew remains unclear to me.

The boy was unconscious, bleeding from the head and face from wounds inflicted by repeated kicks. His shoulder was twisted, obviously broken. His clothes, when whole scarcely adequate, were now gaping, torn, and bloody. He lay in a foetal curve, clutching his groin. The expression on what was left of his features was of anguished surprise, the lips drawn back, mortal fear apparent. The smell of fear and violence, of sweat and vomit, was pervasive.

Resentfully they stood back to allow me to inspect him. Then, not concealing their reluctance, they helped me carry him to the police station, where I telephoned Dr. Veraswami at the nearby hospital. By the time Dr. Veraswami had arrived I knew the outline of the events that led to the brothel boy's beating. Some villagers returning to the fields in the afternoon had heard a girl's screams from a heavily overgrown area near the river customarily used for washing, but not at this time of day. When they reached her the screaming had ceased; she lay, a young girl, naked in the brothel boy's arms. She had been raped. In her struggles she had apparently struck her head violently on a sharp rock. The boy had made no effort to flee.

The girl was taken to her home. More villagers arrived. The boy was attacked. He might or might not have been killed—my arrival may have saved him for the hangman. Or the villagers may have overcome their dislike of the Raj's justice sufficiently to bring him to me. It was, after all, a fairly clear case—a young girl, a virgin, raped and injured by the brothel boy.

And it became an even clearer case when, a few days later, she died from the combined effects of the head wound and sep-

ticaemia. A villainous mixture of local herbs which the villagers
had applied to her head wound probably hastened her death.
Dr. Veraswami had not been called.

The law began its processes. By this time I had been long
enough in the service of the magistracy to know what must be
done to prepare for and carry out a trial in a capital case. In
such cases I usually acted only as judge and prosecutor, avoiding
the further incongruous role of defense counsel I also assumed
in less serious crimes. It was not required, but I had fallen into
the practice of asking one or other of the three Burmese claiming some forensic skill to represent indigent natives accused in
serious cases. But this time my requests were firmly rejected.
There was nothing to be said. He had raped her and she had
died. He had been caught immediately. He did not deny what
he had done. The only question was whether the villagers
would kill him or whether the Raj, with its quaint, imported
formality and pretense of independence, would do so. They
could see no reason in impeding the Raj. So I was judge, prosecutor, and defense counsel, equally untrained in all three roles,
though with developing experience in minor disputes and lesser
criminal matters. Certainly the boy could not do much for himself.

I interviewed him under close gaurd in the hospital. I tried
to talk quietly to him; I didn't hurry, sitting silent for long periods. He would look down and away, immobile, never volun-
teering a word or a gesture. The emanation was of one
cloyingly anxious to please, but not knowing how to. Whenever
I asked him what happened by the river, he would rush to
sweaty verbosity, his head and shoulders bobbing forward with
exaggerated sincerity, "Please Sir, I paid, I'm sorry Sir. . . . Please
Sir, I paid, I'm sorry Sir," the words running on with rising in-
flexion, flooding incoherently into one another, until he would
begin to sob. When the crying stopped he would return to his
motionless silence. And if I again even remotely probed the
events by the riverside, the same miserable routine would be
followed.

If I asked him to do something, to stand up or sit down, to open a window or a door, to bring me that chair, he would leap to obey, diligence gleaming in his eyes, ingratiatingly obedient, like a well-trained dog. But I could achieve no communication with him beyond his prompt obedience to simple order. I tried different tacks to relate to him, asking him about many things, always speaking clearly and slowly, but to little effect. Sometimes he would seem to understand and give a monosyllabic reply, accompanied always by a clipped "Sir," and sometimes would offer a shy and innocent smile, but words and smiles seemed quite random, having little to do with my question. And as soon as I approached the matter of the girl, or washing by the river, or even money, out would spill the "Please Sir, I paid, I'm sorry Sir" flowing to tears, sometimes preceded by the incongruous smile.

"A 'perseveration,' I believe it iss called," Dr. Veraswami told me. "Over and over and over he says the same things in the same words in hiss mind, believing them completely I think, but not an idea what they mean. Sometimes he will say it all, sometimes bits and pieces, you will find, but always in the same sequence, going round and round, exactly the same. You will get very little more from him. It iss all hiss silly mind will let him think about. Perhaps not silly, issn't it. Safer so. But I doubt he pretends; he does not malinger, I think. He tells you all he can tell himself."

So it proved. The boy was obviously stupid. And the meaningless repetition and cringing self-pity became increasingly distasteful.

I went to the brothel to try to learn more of the boy. He had, it seemed, been born there some twenty or so years ago. Who his mother had been was remembered—she had worked for the previous owners of the brothel but had died a few years after the boy's birth. His father was, of course, undiscoverable; any one of the older male population of this or neighbouring villages could be a candidate for that unsought honour. The present brothel keeper, a smarmy lady of large physique, expressed unqualified praise of her own virtue in having let the boy stay when she bought the brothel some years ago. He was, she said, until now an entirely reliable punkah puller, willing to keep the fans moving for the more prosperous clients who wanted them and would pay for them, while he faded into the background.

I could understand how unobtrusive he would have been. As interested in him as I was, I found it hard to see him as a person at all. On any subject apart from the crime, he said only what he thought he ought to say. Otherwise, immobile, slight, turned away, he seemed as present as the furniture.

"How did he keep himself?" I asked the proprietress of the brothel. She was lyrical in her praise of her generosity. She kept him without charge. Actually let him sleep inside. Clothed and fed him. And sometimes, she said, customers, anxious to show off, would give him a few annas. And she would, in her bountiful kindness, let him keep them. This was, I supposed, the source of his savings, which he had tried to give to the girl he killed. "Did he help the girls if they were treated badly by a customer?" I further enquired. Indeed not; that was her job. And, archly, there were always men of the village to whom she could look for assistance if she needed it. But that was very rare. The girls knew they should expect, even encourage, vigour in some customers. They were often the best customers. And the girls knew she would care for them if they were hurt. It would be most improper for the boy to intervene. He was enough trouble to her without that.

All he was expected to do, she explained, was to keep the punkah moving gently to begin with and perhaps later slightly more swiftly so that, by different methods, he and the girl could cool the customer. She laughed with betel-gummed delight at her own wit and then explained to me that the boy's job was very easy, that often he did it on his back, his arms pillowing his head, his heel in the loop of rattan which by regular pressures waved the overhead punkah. She developed this theme of his sloth and her generosity at some length.

"What of his schooling?" I asked. And this confirmed her view of the idiocy of the white servants of the Raj. Powerful eye-rolling laughter was her response, so that I had that often recurring sense of how alien and useless I was in this Burmese setting. A brothel boy at school would be more at home than this assistant police magistrate in Upper Burma. And about as useful, I suppose, in her view.

I asked the brothel keeper if she knew how the boy had met the girl he killed. Her already ample bosom rose, swelled, and trembled with indignation. He had met the girl when he helped her with her parents' laundry. Washing was men's work, but the girl's father was often unwell and the girl did it for him. It was, of course, the brothel boy's duty, in return for the brothel keeper's munificence towards him, to do the washing for the brothel, which took him daily to the river. The boy had, she thought, on occasion assisted the girl by helping her carry some of her parents' laundry to and from the river. She had, it appeared, most unwisely chatted and played with him in a friendly way when they met. The proprietress had on one occasion made it her business, indeed gone out of her way, to warn the girl that the boy was a fool, a simpleton, not to be trusted, and that she should behave towards him like everyone else, not talk to the stupid boy except to tell him what to do or not to do or to reprimand him. But the girl would not listen. She was only a child of twelve or thirteen, but even so she should have known better, as the younger girls in the brothel all understood, certainly after the kindly but firm warnings so generously given.

I turned to Dr. Veraswami to try to understand the boy and his crime. As usual, Dr. Veraswami was pleased to talk to me about this or any other subject, it seemed. Both of us lacked friends and conversational partners in Moulmein. Dr. Veraswami's children by his first marriage were grown and departed, those by his second were old enough to love but not to talk with. And his present wife would run to hide in the kitchen when she saw me approaching their bungalow. She had, the Doctor told me with a gentle smile, "many fine qualities indeed, indeed, but the confidence in conversation of a particularly timid mouse."

Dr. Veraswami was the only person I enjoyed in Moulmein, certainly the only one I felt at all close to since, try as I would, I could never establish any reciprocal warmth of feeling with any of the natives, though I think some of them knew I respected them. My servants would not talk at all of the crime, looking anxiously resentful and falling silent if I mentioned the boy. By contrast, in the Club, it was a subject of unending, energetic, circumlocutiously salacious chatter, the details of which I spared myself by stressing that since the matter was *sub judice* I should not mention it or receive advice about it. This did no good, of course, but it did give me a further excuse to avoid the Club, and confirmed the prevalent view of me there as a posturing outsider, probably a coolie lover.

Dr. Veraswami had, after all, worked in a mental hospital, and he was closer to the Burmese, certainly in their illnesses, than anyone who was not Burmese. So I turned to him.

The evenings on the porch, the rattan armchairs, the foliage still hanging heavy from the regular late afternoon rainshower, the smells and sounds of the village and the nearby hospital and gaol, the heat abating, and the bottles of Watney's beer with their wired glass stoppers clinking among the few tired lumps of ice in the oval bucket, made an oasis of mind talking to mind profoundly different from the relentless ritual phrases of the Club. And it was good to have the chance to learn from him about matters my reading had neglected.

"The boy iss, I think, quite retarded, but to what level iss hard to tell." Dr. Veraswami seemed perplexed. "Iss not easy to be sure. After all, my friend, he iss quite illiterate. Unlike you, he and books move in different circles, always have and will. Measuring such a mind iss beyond me, and others also isn't it. But he iss certainly far backward, far backward."

The villagers had made much of the girl's virginity; I wondered about the boy's sexual experience. Dr. Veraswami was again hesitant, but did not doubt my speculation that the violence by the river might have been the boy's first experience of intercourse. He had witnessed much, of course, but the brothel girls would certainly see themselves as superior to and distant from the boy. Chastity, in the sense of absence of congress with a woman, may well have been forced on the boy.

"Is he mad? Was he mad?" I asked the doctor.

"To be sure, I don't know at all . . . He iss certainly not normal. But given hiss life, dear friend, how would you know what he thinks . . . if he does think, ass you mean it."

"Mad or not, dear doctor, is he likely to do something like this again, or has he learned his lesson?" Surely the swift and brutal punishment for his venery, then the arrest and everyone condemning him, had instructed even his dull mind.

Dr. Veraswami was not so sure. "One would think so, indeed one would. But I must tell you that there are cases like hiss where even after very severe punishment the act iss repeated. You must not, dear friend, underestimate . . ." and here he grasped wildly in the air for an unembarrassing euphemism, and with triumph found it ". . . the power of the gonads! . . . Of course, if you hold him in prisson for twenty years there would then be little risk—these fires do with the years burn less intensely, believe me—but I doubt he would survive so long in prisson."

Dr. Veraswami's resignation in the matter began to annoy me. "Well, if you can't help with why he did it, or whether he's dangerous, what should be done about him?"

"He will be hanged, of course."

I protested that we both knew the boy meant no harm, no evil. The more I thought about him and his crime, the less wicked it seemed, though the injury to the girl and her family was obviously extreme; but it was a tragedy, not a sin.

Dr. Veraswami was relentless. "You think him retarded, and he iss. You think him ignorant of what he should and should not do, and he iss. You think he meant no harm, just like an animal, a reaction to the girl. But don't you see, dear friend, all your English colleagues see him ass just the same ass other Burmese, indistinguishable from all other native boys. All look alike. All are stupid, ignorant, cunning, untrustworthy, dirty, smelly, sexually uncontrolled. All the same. To excuse him because he iss just like the rest would in their minds be madness in you, not in him.

I had no answer. "And," he continued, glancing towards the village, "so I fear iss the view of the Burmese. A brothel boy, yes, but in no other way different. They don't let mind speed worry them. You think he iss different and therefore innocent where others would be guilty, you may be right, probably so, but the villagers don't agree! You must do what your British friends at the Club and the villagers both expect you to do."

My testiness increased. "You seem so content in this, Doctor. The boy is surely *less* responsible than most killers; he meant no harm insofar as he understood what was happening; and you seem so swiftly to accept his hanging. Surely he is *less* worthy of being hanged than most murderers."

Dr. Veraswami was waving his head vigorously from side to side as I spoke. This, I had earlier discovered, was a frequent Indian gesture easily mistaken for dissent, but having the larger meaning of a qualified assent, in effect—you are nearly right but not quite. "The gaol, the prisson, perhaps," he said, waving to the nearby dingy walls. "He could sit there on the other side of the wall with the others until he died perhaps. He will learn nothing there, ass you know. Have even less to do than in the brothel. If anything he will become even more idiot than now. And they will prey on him." Then, after a pause to acknowledge my troubled silence, "Or perhaps the place where we lock up the mad. Have you seen it? . . . Worse, I think, than the prisson. Have you been there?"

I had and it was. No psychiatrist could possibly wish to work in such circumstances and none did. It was indeed the least desirable service for any doctor, Burmese or Indian—and no English doctor had as yet ever drunk enough to find himself posted there.

"But iss it not much the same, . . . even in England?" Dr. Veraswami asked. It was not really a question. He knew. I did not know. What he implied was probably the truth.

"So what, dear police magistrate friend, would you have
us do with the boy? Shall I take him home with me? Keep him
here to serve us beer? Iss it not difficult enough for me to live
in this dreadful place without taking him ass a son to my
bosom? The villagers would indeed then reject me entirely
quite. Or iss he to be a part of the police magistracy? You
would be more doubted and even less respected—a most un-
wise move indeed, indeed . . ." And he trailed off to vague head
wavings.

"I wonder, Doctor, if one of us could have talked to the
girl before she died, what would she have wanted me to do?"

"She would have been more scared of me than of you—
Indian doctors, ass you know, bewitch village maidens and turn
them into hyenas or other horrible animals; English policemen
merely steal them! I doubt either of uss could have made her
understand very much about the boy. But what if we could?
How could she forgive him? How tell him? Take the money
from him, perhaps . . . ? It iss offensive. No, you will get no help
from such thoughts, my friend. It could not in any way have
been her problem. It iss yours."

Later, reflecting on the realities Dr. Veraswami had held up
to me, I found myself dreaming the reformer's dreams, sum-
moning resources of medicine, psychiatry, prisons without brutality, and a political caring ages removed from Burma under the
Raj.

Did much change? I was not sure. Certainly, the boy
would not be executed, since with the movement towards minimum social decencies the executioner is one of the first functionaries to be retired. But others tend to take his place. A
larger self-caring often accompanies a larger caring for others.
The boy might well be held until cured. And how would one
ever know that? Only by letting him out. And one can't do that
until he is cured. So he must be held. The false language of
treatment and cure would replace the Burmese bluntness of
condign punishment—and who could tell which is to be preferred? If the boy could choose he would choose to avoid the

17

hangman, but there would be other whips and torments waiting for him even in my dream of the all-loving State.

My daydreams of the boy and I being elsewhere and at another time, rather than here and now in Moulmein, were understandable but gave me no comfort. My decision would have been cruelly lonely had not Dr. Veraswami seemed to enjoy our discussions and to wish to help me in my thrashings around to avoid hanging the boy. Sometimes, however, he struck home hurtfully. I was pressing him for his opinion of how the boy felt in killing—caring, cruel, lost, bewildered? I suggested confusion and a sense of isolation. Dr. Veraswami looked incredibly embarrassed. "Did you not tell me, dear friend, of some difficulties you and some of your distinguished young friends . . . ass it were . . . experienced at that fine English preparatory school you attended before Eton? St. Cyprian's, issn't it?" I had no idea what he was talking about and remained silent. He blushed. Indians do blush, though less obviously of course than Englishmen. "Enuresis, issn't it, I believe . . . Flogged for what you did not know how to avoid, I think you said." And I knew that I too suddenly was blushing, the lobes of my ears scarlet, the guilt of my childhood bed-wetting still upon me. Dr. Veraswami was sure he had offended me; his agitation increased. He got up, fussing about with bottles of beer, now warming as the bits of ice he had somewhere found melted to fragments.

He was, of course, quite right. In a sense I had been where the brothel boy found himself. I had been beaten for my sins, sins which were clearly both wicked and outside my control, yet nevertheless sins, or so they seemed to me and to Bingo and to Sim, who wielded the cane and broke the riding crop on me.

It was possible, therefore, to commit a sin without knowing you committed it and without being able to avoid it. So it had seemed then, and the feeling of guilt undeniably remained, and strong. Sin was thus sometimes something that happened—to me as to the brothel boy. You did not properly speaking *do* the deed; you merely woke up in the morning to find in anguish that the sheets were wringing wet.

I tried to calm Dr. Veraswami, to assure him that he had
not offended me, that I appreciated his directness, that I needed
his help. This led me to an excessive confession, one I had
made to no one else, and probably no one else knew about it,
not even Sim. The last time Sim had flogged me for bed-wetting
I remember with great pain a further loss of control of my
bladder and a warm flow inside my short pants, down the inside of my left knee, onto my long socks and into my left shoe.
Sim had me bent over a desk, posterior protruding; but I hoped
most desperately and still in misery believe that the desk
shielded his eyes from my pants and the pool which may have
formed at my feet. The shame, had the puddle been seen and
almost surely commented on, would have been beyond bearing.
But I still don't know if it was.

Dr. Veraswami's hands were flying about in near frenzy. I
tried hurriedly to make the link to the case of the brothel boy,
straining thus to calm him. I thought he feared a breach in our
friendship, but that is unfair; on reflection I think his only anxiety was that he was troubling me too deeply. Perhaps he was.

Were my feelings then, and the brothel boy's now, at all
comparable? Had I become a ponderous, unfeeling mixture of
Bingo and Sim, punishing the boy by death because of the
harshness of the environment into which he had been flung,
compared to which my trials at St. Cyprian's were trivial?

Dr. Veraswami would have none of it. "Dear friend, bed-
wetting and rape which kills . . . how can you compare them at
all? . . . misplaced guilt . . . childish fears and adversities loom
ever large, but no, not at all, not in any way like the brothel
boy's guilt."

Perhaps gallows humor would reassure the Doctor that he
had not wounded me. "At all events, Dr. Veraswami, after that
beating, when I wet my sock and shoe, I did not wet my bed
again. I was cured. Sim cured me. The hangman will surely cure
any lack of control our brothel boy may have over his burgeon-
ing sexual instincts!"

But Dr. Veraswami was hardly listening, "No, no, no, dear
Sir . . . enuresis while you sleep; sexual attack while awake;
nothing similar."

So I pressed the analogy, suggesting that precautions might be taken to empty the bladder. One might arrange to be awakened during the night if others would help. What were the precautions the brothel boy should have taken against copying what he had seen, and seen as acceptable, to be purchased when the flesh engorged? The brothel boy could hardly be justly punished for the desire. Obviously he had had nothing to do with it, less than I had with the springs of enuresis. And whence was he to find the wisdom and control, in unsought and unexpected heat, not to do what probably seemed to him an obvious and acceptable act. He had observed in the brothel apparent gratitude by both parties, simulation and true appreciation being indistinguishable by him. Where were the differences between him and me in sinning? The distinctions seemed to favour him.

Dr. Veraswami's intensity increased. "No, you are very wrong, forgive me contradicting you, but you are off a lot. The boy must have known he wass hurting her, dull though he iss. The girls in the brothel fear and complain of violence, they talk to each other about it often, the boy must have known. Once he came close upon her, he knew, he knew, believe me my friend. The cases are quite different. You do yourself too much injustice. You did not sin, he did, and most grievously. Your comparison with your bed-wetting misses the essential difference, issn't it—he was conscious of what he wass doing, you were not. And being conscious, backward and confused though he iss, mistreated and bewildered though he wass, he must be held responsible. You must convict him, punish him, hang him! He iss a citizen of Burma, a subject of your Imperial Majesty, but you must treat him ass a responsible adult and punish him. That iss what citizenship iss."

I had never before heard such a lengthy, passionately sibilant speech from Dr. Veraswami. It seemed to have calmed him. Again, it didn't help me.

It seemed to me that the discussion had tilted crazily against the brothel boy. Responsibility . . . citizenship . . . consciousness of what he was doing . . . were these sensible standards for a youth of his darkly clouded intelligence and blighted situation? And, if not, what standard should be applied, to what end, with what results?

An all-wise God could by definition draw these fine distinctions, but it was hard to think of the brothel boy and an omniscient God as in any way related, hardly an omnibenevolent God to be sure. And I knew that I was no plenipotentiary of such a divinity; a minor agent of the Raj was enough for me. My employers had never distinguished themselves in drawing delicately generous moral distinctions; indeed, they seemed to judge entirely by the results and not by the intentions, which surely must inhibit any fine gradations in attributing responsibility.

Did this mean that there was no room at all in my jurisdiction for mercy, for clemency? I decided to put the question to Dr. Veraswami.

Unlike my fellow members of the Club, Dr. Veraswami enjoyed my skill in rolling cigarettes. He rarely smoked but occasionally would accept one of my home-grown cigarettes. He preferred to moisten the paper himself, I holding the enfolded tobacco out to him; but he also cheerfully accepted those the product of my own hands and tongue.

When talking with Dr. Veraswami, I found I sometimes rolled a cigarette to give me time to phrase a point of delicacy or difficulty, as many who smoke a pipe use the ritual of filling, lighting, and tamping as time for meditation. On this occasion, the cigarette rolling was a preamble to an effort to seek Dr. Veraswami's views on the moral aspects of the problem of the brothel boy. And, if he agreed that the boy was less culpable, to press him why he was so adamant about the hanging.

"Do you know a painting by Peter Paul Rubens of the Last Judgment?" I asked Dr. Veraswami. "It is a huge painting with lovely though overweight naked ladies and gentlemen going up to unclothed inactivity above the right hand of Christ. Just below His left hand there is an interesting Prince of Darkness in control of a lecherous team dragging the damned off to unpainted horrors, with a face at the bottom of the Devil's side of the painting screaming in agony."

Dr. Veraswami said he had seen a poor print of it once, he thought, but in any event he plunged ahead of my circumlocution to the heart of the question. "You ask, I suppose, my friend, where will the boy be if the admirable Mr. Rubens paints truth? Of course, I don't know. I am not a Christian but, if I were, I would guess he will not be among those damned."

"Well, then, how can you tell me to hang him?" I asked, pressing Dr. Veraswami for reconciliation of what some would see as conflicting positions.

Dr. Veraswami yielded to no difficulty in the reconciliation. Mercy, a full and forgiving understanding of behaviour, was the prerogative of whoever was God, if there was one, and if he had so little to do that he interested himself in us after we died—which Dr. Veraswami doubted. Nor did he believe, as did some Hindus, that we came back in some other form; but if we did the boy was as likely to ascend as to descend in the hierarchy—whatever it was. All in all, if God had made the boy as he was, and put him where he was, it was hard to see that the boy had behaved any better or worse than God must have expected. But all that, he argued most vigorously, had nothing to do with Assistant Police Magistrate Blair, who, admirable though Dr. Veraswami knew he was, educated and wise beyond his years, could not now help the boy. "Justice, my friend, iss your job. Justice, not mercy." And his gesturing hand fell and was still, simulating the fall of the gallows.

"Surely, Doctor, mercy can be a part of justice. They are hardly in opposition. Cannot mercy infuse justice, shape it, direct it?"

"Sometimes, sometimes, but often it iss beyond our competence." And he launched again into a lengthy speech, his plump white-clad behind balanced against the veranda rail, his black thumb and forefinger nipping at the air as if to capture ideas as they floated by. The tenor of his argument was, so far as I followed it, Freudian. If we knew all we could about any murderer, including the brothel boy, all about his inherited capacities and all his life experiences, we would find more than sufficient explanation for all his actions including the killing.

Conduct was apparently "overdetermined," once you included
the unconscious and the subconscious. And for most of these
pressures, which collectively and massively determine everyone's
behaviour, it would seem unfair to hold anyone responsible.
"But, my dear friend, fair or not, it iss essential to do so!
Within justice there may be room for clemency, for mercy, for
human understanding, providing only the essential purposes of
punishment under law are not frustrated. Here they would be.
He hass killed while deliberately doing what iss a very serious
crime. There iss no room for mercy, no room at all." And then
as if he thought it would clinch the matter: "Why even the
good Viennese doctor himself, Sigismund Freud, said you are responsible for your unconscious. There it iss!"

"But, dear Doctor, if we can assess differences of fault, or
think we can, sufficiently to reduce or increase the punishment
of the guilty, to be merciful or to be severe, why can't we, why
can't I, by the same means reduce guilt itself? After all, sometimes we do that—when people kill accidentally we call it manslaughter, if they have been very careless indeed; and if they
have not been careless and yet have killed it is usually no crime
and never murder. We may not be very good at judging moral
fault; but in a rough and ready way we can. And surely the boy
is nearer innocence than guilt."

"No, no, my magistrate friend, you make the same mistake, forgive me please. We are talking only of intentional acts,
not of acts of carelessness—they are quite different. That iss
what distinguishes the boy's act from your enuresis, issn't it.
And for such acts . . ." and here Dr. Veraswami grabbed two
handfuls of ideas from the air around him ". . . the boy iss
either to be treated ass a responsible man or he issn't. There are
no half-men for guilt in the eyes of the law. If there were a
choice of punishments for what he hass done, perhaps you
could be merciful, because he hass been much abused and iss of
weak mind. But there issn't, there issn't. It iss circular you see,
dear friend."

I didn't see at all, but he pressed on, now almost skipping
about with the released energy of uninhibited talk, which I sud-

denly realised was an even more cherished luxury for him than for me—"Man iss defined by hiss capacity for moral choice. That iss what man iss, nothing else, otherwise an animal." And then, chuckling at the cruel pointedness of the joke: "Dr. Freud and the law agree, you see. For his unconscious mind and for hiss conscious mind, such ass they are, the brothel boy iss twice responsible. Otherwise you would have to excuse everyone, certainly everyone you took the trouble to understand."

Though an elusive conclusion, the point was strong. Justice cannot excuse everyone, obviously. And if our judgment of moral guilt reflects mainly our degree of ignorance of the relevant moral facts, then all we would do in a mercy controlled system of punishment would, in effect, be to excuse or be merciful towards those we know a lot about or decided to find out about—and not the others. To my dismay it seemed to me, therefore, that if Justice stands in opposition to Mercy, we are damned (or, certainly, this Assistant Police Magistrate is); and if Mercy is to infuse Justice, to be a part of it, we probably claim beyond our competence.

Dr. Veraswami understood my difficulty in this whole matter, my search for some principle to guide me. "I think a lot about it, my friend, since it iss such a worry to you. And, if I may please, I hope you agree, here iss my conclusion." And after a pause, a thumb and forefinger, tweezer-like nip in the air to catch his words, "There iss no steady principle to guide you, none at all. You must be a man of principles, not of principle."

Dr. Veraswami seemed to be becoming more elliptic than before, and in annoyance I told him so. "No, you misunderstand me," he replied, "I mean there iss no moral principle to guide you, moral, moral . . . There are, of course, other guides, other principles. The main one iss that you English should use the executioner ass little ass you can—rarely, if you use him at all. And how to know how little iss ass little ass you can?" Here he paused again, hands still, achieving impressive rhetorical effect. "I have it: if the British do not wish him killed, there iss no problem unless the natives want him killed very much, and the British think they should let them have their way. If it iss a native to be executed they will not care too much. But if the British and the natives *both* want him killed, ass with the brothel boy, unless he iss so very mad ass to be obviously mad to all, natives and British, you can do nothing unless you also wish to leave the service of the Raj and be seen by all ass a treasonable fool."

Hesitantly, regretting the force of "treasonable fool," he added: "I would like to help you, but I can't. Perhaps you should leave here . . . I would miss you. You would be happier in England I think. But iss this the way? Iss this the way to go? And even if you do save the boy what can we do with him? Ass I said, the gaol? the madhouse?"

It appalled me to realise that I was in Pilate's role, at least as Pilate may have seen it, though otherwise the comparison made no sense. Nor, increasingly it seemed to me, did I. Perhaps it was me for the madhouse that Dr. Veraswami saw as useless for the boy. No; I understood the issue all too well; it was now clear and I was not confused. Dr. Veraswami was right. As a moral issue, the boy was nearer to innocence than most of us; at the Last Judgment I would back his chances over most. But as a political matter, what a weak reed he had in me to sustain his life.

I recalled another recent occasion in Moulmein when I had failed to stand for the right against public pressures. Was it to become a habit? A recidivist Pilate indeed! A few months ago, very much against my better judgment and every inclination, I had shot a working elephant that had recovered from a period of "must" in which he had damaged some property and killed a native. As soon as I saw the elephant I knew with perfect certainty that I ought not to shoot him; but the natives expected it of me and I had to do it; I could feel their dark, sweaty wills pressing me forward, irresistibly. If I did nothing it was quite probable that some of them would laugh. So I shot the elephant.

I had to contend then only with native opinion; the Europeans would have divided on the question, some holding it to be a damn shame to shoot an elephant for killing a coolie, because an elephant was worth more than any damn Coringhee coolie. Now, with the brothel boy, the forces pressing on me were different and probably greater. No one would laugh if I did not hang the boy, but both European and native opinion was agreed and vehement: that is what I ought to do, what I must do.

Memories of St. Cyprian again swept in. I remembered how Latin was beaten into me and I still doubted that a classical education could be successfully carried on without corporal punishment. Bingo, Sim, and the boys all believed in its efficacy; as in Moulmein, public opinion was unanimous about the value of physical punishment. I recalled Beacham, a boy of dull mind, not as dull as the brothel boy but certainly not bright, whom Sim flogged towards their joint goal of a scholarship for Beacham, as the heartless might flog a floundered horse. And when Beacham was severely beaten yet again for his failure in the scholarship exam, his words of poignant regret came back to me: "I wish I'd had that caning before I went up for the exam."

[Here there are pages missing in the manuscript. It leaps to a few concluding paragraphs.]

As I walked with Dr. Veraswami into the gaol yard I caught sight of him. Six gaurds were getting him ready for the gallows. He stood, surrounded by the gaurds, slim and muscular, with shaven head and vague liquid eyes. He seemed genuinely bewildered, puzzled, uncomprehending though deeply fearful. The gaurds crowded close to him, with their hands always on him in a careful, caressing grip, as though all the while feeling him to make sure he was there. He seemed hardly to notice what was happening. His eye caught mine and paused while it dawned on him that he knew me and that I had been gentle with him. The vague eyes developed a semblance of communication.

By the time he stood by the scaffold no marks remained of the beating. His body had repaired itself, but the intervening weeks had not helped my mind to repair its anguish.

I walked behind him to the gallows. Though his arms were bound, he walked quite steadily. And once, in spite of the men who gripped him by each shoulder, he stepped lightly aside to avoid a puddle on the path. The puddle—and I understood why—brought me back to the unreasoning St. Cyprian guilt. That I should be destroying a healthy conscious man, dull and dangerous though he may be. The unspeakable wrongness of cutting short a life in full tide. The struggle for rational judgment came as a minor anodyne. How can I refashion the world of the just and the unjust, of the forgiving and of the prejudiced, myself an uncertain observer rather than a shaper of justice, a player without influence on the rules. Only by my own death would I escape the pain of these cruel games. I must leave Burma.

So that when he was dead, and the Superintendent of the gaol asked Dr. Veraswami and me and the rest of the little procession to join him in a drink—"I've got a bottle of whiskey in the car. We could do with it."—I found myself drinking and laughing, perhaps too loudly, with the rest of them, quite amicably, natives and Europeans alike.

Veraswami was right; I must leave Burma.

TWO

The Criminal Responsibility of the Mentally Ill

Progress in medicine having set aside quarantine as rare, brief, and hence inconsequential, there remain only two legal powers for compulsory incarceration: jail or imprisonment under the criminal law and commitment to a mental hospital under the mental health law. It is my aim in this chapter to offer some principles in relation to two areas of overlap of the criminal-law power and the mental health power of the state.

The analysis is based on Anglo-American law and practice, but the principles should be relevant to all developed legal systems. Jails, prisons, and mental hospitals are present in all cultures, though different societies use them very differently. But in all societies, some persons who are mentally ill also commit crimes and some persons who are criminals are also mentally ill.

I shall not discuss criminal-law controls or compulsory treatment alternatives to jails, prisons, or mental hospitals. The lesser armamentarium of the criminal law—fines, probation, and so on— is, of course, of great practical importance, as is the range of lesser treatment alternatives in the community available for the mentally ill; but if principles can be applied to the state's greater powers, the lesser powers will more easily fall into place.

The literature on the several issues to be considered in this chapter is extensive. A certain dogmatism should not be mistaken for a failure to appreciate either the complexity of the issues or the extent of my dependence on the work of others; precisely because of the multitude of doctrines, practices, and commentators some blunt hacking away is necessary. Libraries are stuffed with discussions of the trees; the forest has been neglected.

What then are the broad prerequisites for invocation of these two great powers of the state to separate the citizen from his family, his friends, and his community? Leaving aside the nuances, here they are:

> To imprison—that he has been convicted of a crime and that his imprisonment is both deserved and socially desirable;

> To commit to a mental hospital—that he is mentally ill or retarded and that he is a danger to others or to himself or is incapable of caring for himself.

These two powers thus differ both in the subjective conditions for their invocation (the commission of a crime as distinct from the presence of a mental state) and in their objective purposes (crime control by punishment as distinct from individual and societal protection). Different concepts also limit these two powers of the state: the concept of the maximum deserved punishment for what the offender did limits the criminal-law power of the state; the concept of continuing dangerousness to the patient or to others (or continuing inability to care for himself) limits the mental health power of the state. It will be demonstrated later that when these two limiting principles are confused, as they often are in current law and practice, injustice and inefficiency result; but it is worth noting now that the mental health power is more extensive and longer enduring than the criminal-law power. Capital punishment is an obvious exception to that proposition, but in all developed criminal-law systems capital punishment is a sensational rarity, and even where it continues on the law books, it should not be seen as part of the mainstream of punishments for crime.

In recent years, improved drug therapy, developments in psychiatric treatment, and changing community attitudes have largely emptied the long-term back wards of the mental hospitals. Those committed to mental hospitals stay, in the main, much shorter periods than they used to, although they not infrequently return for further relatively brief visits. And psychiatrists have become increasingly reluctant to predict the dangerousness of a patient, except for limited periods and in social circumstances that are well known and reasonably likely to remain constant. But the point remains: in principle the criminal-law power of the state is limited by what the criminal deserves for what he did whereas the mental health power of the state is limited only by the patient's death.

Insofar as the protection of society from a particular convicted criminal—incapacitation—is a legitimate purpose of punishment[1] one may take a slightly different perspective on this relationship between the criminal-law power and the mental health power. Given mental illness or retardation, dangerousness to self or others limits the mental health power, defines its coercive invocation, and limits its duration. Given conviction of a crime, dangerousness to others may lead to imprisonment when it otherwise might not have been imposed and may extend its duration, but it does not limit that duration, that limit being set by legislative, judicial, or parole board decisions as to the maximum deserved punishment for the crime. Desert limits the criminal-law power; it does not limit the mental health power. When the two powers are blended, the "criminal patient" may suffer the worst of both worlds, imprisonment for what he did with its duration limited only by predictions of his continuing dangerousness.

It is the overarching theme of this book that injustice and inefficiency invariably flow from any blending of the criminal-law and mental health powers of the state. Each is sufficient unto itself

1. See A. Blumstein, ed., *Deterrence and Incapacitation: Estimating the Effects of Criminal Sanctions on Crime Rates*, National Academy of Sciences (1978).

31

to achieve a just balance between freedom and authority; each has its own interested constituency; when they are mixed together, only the likelihood of injustice is added. In chapter 4 this theme will be analyzed in relation to sentencing the mentally ill; I now wish to consider it in relation to bringing the mentally ill to trial and to holding them responsible for their criminal acts. In these two areas, the consequence of applying the principle I advocate would be, first, that there would be no special plea of unfitness or incompetency to stand trial—when socially necessary the mentally ill and retarded would be charged and tried by criminal process—and secondly, there would be no special defense of insanity to a criminal charge. Obviously, these two propositions require more than affirmations if they are to be accepted.

These propositions, I had better confess, fly in the face not only of conventional wisdom but also of much current practice. They also confront a substantial body of powerful commentary by leading scholars, although, fortunately, opinions are divided.

My belief is that practice and scholarship have been led astray by the following ambivalent and corruptive reaction: though he has done a criminal act, being mentally abnormal he is less guilty in moral terms; St. Peter may indeed hold him morally faultless or at least less blameworthy and so should we; but also he is different from the rest of us, strange and probably more dangerous, and therefore, since he has committed a crime, we had better for his sake and ours separate him from the community or prolong his separation, for his treatment and our protection. We are at the same time more forgiving and more fearful, less punitive and more self-protective; we wish to have it both ways.

A final introductory comment: It should not be assumed that the principle I recommend, of keeping distinct the criminal law and mental health powers of the state, favors more punitive practices than currently obtain. In my view the contrary is the case; and certainly the principle need not lead to greater severity. But, equally, the principle is not reformist in the sense that it is shaped to respond to present practical and political problems. It represents a struggle toward justice and, one may fairly note, applies a concept that is accepted in the treatment of all mental illness—that of invoking to the limit of his capacity the patient's responsibility for his own cure.

The sequence of topics to be discussed in this chapter is as follows:

I. Political Conflicts and Current Compromises
II. The Trial of the Mentally Ill
III. The Abolition of the Special Defense of Insanity
IV. Incarcerating the "Not Innocent"

The case to be made is that there should be no special plea of unfitness or incompetency and no special plea of insanity, that well-established criminal-law principles can better handle the problems now dealt with by these two special pleas.

I. Political Conflicts and Current Compromises

Tensions have developed in public acceptance of both the incompetency and the insanity pleas, and compromise legislation has been developed to meet public and professional concerns. The details vary from state to state but the broad themes are clear.

As to incompetency: This plea is more common than the special defense of insanity and is sometimes a trial tactic en route to the insanity defense. Turning on the accused's ability to play the role of one charged in a criminal trial, to understand what is at issue and to advise his counsel, it has a clear shape and there is no substantial debate as to what are the appropriate criteria of incompetency to stand trial. Difficulties have arisen in the definition of the tests to be used to find the presence or absence of those criteria, in the roles of the psychologist and the psychiatrist in those tests, in the propriety of trying an accused while he is under drug therapy, and, in particular, on the period that one found unfit to stand trial may be held. It is this last problem that has led to compromise legislation. The details of these compromises will be discussed later; here all that is intended is that their outline be understood.

Massachusetts gave the legislative clue; other states have followed but have pursued different purposes. The pioneer Massachusetts legislation was directed to allowing an incompetent accused to assert some defenses and bars to prosecution, to make some preliminary motions without losing his status as one incompetent to stand trial if his assertions failed.[2] Recent legislation has been designed to put the incompetent to a qualified, "innocent only" trial, varying his status for purposes of compulsory detention in a mental hospital and allowing him to be held for the period he might have been held had he been convicted of the crime.

The "innocent only" trial is a compromise to avoid the constitutional prohibition, expressed in *Jackson v. Indiana*, of the indeterminate detention of those found incompetent to stand trial. It is also a compromise designed to reassure a properly anxious community that those who because of mental illness or retardation cannot be tried for what they in fact did will not be prematurely released to do it again.

I will submit that the abolition of the incompetency plea, with some consequential changes in rules of courts concerning continuances and the trial of the mentally disabled, would better achieve both justice and social protection than the presently spreading legislative compromises.

As to the special plea of insanity: psychiatric practice and constitutional decisions have facilitated the earlier release of those found not guilty by reason of insanity than when the back wards of mental hospitals held them for periods longer, on the average, than they would have served had they been convicted of their crimes. Again, public anxiety fueled political concern that this defense was becoming a contrivance, a subterfuge, and that even where it was validly pleaded the public should not be expected

2. In *Jackson v. Indiana* the Supreme Court referred with approval to states providing "some proceedings to go forward despite the defendant's incompetency" and cited the American Law Institute's Model Penal Code recommendation permitting the court to determine any issue "susceptible of fair determination prior to trial and without the personal participation of the defendant" (§§4.06(3) and 4.06(4)). The Court further referred with approval to "statutory provisions permitting pretrial motions to be made or even allowing the incompetent defendant a trial at which to establish his innocence, without permitting a conviction" and cited Wisconsin, New York, Massachusetts, Montana, and Maryland statutes. 406 U.S. 715 (1971) at 740–41.

to bear the risk of further criminal acts by those who had escaped punishment because of their mental illness.

Compromise here has taken two forms: First, legislation has been enacted providing for the exercise of judicial control over the discretion, held under normal mental health law by the psychiatrist, as to the release (including the trial release) of those found not guilty by reason of insanity. The consequence has been the prolongation of their detention beyond what it would have been under mental health law and this consequence has been held to be constitutionally acceptable. Secondly, Michigan, Indiana, Illinois, and several other states have established a new verdict lying between conviction and acquittal by reason of insanity.[3] The new verdict is "guilty but mentally ill." This is no mere verbal change. One so found, whether or not he is restored to sanity, will serve in a prison or a mental hospital the time he would have served had he been convicted and sentenced, and thereafter may be considered for civil commitment.

I submit that the abolition of the special plea of insanity would better achieve both justice and social protection than these presently spreading legislative compromises.

These compromises in relation both to incompetency and insanity reveal strong public and political pressure for legislative reform. They confront established doctrine which is not secure enough to draw lines of principle so that practical expediency dominates. Let us therefore turn to those issues of principle, first concerning the incompetency plea and then the special defense of insanity.

II. The Trial of the Mentally Ill

At first blush, to advocate the abolition of the plea of unfitness for trial, and hence to favor the trial of some mentally ill, retarded, or otherwise gravely disadvantaged accused persons, seems heartless, useless, and unconstitutional. Paradoxically, it is one situation of overlap between the mental health power of the state and the

3. Attorney General's Task Force on Violent Crime, Final Report, 17 August 1981, p. 54.

criminal-law power where the case for reform in the general direction I favor is compelling—and is being pursued.

Widespread legislative reforms are moving in the direction of the principle here recommended, though uneasy compromise is all that has, as yet, been legislatively achieved.[4] The American Bar Association (ABA) Commission on the Mentally Disabled (1978)[5] expressly accepted the proposal Robert Burt and I had earlier advanced,[6] as did a Home Office Committee under the chairmanship of Lord Butler,[7] though varying the form of verdict for the "convicted" incompetent; but their recommendations have not yet won legislative acceptance.

Setting aside problems in the definition of unfitness to plead and in the procedures and processes of its proof, here is the proposal: The plea of incompetence to stand trial should be changed. A motion for trial continuance by reason of disability should be allowed up to a maximum of six months for the accused to maximize his fitness for trial. Psychiatric and psychological (or other) treatment where appropriate should be made available to him to this end during this period in the least restrictive setting properly determined by the court. Thereafter, at the election of the prosecution, either the trial should proceed under rules of court designed so far as practicable to redress the trial disadvantages under which the accused labors or a *nolle prosequi* should be entered. In making this election there would be no impropriety in the state's first pursuing civil commitment processes against the accused, it being understood that the prosecution will proceed to trial only if the accused is not civilly committed.

4. See, e.g., Ill. Rev. Stat., ch. 38, §§104-10–11 (Supp. 1980); Cal. Penal Code, §§1367, 1368 (West 1981).

5. 2 *Mental Disability Law Reporter* 617 (1978).

6. "A Proposal for the Abolition of the Incompetency Plea," 40 *U. Chi. L. Rev.* 66 (1972). In this chapter I have relied on that article to a considerable extent and express gratitude to Professor Burt for the demi-plagiarism thus committed.

7. Report of the Committee on Mentally Abnormal Offenders, Cmnd. 6244 (1975).

There are many other problems in present law and practice concerning fitness to plead which I wish to skirt here so as directly to confront the difficult problem of the unrestorable incompetent: what to do about those who protractedly or permanently suffer serious psychological or physical (deaf-mutism) disadvantages as defendants in a criminal trial?[8] But some brief ground-clearing is necessary.

Unfitness to stand trial is a frequent plea as compared to the insanity plea, the ABA Commission on the Mentally Disabled[9] suggesting that "more than a hundred times as many defendants are found incompetent to stand trial ... [as] are acquitted on grounds of insanity,"[10] yet it has received scant scholarly attention compared to the prodigious academic wrestling with the criminal responsibility of the mentally ill.

The test of unfitness for trial as established by the Supreme Court is whether the accused "has sufficient present ability to consult with his lawyer with a reasonable degree of rational understanding—and whether he has a rational as well as factual understanding of the proceedings against him."[11] It is an old rule that persons who cannot meet that test should not be tried: they are not really present at trial; they may not be able properly to play the role of an accused person, to recall relevant events, to produce evidence and witnesses, to testify effectively on their own behalf, to help confront hostile witnesses, and to project to the trier of facts a sense of their innocence.

Without special procedural and evidentiary safeguards their trial would clearly violate the due process clause of the Fifth

8. For a comprehensive and thoughtful analysis of the problems in the unfitness plea with recommendations for their resolution, see the ABA Report referred to in note 5 *supra*.

9. *Supra* note 5.

10. *Ibid.*

11. Dusky v. United States, 362 U.S. 402 (1960).

Amendment;[12] and even with such safeguards the question is not free from doubt. Hale put the matter well in 1736:

> If a man in his sound memory commits a capital offense, and before his arraignment he becomes absolutely mad, he ought not by law to be arraigned during such his phrenzy, but be remitted to prison until that incapacity be removed; the reason is, because he cannot advisedly plead to the indictment. . . . And if such person after his plea and before his trial, become of *non sane memory*, he shall not be tried; or, if after his trial he become of *non sane memory*, he shall not receive judgment; or, if after judgment he become of *non sane memory*, his execution shall be spared; for were he of sound memory, he might allege somewhat in stay of judgment of execution.[13]

It is no small suggestion that such a long-established plea should be changed into a mere motion for a continuance; but practice, principle, and Occam's Razor all cut in that direction. The cases of Theon Jackson and Donald Lang will take us to the heart of this thorny problem.

When Theon Jackson was aged twenty-seven, supporting himself reasonably well in an Indiana community, he was arrested for a purse snatching involving property of the value of $4.00 (the purse and its contents) and a robbery of $5.00 in cash. The record is unclear whether any actual violence accompanied these crimes—whoever committed them. Jackson was a deaf-mute, with very little capacity to communicate, being unable to read, to write, or to use sign language. He was found unfit to plead. Jackson's counsel wanted him to be committed to the state school for the deaf, but the school refused to accept the "mentally retarded deaf," though there was no evidence of Jackson's mental retardation. Jackson was therefore committed to the custody of the Department of Mental Health to be held secure until, as the law then provided,

12. Cf. Pate v. Robinson, 383 U.S. 375, 378 (1966); Bishop v. United States, 350 U.S. 961 (1956).

13. 1 Hale, *Historia Placitorum Coronae* 34–35 (1736) (citations omitted).

he was fit for trial. Psychiatric testimony to the court hearing the plea of incompetency had been firm and uncontradicted that Jackson was most unlikely ever to become competent to stand trial; in effect, he would forever be unfit for trial. He thus faced detention for the term of his natural life.

Prior to the charge of purse snatching Jackson was free, civil commitment not having been pursued against (or for) him for twenty-seven years; after the charge and the incompetency plea, he was indeterminately incarcerated, the safeguards of freedoms in both the criminal law and the law of mental health having been abrogated in his case. The manifest injustice of this result led the Supreme Court to the narrow conclusion that "Indiana cannot constitutionally commit the petitioner for an indefinite period simply on account of his incompetency to stand trial on the charges filed against him,"[14] the more ample holding being that

> a person charged by a State with a criminal offense who is committed solely on account of his incapacity to proceed to trial cannot be held more than the reasonable period of time necessary to determine whether there is a substantial probability that he will attain that capacity in the foreseeable future. If it is determined that this is not the case, then the State must either institute the customary civil commitment proceeding that would be required to commit indefinitely any other citizen, or release the defendant. Furthermore, even if it is determined that the defendant probably soon will be able to stand trial, his continued commitment must be justified by progress toward that goal.[15]

The Court reached this conclusion on grounds of the denial to Theon Jackson both of equal protection and of due process, equal protection since he lacked the protections accorded civilly committed patients, due process since the "nature and duration" of his confinement bore no "reasonable relation to the purpose for which" he was committed, that is, to make him competent to stand trial. Given the evidence of Jackson's unrestorable incom-

14. Jackson v. Indiana, 406 U.S. 715 (1971) at 720.
15. *Id.* at 738.

petency, no period of commitment at all could be justified by the supposed purpose of helping him to become fit for trial, though, of course, under the mental health law a temporary detention pending a hearing on his civil commitment would be justified— but not the three and a half years between Jackson's arrest and the decision of the Supreme Court![16]

Jackson v. Indiana was an important step forward but, quite properly, it left unsettled the best legislative solution to the problem of the unrestorably incompetent defendant.

One case on which the Supreme Court relied in *Jackson* has had an extraordinary and troubling sequel—*People ex rel. Myers v. Briggs.*[17] Donald Lang, the subject of the litigation in *Myers v. Briggs*, was and is an illiterate deaf-mute. After a tavern pick-up, a lady of mercenary virtue had been killed; the state alleged that Donald Lang did the killing and had some evidence to support the charge. Lang's counsel expressed belief to the contrary and wished to take the matter to trial, but under the Illinois statute the question of the accused's incompetency for trial could and can be raised by the prosecution, or the defense, or the trial judge. Over defense counsel's vigorous objections, Lang was in 1967 found unfit to stand trial, was committed to the custody of the Department of Mental Health, and was sent for treatment to the Dixon institution for the retarded. Two years later the superintendent of that institution wrote the following letter to the special counsel to the Department of Mental Health:

> Based on our experience with Donald Lang, it now appears that he will never acquire the necessary communication skills needed to participate and cooperate in his trial. He has rejected all of our efforts to instruct him and has refused to participate and cooperate with his instructor. The probability for his acquiring the necessary communication skills at any future date is unlikely. However, it is our impression that Donald is functioning at a

16. Theon Jackson was discharged from Indiana Central State Hospital on 6 September 1972 as "improved." I have without much effort traced him until late 1979. He remained at large, apparently getting by in the community with some social work and financial help.

17. 46 Ill.2d 281; 263 N.E.2d 109 (1970).

nearly normal level of performance in areas other than communication. He is capable of fairly complex operations which
would tend to support our opinions concerning his over-all abil-
ities.

Since Donald's commitment to the Department of Mental
Health is based on physical and mental incompetence and the
probability of appropriate functioning in the former area is
doubtful, we wonder if you would consider contacting Donald's
lawyer in order that appropriate legal action be initiated. Re-
viewing his lawyer's previous correspondence, it would seem
that if his case came to court, sufficient evidence could be produced which would clear him of all charges.

In regard to a home visit, it is our feeling that if one of Donald's brothers assumes the responsibility of supervising him in
the community, we will consider this after re-evaluating his current adjustment and behavior.

It is apparent now that Donald's future must be decided in a
court of law. He will not be able to communicate even in the
limited sense as we had first anticipated.[18]

The Illinois Supreme Court concluded that Donald Lang
"should be given an opportunity to obtain a trial to determine
whether or not he is guilty as charged or should be released."[19]
But this, unhappily, did not conclude the case of Donald Lang; he
is still before the courts of Illinois.

The principal witness the state proposed to present to testify
to Lang's involvement in the 1965 murder had died by the time
Lang was released in February 1971; he was, therefore, not again
indicted. In July 1971 Lang was again arrested and charged with
the murder of another woman, a crime of similar pattern to the
1965 crime, it being alleged that Lang was similarly related to it.
Lang's lawyer again requested a trial. The trial court, guided by
the opinion in *Myers v. Briggs*, proceeded to trial, trying to com-

18. This letter is mentioned in several of the *Lang* opinions; the original
has been lost with a substantial amount of other records transferred to the
courts from the Department of Mental Health and Developmental Disabilities.

19. People ex rel. Myers v. Briggs, 46 Ill.2d 281, 288; 263 N.E.2d 109,
113 (1970).

pensate so far as possible for Lang's incapacity to communicate. Lang was convicted and sentenced to fourteen to twenty-five years' imprisonment. The appellate court reversed, holding that no trial procedures could sufficiently compensate for Lang's inability to communicate, and ordered a hearing on Lang's fitness to stand trial.

At the time of writing, Donald Lang is still held in custody by the Department of Mental Health, the courts being in a state of repeated activity, confusion, and disagreement on the grounds for his detention. *Jackson* would seem to preclude his indeterminate detention as unfit for trial; after all, the reason for detaining those so found can only be to make them fit for trial and if progress ceases to that end, or if at any time the patient is seen as unrestorable, *Jackson* would seem to compel release or civil commitment. And the problem is that Lang is also probably not civilly committable unless the standards of civil commitment are crudely extended, a course followed by the Supreme Court of Illinois the last time it confronted this matter.[20]

Let us try to cut through to the heart of the matter before considering the several compromise solutions that have been offered. To know how to handle, whether to confine, and for how long to confine Theon Jackson and Donald Lang, it is essential to do one's best to decide whether the former robbed and whether the latter killed. Even if we assume mental retardation in both (which was unlikely in the former and clearly not so in the latter), it remains necessary to determine the essential facts of the criminal acts and the "accused-patient's" relation to them—for civil commitment as well as for criminal guilt. In which forum, civil or criminal, will the "accused-patient" have larger protections, more ample process, in relation to his involvement in the robbery or the murders? Without doubt, in the criminal trial.

There is surely a strong community interest in finding these facts by due process. Apart from other legitimate community values, there is the question of whether the actual perpetrator of the

20. Illinois v. Lang, 76 Ill.2d 311; 391 N.E.2d 350 (1979).

crime has indeed been arrested; he may still be at large. Particularly in relation to sexual offenses against children there is a long record of the arrest of innocent though mentally retarded boys and men.

Apart from community interests, it seems clear that it is to the advantage of the accused to go to trial, though mentally ill or retarded, if the consequence of a finding of incompetency is his detention for a period longer than would or could have been imposed pursuant to conviction of the criminal offense. Hence the movement in several states, to which we shall soon turn, to limit such commitments to fixed maximum periods related to the gravity of the original charge. Put at its lowest, this would appear to be a strong argument for the criminal trial of the incompetent, at least when they or their counsel so elect, though there is obvious incongruity in giving such an election to the accused, in effect finding him unfit for trial but fit to waive an unfitness hearing.

Cases like Jackson's and Lang's, as well as observation of the operation both of the unfitness plea and of the conditions and duration of detention of those found unfit, have led me to the view that, where necessary, when they are as fit as we can help them to be, we should take those accused of crimes to trial, despite their mental illness or retardation, under special rules of court dealing with pretrial disclosure, onus and burden of proof, corroboration, jury directions, and new trials appropriate to their particular circumstances. We should cease to detain the mentally ill or retarded because they are charged with crimes.

All states, the District of Columbia, and the federal system prohibit the trial of an incompetent and have broadly similar criteria of incompetency.[21] All these systems were, as a result of the *Jackson* decision, compelled to confront the problem of the unrestorable

21. A convenient catalog of this legislation appears as note 1 to a thoughtful article by N. Richard Janis, "Incompetency Commitment: The Need for Procedural Safeguards and a Proposed Statutory Scheme," 23 *Catholic U. L. Rev.* 720 (1974).

incompetent.[22] There has been much legislative experimentation. Most states have provided for the hearing of pretrial motions though the accused be unfit for trial, if, for example, in the words of the Illinois statute, "the defendant's presence is not essential to a fair determination of the issues";[23] but such motions leave the central problem of the unrestorable incompetent unresolved.

There are three possible solutions. The details of the legislative experiments and the recommendations of the commentators vary greatly, but the possibilities may be fairly stated as follows: (a) civil commitment (the rule in *Jackson*), (b) trial of the unrestorable incompetent (the Burt-Morris recommendation), and (c) the "innocent only" trial. Let us consider the advantages and disadvantages of each.

The ruling in *Jackson v. Indiana* was plain. The only warrant for holding the accused who is unfit for trial is to make him fit for trial. Lacking movement in that direction, he must be released unless, of course, quite apart from the charge, he can be civilly committed. For most cases, such a direct, clear, and simple principle suffices; it certainly would have sufficed in Jackson's case. But it is less satisfactory in cases like, for example, *Lang*, or others where if the "accused-patient" did the act with which he is charged, the grounds for his civil commitment as dangerous to others are strong, both in theory and practice, and if he did not they are not. It needs no extensive commentary to make the point that the base expectancy rate for Lang's dangerousness to others increases drastically if he killed the first woman as distinct from if he was not with her when she died.

22. By "unrestorable incompetent" I mean an accused found unfit for whom the court hearing that plea also finds that there is no reasonable likelihood of his ever becoming fit for trial or a person found unfit and sent for treatment to a mental hospital (or school for the deaf or similar special training facility) who does not respond to treatment or who at some point is seen as unlikely ever to be fit for trial, or who is treated for the maximum period authorized by the unfitness to plead statute and remains incompetent. The same problem arises in all these situations; for brevity of presentation all this is embraced in the phrase "unrestorable incompetent."

23. Ill. Rev. Stat., ch. 38, §§104–11.

Thus the *Jackson* rule, in a few serious cases of unrestorable incompetents, puts very great weight on the fact-finding processes in the civil commitment hearing. For this reason, in our 1967 article, which the ABA Commission on the Mentally Disabled relied on, Professor Burt and I argued that there were a few exceptional cases which the *Jackson* solution did not address satisfactorily and which should be taken to criminal trial under special rules of court.

Nevertheless, some states,[24] and some commentators[25] have rested content with the *Jackson* rule as dispositive of all cases, and the ABA Commission recommended this rule as its second preferred solution to the problem of the unrestorable incompetent.[26]

State legislatures may of course extend the rules of civil commitment to encompass the particular problems of the unrestorable incompetent. California, for example, has done this, meeting the terms of the *Jackson* ruling but so distorting its law relating to civil commitment as to evade the thrust of *Jackson*. California's Lankerman-Petris-Short Act (hereafter LPS) was amended in 1974 to add a new class of candidates for civil commitment,[27] namely, those who have been found incompetent to stand trial under the Penal Code and who have also been charged with a felony involving death, great bodily harm, or a serious threat to the physical well-being of another person. For these, year-to-year hearings may preserve their civil commitment status while the charge remains pending and their incompetency endures. The constitutionality of this scheme must remain in doubt;[28] but in any event it is a transparent and unprincipled legislative effort to avoid the clear

24. Va. Code Ann., §19.2-181 (Supp. 1976); W. Va. Code Ann., §27-6A-2 (Supp. 1974). Cf. Fla. Rev. Crim. Pro., §3.210 (1975); *In re* Florida Rules of Criminal Procedure, 272 So.2d 65 (Fla. 1972).

25. Group for the Advancement of Psychiatry, "Misuse of Psychiatry in the Criminal Courts: Competency to Stand Trial," Report No. 89, at 906–08 (February 1974); National Advisory Commission on Criminal Justice Standards and Goals, *Corrections* 131 (1973).

26. *Supra* note 5, at 631 and 645–46.

27. Cal. Stat., ch. 1511 (1974).

28. See Marjory Winston Parker, "California's New Scheme for the Commitment of Individuals Found Incompetent to Stand Trial," 6 *Pacific L. J.* 484 (1975).

moral precept of *Jackson* without interposing a full and public hearing of the facts relied on to justify the detention of the unrestorable incompetent.

To summarize concerning the first solution to our problem: the *Jackson* ruling, civil commitment or release, solves all but a few cases of unrestorable incompetents who may be serious dangers to others if they did indeed do the acts with which they are charged. It is a fair but perhaps insufficient response, placing too heavy a burden on civil commitment processes.

Because of that gap in the *Jackson* ruling and pursuant to the invitation in Mr. Justice Blackmun's opinion in *Jackson* for experimentation with this problem, Professor Burt and I recommended that the unrestorable incompetent thought to be a danger to others should be taken to trial under special rules of court designed so far as practicable to compensate for his physical or psychological adversities. I will not rehearse here the details of this recommendation, for they are amply analyzed in the report of the ABA Commission on the Mentally Disabled;[29] the broad contours of the argument will suffice.

A consequence of this solution to the problem of the unrestorable incompetent is that it fundamentally changes and simplifies the incompetency plea itself. Given this as the ultimate solution to the Jackson problem, Occam's Razor requires abrogation of the incompetency plea itself. It now has nothing to offer; it is pejorative and injurious without influence on the balance of authority and autonomy between the state and the citizen. The accused citizen has a right to be tried at his maximum level of competence to play the role of an accused person, provided he does not unduly delay trial. The state has the right to the best available fact-finding at criminal trials and to as competent an accused as possible for this purpose, subject to the accused's rights to bail and to a speedy trial. And both bail and speedy trial will have to bend to a degree to the need sometimes to treat in custody the psychologically or physically less competent accused to help him reach his maximum competence. All this can be conveniently and sensibly incorporated

29. *Supra* note 5, at 629–31 and 644–45.

into rules of court dealing with continuances. And a six-month continuance should define the normal outer limits for such a delay.[30] Thereafter, civil commitment or trial would ensue, with the state having the right to a deferred election on this question; so that if the "accused-patient" is civilly committed, a *nolle prosequi* follows as of right, and if he is not civilly committed, the state may proceed with the prosecution if it thinks this course socially desirable— and in some cases, such as Lang's, it would be.

Is this argument for the trial of the mentally ill meant to suggest that the accused's mental illness or retardation is irrelevant to the efficiency and fairness of a trial? Not at all. It goes no further than to urge that trial should be deferred to allow the mentally ill or retarded accused to be as fit mentally for trial as treatment in or out of a mental hospital (on bail or not) can make him, and that it may then be socially desirable to take him to trial with special rules of discovery, corroboration, jury warnings, and new trials designed to minimize his personal physical or mental disadvantages. If, after the continuance for treatment, he remains gravely impaired, civil commitment will normally adequately meet all society's needs for protection and the accused's needs for treatment; but in exceptional cases it will not be adequate, and then a criminal trial should follow, with a conviction, if it ensues, leading to sentencing cognizant of the special problems of sentencing the mentally ill discussed in chapter 4.

Putting aside questions of justice and social protection for a moment, are such trials unseemly and should they be repudiated

30. The Burt-Morris article, note 6 *supra*, makes the case for the six-month limitation on such a continuance. There are a very few cases where this would not suffice and which would meet the spirit of the *Jackson* rule for further training in custody. Assume a deaf-mute who was making steady progress in learning improved communication by sign language or other means; here a further continuance beyond six months would be in the interests of the state and of the accused. Legislation abolishing the incompetency plea, converting it into a new continuance, and providing for the trial of the unresolvable incompetent under special rules of court should encompass this rare case. One way would be to provide for an extension of the continuance period on the agreement of both prosecution and defense to such an extension.

on that ground alone? The vision of the idiot drooling before the court is conjured up (the accused in the Reichstag Fire), but it is unreal. The *nolle prosequi* remains in the discretion of the prosecutor. Where civil commitment is obvious and will clearly be for a protracted period quite apart from the alleged crime, the prosecutor should abandon the criminal charge, and thus dispose of the specter of the unseemly criminal trial. In that the competence of a defense rests more with the competence of the defense counsel than in any words by the accused, it will be in only the most exceptional case that seemliness will present a problem. And where it does—as perhaps it did in the case of Donald Lang, though I doubt it—there may be no proper avoidance of the necessity for a criminal trial. Further, it is well to remember that a civil commitment hearing is also a trial and that the seemliness problem is more frequent there—and tolerated.

Hence, just as in exceptional cases we take the amnesiac to criminal trial, and those whose memory fails them because of the long time between the events at issue and the trial (in the charming conceit of an English judge, "he is a man who has lost his diary or doesn't have one"), just as we take to trial one whose disruptive behavior precludes his physical presence (or run the trial with him in restraint), or as we pursue a criminal trial though important witnesses are dead or unavailable, so in exceptional circumstances and by carefully adapted means we should take some unrestorable incompetents to trial.

The argument for this course is strong; the impediment is constitutional. In *Pate v. Robinson*[31] the Supreme Court said that "the conviction of an accused person while he is legally incompetent violates due process," being inconsistent with the "constitutional right to a fair trial."[32] It seems somewhat more unfair to the accused to subject him to indeterminate civil commitment because he is unfit for trial, and hence the development of the third solution to the problem of the unrestorable incompetent which we will

31. 383 U.S. 375 (1966).
32. *Id.* at 378–85.

soon address. But is the *Pate v. Robinson* barrier as high as it at first seems? I think not.

In the first place the constitutional issue was clearly *obiter* in *Pate;* the statement in the previous paragraph that the trial of the legally incompetent is unconstitutional was clearly *dictum*. The ABA Commission is compelling on this point: "That the statement is *dictum*, not a holding, is certain because the state had conceded that issue."[33] The holding in *Pate* was that evidence raising the issue of incompetence entitled the defendant to a hearing on the issue— "failure to make such inquiry thus deprived Robinson of his constitutional right to a fair trial."[34] Providing for the trial of an incompetent would, therefore, not be inconsistent with the *Pate* holding. If such trials are held, *Pate* should apply and the right to a hearing on incompetency should be conducted. Upon a finding of unrestorable incompetence, the question should be whether the conduct of the trial is fair. The position taken herein is that, with appropriate safeguards, the conduct of the trial would be fair.[35]

In *Jackson* the Supreme Court hinted that the criminal trial of an unrestorable incompetent may be constitutionally acceptable: "We do not read this Court's previous decisions [citing *Pate v. Robinson*] to preclude the States from allowing, *at a minimum*, an incompetent defendant to raise certain defenses such as insufficiency of the indictment, or to make certain pretrial motions, through counsel."[36]

Hence, only *dicta* stand in the way; fairness, arguments by analogy, and a decent balance between the interests of the state and the accused speak strongly in some cases for the trial of the unrestorable incompetent. It is unlikely that the Supreme Court will stand in the way of such a sensible solution to a problem whose considerable difficulty the Court has so clearly recognized.

Before abandoning this preferred solution to the problem of the unrestorable incompetent, the report of the English Committee

33. *Id.* at 378.
34. *Id.* at 385.
35. *Supra* note 5, at 630 n.135.
36. 406 U.S. at 741 (emphasis added).

on Mentally Abnormal Offenders of October 1975,[37] the Butler Committee Report, merits consideration. That committee took the same view of the problem as did the ABA Commission on the Mentally Disabled, following the recommendation of the Burt-Morris article.[38] They recommended that a trial of the incompetent be deferred for a maximum of six months (actually, two periods of three months, an interstitial further hearing on incompetence to justify further deferment of trial being required after three months) and if the incompetence remains and the prosecution wishes to proceed, a trial should be conducted "to the fullest extent possible having regard to the medical condition of the defendant."[39]

The Butler Committee addressed one common objection to such a trial:

> It may be asked how the prosecution can establish their case if the defendant is unable to make a proper defense and in particular how they can prove intention in these circumstances. The answer is that intention is proved as it almost always is in court: by inference from the evidence of what the defendant did.[40]

If an acquittal followed such a trial the only possibility for detaining the defendant would be by civil commitment. What should follow a conviction? In my submission and that of the ABA Commission, ordinary sentencing powers, not including capital punishment, should apply, sensitized, one would hope, to the particular problems of sentencing the mentally ill. The Butler Committee took a different view and followed a path which as yet is, unfortunately, not available to my knowledge in this country.

In England and Wales, when a criminal is convicted and there is evidence that he is mentally ill or retarded, the sentencing court may make an order for his in-patient or out-patient treatment in a mental hospital "with or without a restriction order." The "re-

37. *Supra* note 7.
38. *Supra* note 6.
39. *Supra* note 7, at 150.
40. *Ibid.*

striction order" gives power to the home secretary to control trial and final release of the convicted person. The Butler Committee adapted these processes to convictions following trials of unrestorable incompetents, and recommended that the court be given "power to make any of the following social or medical orders":

(a) an order for in-patient treatment in a hospital with or without a restriction order;

(b) an order for hospital out-patient treatment;

(c) an order for forfeiture of any firearm, motor vehicle, etc., used in crime;

(d) a guardianship order;

(e) any disqualification (e.g., from driving) normally open to the court to make on conviction;

(f) discharge without any order.[41]

The differences between English and American practice in sentencing the mentally ill become apparent. The trial recommended by the Butler Committee is the same as that recommended in this chapter as the best solution to the problem of the unrestorable incompetent in this country; but the English committee varies its sentencing recommendation because: "[W]e cannot envisage any circumstances in which an overtly penal disposal— prison, borstal, or fine—would be suitable for such a defendant."[42] This difference in the recommendations of the two main committees, in the United States and in England, that have considered the problem of the unrestorable incompetent is of interest: they agree in principle to the necessity for criminal trials in some such cases, diverging in sentencing powers which reflect the more sophisticated powers given to the English judge in sentencing mentally ill criminals.

Let us turn now to the third and final solution offered to the problem of the unrestorable incompetent: the "innocent only" trial. The most extreme form of "innocent only" trial is that developed in Illinois, there called a "discharge hearing" and discussed in some detail in part IV(A) of this chapter. A more modest

41. *Id.* at 151.
42. *Ibid.*

form of "innocent only" trial was recommended as their third and least preferred alternative by the ABA Commission on the Mentally Disabled. Their reasons for offering this alternative were to "avoid both the uncertain constitutionality of proceeding to trial and distortion of the civil commitment process."[43] It is a *faute de mieux* solution, an unsatisfactory compromise; but it is finding acceptance in some states and must be considered even though it suffers what I regard as the fatal taint of intermingling the criminal-law and mental health powers of the state.

Here, in summary, is the procedure proposed: trial postponement up to 180 days to achieve competency; then, or earlier if competency is unlikely to be restored, the state must either dismiss with prejudice the charges against the defendant or file "a petition for evaluation." A petition for evaluation can be filed only if the defendant was charged with a crime involving serious bodily harm to another. Pursuant to the petition for evaluation a special commitment hearing will be held at which it must be established beyond reasonable doubt, that

> (a) the person sought to be committed did indeed perform the criminal act or acts specified (no mental disorder at the time of such act or acts is relevant to this finding)—this is the ABA version of the "innocent only" trial; and
>
> (b) that he "presents a substantial risk of serious bodily harm to others, such risk being defined as a substantial probability that in the foreseeable future he will inflict serious unjustified bodily harm on others as evidenced by conduct attempting, threatening, or inflicting such harm."[44]

This is, of course, a manifest blending of the two powers, dodging the safeguards of each. The ABA's proposal is cautious in that it limits the special commitment to a period of 90 days, with subsequent renewals for 180 days each, the total period of commitment not to exceed three years or to extend beyond the date the defendant would have become eligible for parole had he been convicted and given the maximum sentence. This three-year lim-

43. *Supra* note 5, at 631.
44. *Id*. at 646.

itation is not found in the Illinois legislation (see below) or in other states that have followed this path.[45]

It would be burdensome to rehash the arguments. The "innocent only" trial leading to detention related to the term imposable pursuant to the original charge against the unrestorable incompetent may succeed in avoiding the constitutional obstacle on which Indiana foundered in *Jackson*, but it skirts the spirit of that decision and is an unprincipled blending of two great powers of the state leading to the protracted incarceration of one who has been neither found guilty of a crime nor found to be mentally ill at a level to justify civil commitment.

A short reply might be: if the "innocent only" trial protects the citizen as well as your preferred criminal trial with special rules of court to compensate for the defendant's disabilities, of what do you complain? Is this not straining at a gnat? I think not. I doubt that the "innocent only" trial can be made as fair as the customary trial procedures varied to compensate for the accused's disabilities, and, in the last resort, I believe, the combination of evidence of the crime and prediction of future dangerousness will be devastating. Strongly supportive of this view is the fact that the ABA Commission recommends these identical commitment processes—petitioning for evaluation and a special commitment hearing—with identical standards of proof and evidentiary rules for one found unrestorably incompetent and one found not guilty by reason of insanity.

III. The Abolition of the Special Defense of Insanity

Abolition of the defense of insanity has received exhaustive attention in the literature; the informed reader is entitled, therefore, to be notified of where the argument leads so that he may avoid the sharper irritations of redundancy. In accordance with the thesis of separation of the mental health law and the criminal-law powers to incarcerate, I propose the abolition of the special defense of insanity. A fall-back alternative position, in no way conflicting with the separation thesis, is for the abolition of the special defense and

45. Ill. Rev. Stat., ch. 38, §§104-17–18 (Supp. 1980).

for legislative substitution of a qualified defense of diminished responsibility to a charge of murder having the effect, if successful, of a conviction of manslaughter with the usual sentencing discretion attached to that crime.

The argument will be presented in broad perspective, the nuances of difference between the competing defenses of insanity being glossed over. The sequence will be (a) the general argument for abolition, (b) an analysis of how the law would operate under the proposed abolition and the alternative substitution of diminished responsibility, and (c) a consideration and repudiation of the main criticisms of the abolition proposal.

The problem is to cut through the accumulated cases, commentaries, and confusions to the issues of principle underlying the responsibility of the mentally ill for conduct otherwise criminal. The issues are basically legal, moral, and political, not medical or psychological, though, of course, the developing insights of psychiatry and psychology are of close relevance to those legal, moral, and political issues.

A glance at the history of the common-law relationship between guilt and mental illness may help to structure the discussion. Until the nineteenth century, criminal-law doctrines of *mens rea* (criminal intent) handled the entire problem. Evidence of mental illness was admitted on the question of intent, and as the infant discipline of psychiatry claimed an increased understanding of mental processes such evidence on the question of intent grew in importance. Psychiatrists, then generally known as "alienists" (separating, alienating, the citizen from the community because of mental illness), claimed increasing competence to classify, explain the origins, and predict the course of mental illnesses, with and without diverse treatment interventions. The dramatic events of major criminal trials became important battlegrounds for psychiatry and psychiatrists, public dramatic ceremonials in which professional standing was proclaimed and tested. Inexorably, conflict developed between the disciplines of law and psychiatry with their distinct supporting epistemologies, the language and concepts of the law—free will, moral choice, guilt, and innocence—confronting those of psychiatry—determinism, degrees of cognitive and volitional control, classification of diseases, and definition of treatments. Complicating these inherent confrontations were the different consequences of the application of the two competing systems: the binary system of the law, guilt or innocence, and, if the former, punishment to close the equation; the continuum of psychiatry, degrees of illness and opportunities for "cure," to be determined in the last resort only by the fact of nondestructive life in the community.

In a multipurposive society these epistemological and purposive differences between law and psychiatry are to be welcomed but they carried, and still carry, the seeds of confusion. The pre-*McNaughtan* position was correct and clear: the psychiatrist could contribute useful evidentiary insights to the issues correctly defined by the common law of crime—did the accused intend the prohibited harm? But by the time of *McNaughtan* (1843) this clear position was frustrated by the increasing tendency of lawyers, psychiatrists, public opinion, and legislators to turn questions of evidence into matters of substance, to transmute medical evidence about legal issues into substantive legal rules. *McNaughtan* was just such a substantive rule, confusing the evidence for a proposition with the proposition itself.

How would the pre-nineteenth-century position now stand, taking into account advances in the discipline of psychiatry? The sick mind of the accused would be relevant to his guilt since he may, because of sickness, have lacked the state of mind required for conviction of the offense with which he has been charged or of any other offense of which he may be convicted on such a charge (in the language of the trade, "lesser included offenses"). If guilty of such a crime, his sick mind is relevant to fair sentencing.[46] If innocent, that is all the criminal law has to do with the matter though, of course, like any other citizen he may be civilly committed if he is mentally ill and is a danger to himself or others or is incapable of caring for himself. On many of these issues the psychiatrist has useful insights; on none should psychiatry frame the operative rule, define the dividing line between guilt and

46. See chap. 4, *infra*.

innocence, between detention and freedom. Whenever this happens, the law is perverted in practice, and psychiatry is brought into disrepute. The English and American judges went wrong in the nineteenth century; it is time we returned to older and truer principles.

I must stress that in advocating the abolition of the special defense of insanity, the nuances of difference among the *McNaughtan* Rules, the *Durham* Rule, the rules offered by the American Law Institute and accepted in *Brawner* and in many state criminal codes, the irresistible impulse test, the recommendations of the Group for the Advancement of Psychiatry, and other suggested special defenses, though important in practice and meriting close analysis, are not essential to the present discussion. All vary around the following structure: a definition of mental illness, as a threshold to the invocation of the defense, and a statement of a required causal relationship between that "mental illness" and the otherwise criminal behavior of the accused. My thesis stands, whatever definition of illness and whatever language to capture a causal relationship are offered. And, of course, variations on where the burdens of proof are placed on those two issues, and on how heavy are those burdens, are also irrelevant.

It would be a mistake to read these dogmatisms as an attack on psychiatry. The lawyers have been quite content to strap a mattress to the back of any psychiatrist willing to appear in court to answer questions like: at the time of the killing did the accused "know the nature and quality of the act"? did he "know that it was wrong"? did he have "substantial capacity to appreciate the criminality of his conduct"? did he have "substantial capacity to control his conduct"? Wiser psychiatrists and those not tempted by the bright focus of public interest have avoided these philosophically impossible questions. Nor does it assist materially to direct the psychiatrist to give information to the jury to help them answer these elusive questions but to avoid offering answers himself,[47] since it is the questions themselves that are philosophically

47. See Washington v. U.S., 390 F.2d 444 (1967) and Judge Bazelon's directions to the psychiatrist later expressly approved in U.S. v. Brawner, 471 F.2d 969.

in error that pretend to a precision beyond present knowledge.

Why, then, go beyond the simple rule, to give mental illness the same exculpatory effect as, say, blindness or deafness? Evidence of the latter afflictions may be admitted as indicative of lack of both the *actus reus* (prohibited act)[48] and the *mens rea* of a crime. Why go further? The answer lies in the pervasive moral sense that when choice to do ill is lacking, it is improper to impute guilt.[49] And hence there is pressure for a special defense of insanity, just as there is pressure for a special defense of infancy or duress. Let us consider what has been offered by way of larger statements of the ends to be served by a special defense of insanity.

The major commissions of inquiry in the United States and in England have been less than compelling on the underlying justifications of this defense. Here is the American Law Institute's rationale for the special defense of insanity which now dominates the field:

> What is involved specifically is the drawing of a line between the use of public agencies and public force to *condemn* the offender by conviction, with resultant sanctions in which there is inescapably a punitive ingredient (however constructive we may attempt to make the process of correction) and modes of disposition in which that ingredient is absent, even though restraint may be involved. To put the matter differently, the problem is to discriminate between the cases where a punitive-correctional disposition is appropriate and those in which a medical-custodial disposition is the only kind that the law should allow.[50]

This seems to me descriptive of what is to be done and not at all a justification of the doing.

The justification for the special defense of insanity offered by the English Royal Commission on Capital Punishment carries the matter no further. It says it has long been so; therefore it should continue to be. Should you doubt me, here are the commission's words:

48. See chap. 3, *infra*.

49. See Leventhal, J., in Brawner, 471 F.2d 969, 984 (1972).

50. American Law Institute, Model Penal Code, §4.01 Comment (Tentative Draft 4, 1955).

It has for centuries been recognized that, if a person was, at the time of his unlawful act, mentally so disordered that it would be unreasonable to impute guilt to him, he ought not to be held liable to conviction and punishment under the criminal law. Views have changed and opinions have differed, as they differ now, about the standards to be applied in deciding whether an individual should be exempted from criminal responsibility for this reason; but the principle has been accepted without question.[51]

The Butler Committee Report[52] in 1975 expressly accepted this "reason is since reason long has been" argument[53] even though, in their words, "the insanity defense is in fact almost unheard of nowadays," which, as we shall see, is the present situation in England. They regarded retention of a special defense as "right in principle"[54] though they carefully eschewed any definition of that principle, but they so whittled away the defense in practice in England as to make it a quaint historical survival rather than a contemporary and operative rule of law.

In *Durham*, Judge Bazelon put the matter curtly and clearly: "Our collective conscience does not allow punishment where it cannot impose blame."[55] Such a rationale claims too much, assumes our possession of finely calibrated moral scales, and flies in the face of observation of the dross daily work of our criminal courts. It is hortatory rather than descriptive but it does state a justification that a generous mind may accept as an aim though doubt as a reality.

Historically, of course, the special defense made good sense in relation to one punishment. Capital punishment infused it with meaning. But even perfervid advocates of capital punishment do not favor the execution of the mentally ill, and this justification

51. Royal Commission on Capital Punishment, 1949–53 Report, Cmd. 8932, at 98 (1953).

52. *Supra* note 7.

53. *Id.*, §18.2 at 216 and §18.10 at 219.

54. *Id.*, §18.10 at 219.

55. 214 F.2d 862, 876 (D.C. Cir. 1954).

for the special defense is now sufficiently covered by the rules and practices of sentencing.

One is left, therefore, with the feeling that the special defense is a genuflection to a deep-seated moral sense that the mentally ill lack freedom of choice to guide and govern their conduct and that therefore blame should not be imputed to them for their otherwise criminal acts nor should punishment be imposed. To the validity of this argument we will several times return, but it is important not to assume that those who advocate the abolition of the special defense of insanity are recommending the wholesale punishment of the sick. They are urging rather that mental illness be given the same exculpatory effect as other adversities that bear upon criminal guilt. And they add the not unfair criticism of the conventional position that they observe the widespread conviction and punishment of the mentally ill, the special defense being an ornate rarity, a tribute to our capacity to pretend to a moral position while pursuing profoundly different practices.

The number held as not guilty by reason of insanity in the United States as a whole and in some states will illustrate the relative rarity of the special defense. Nationally, in the 1978 census of state and federal facilities, 3,140 persons were being held as not guilty by reason of insanity.[56] In Illinois, at the time of writing, 127 are so held. In New York, between 1965 and 1976 inclusive, 278 persons were found not guilty by reason of insanity (53 in the first five years, 225 in the second six years—the increase being explicable presumably by constitutionally imposed relaxation of the *Brawner* rules for, and processes of, releasing those found not guilty by reason of insanity). No one acquainted with the work of the criminal courts can think that these numbers remotely approximate the relationship between serious mental illness and criminal conduct. The defense is pleaded only where it may be advantageous to the accused and that balance of advantage fluctuates with sentencing practice and rules and practices relating to

56. Steadman, Monahan, Hartstone, Davis & Clark, "Mentally Disordered Offenders: A National Survey of Patients and Facilities," *Law and Human Behavior* (in press).

the release of those found not guilty by reason of insanity. Hence statistics will not lead us to principle in this matter; a more fundamental inquiry is necessary.

A useful entering wedge to principle is to inquire, What is the irreducible minimum relationship between mental illness and criminal guilt? What is the least the criminal law could do in this matter?

It is unthinkable that mental illness should be given a lesser reach than drunkenness. If a given mental condition (intent, recklessness) is required for the conviction of a criminal offense, then, as a proposition requiring no discussion, in the absence of that mental condition there can be no conviction. This holds true whether the absence of that condition is attributable to blindness, deafness, drunkenness, mental illness or retardation, linguistic difficulties, or, if it could be established, hypnotic control. But this states basic principles of criminal law, not a special defense. The main reasons for defining a "special defense" beyond the traditional common-law relationship between mental illness and the *actus reus* and *mens rea* of crime are, I think, twofold: expediency in crime control and fairness.

The expediency rationale can be quickly advanced and disposed of; the fairness rationale is more difficult.

In an important article in 1963, "Abolish 'The Insanity Defense'—Why Not?"[57] J. Goldstein and J. Katz accurately perceived that "the insanity defense is not a defense, it is a device for triggering indeterminate restraint"[58] of those who were mentally ill at the time of the crime but are not civilly committable now. In considerable part, that has been its role since 1800 when the emergence of the special defense in England led to the Criminal Lunatics Act of 1800,[59] which provided indeterminate custody for those found not guilty by reason of insanity, with similar legislation spreading in the states and federal systems in this country.

57. 72 *Yale L. J.* 853 (1963).
58. *Id.* at 868.
59. 39 & 40 Geo. 3, c.94.

Few are prepared any longer to justify the special defense on this crime control basis, as a means of confining the dangerous though not civilly committable. It would be a strange "defense," an unusual benevolence, whose purpose is confinement of those who could not otherwise be confined.

Hence we are brought to the central issue—the question of fairness, the sense that it is unjust and unfair to stigmatize the mentally ill as criminals and to punish them for their crimes. The criminal law exists to deter and to punish those who would or who do choose to do wrong. If they cannot exercise choice, they cannot be deterred and it is a moral outrage to punish them.[60] The argument sounds powerful but its premise is weak.

Choice is neither present nor absent in the typical case where the insanity defense is currently pleaded; what is at issue is the degree of freedom of choice on a continuum from the hypothetically entirely rational to the hypothetically pathologically determined—in states of consciousness neither polar condition exists.

The moral issue sinks into the sands of reality. Certainly it is true that in a situation of total absence of choice it is outrageous to inflict punishment; but the frequency of such situations to the problems of criminal responsibility becomes an issue of fact in which tradition and clinical knowledge and practice are in conflict. The traditions of being possessed of evil spirits, of being bewitched, confront the practices of a mental health system which increasingly

60. Arguments for the retention of the special defense of insanity as a moral foundation of the criminal law are offered by Herbert Wechsler (see, for example, 37 F.R.D. 365 (2d Cir. 1964)) and by Sanford Kadish ("The Decline of Innocence," 26 Camb. L. J. 273 (1968)). A more cautious support of retention is advanced by Francis A. Allen (Law, Intellect and Education, at 114–18 (1979)). Contrary views, generally supporting the abolitionist position taken in this chapter, are advanced by H. L. A. Hart, Chief Justice Weintraub, Lady Barbara Wooton, Joel Feinberg, Dr. Seymour Halleck, and Dr. Thomas Szasz. (Their views are summarized in the appendix to N. Morris, "Psychiatry and the Dangerous Criminal," 41 S. Cal. L. Rev. 514 (1968), prepared by Gary Lowenthal; see n.13 of that article). The lists of those favoring abolition lengthens with the Butler Committee Report (see note 7 supra) and the Carnahan Report (see note 69 infra), as well as the apparently unending debates of the various proposals for a Federal Criminal Code.

fashions therapeutic practices to hold patients responsible for their conduct. And suppose we took the moral argument seriously and eliminated responsibility in those situations where we thought there had been a substantial impairment of the capacity to choose between crime and no crime (I set aside problems of strict liability and of negligence for the time being). Would we not have to, as a matter of moral fairness, fashion a special defense of gross social adversity? The matter might be tested by asking which is the more criminogenic, psychosis or serious social deprivation? In an article in 1968 on this topic I raised the question of whether there should be a special defense of dwelling in a black ghetto.[61] Some literal-minded commentators castigated me severely for such a recommendation, mistaking a form of argument, the *reductio ad absurdum*, for a recommendation. But let me again press the point. If one were asked how to test the criminogenic effect of any factor in man or in the environment, the answer would surely follow empirical lines. One would measure and try to isolate the impact of that factor on behavior, with particular reference to criminal behavior. To isolate genetic pressure toward crime one might pursue twin studies or cohort studies, one might look at patterns of adoption and the criminal behavior of natural fathers and adoptive fathers and see whether they were related to the criminal behavior of their children.[62] Somewhat similar measuring techniques would be followed if one were trying to search out the relationship between unemployment and criminality, or a Bowlby-like study of the effects of maternal separation or maternal deprivation on later criminal behavior. Our answers to the question of the determining effects of such conditions would be found empirically and not in a priori arguing about their relationships to crime, though there may be ample room for argument involved in the empirical studies.

Hence, at first blush, it seems a perfectly legitimate correlational and, I submit, causal inquiry, whether psychosis, or any

61. Morris, note 60 *supra*.
62. Mednick & Volovka, "Biology and Crime," in 2 *Crime and Justice* (N. Morris & M. Tonry, eds., 1980).

particular type of psychosis, is more closely related to criminal behavior than, say, being born to a one-parent family living on welfare in a black inner-city area. And there is no doubt of the empirical answer. Social adversity is grossly more potent in its pressure toward criminality, certainly toward all forms of violence and street crime as distinct from white-collar crime, than is any psychotic condition. As a factual matter, the exogenous pressures are very much stronger than the endogenous.

But the argument feels wrong. Surely there is more to it than the simple calculation of criminogenic impact. Is this unease rationally based? I think not, though the question certainly merits further consideration. As a rational matter it is hard to see why one should be more responsible for what is done to one than for what one is. Yet major contributors to jurisprudence and criminal-law theory insist that it is necessary to maintain the denial of responsibility on grounds of mental illness to preserve the moral infrastructure of the criminal law.[63] For many years I have struggled with this opinion by those whose work I deeply respect, yet I remain unpersuaded. Indeed, they really don't try to persuade, but rather affirm and reaffirm with vehemence and almost mystical sincerity the necessity of retaining the special defense of insanity as a moral prop to the entire criminal law.

And indeed I think that much of the discussion of the defense of insanity is the discussion of a myth rather than of a reality. It is no minor debating point that in fact we lack a defense of insanity as an operating tool of the criminal law other than in relation to a very few particularly heinous and heavily punished offenses. There is not an operating defense of insanity in relation to burglary or theft, or the broad sweep of index crimes generally; the plea of not guilty on the ground of insanity is rarely to be heard in city courts of first instance which handle the grist of the mill of the criminal law—though a great deal of pathology is to be seen in the parade of accused and convicted persons before these courts. As a practical matter we reserve this defense for a few sensational cases where it may be in the interest of the accused either to

63. See note 60 *supra*.

escape the possibility of capital punishment (though in cases where serious mental illness is present, the risk of execution is slight) or where the likely punishment is of a sufficient severity to make the indeterminate commitment of the accused a preferable alternative to a criminal conviction. Operationally the defense of insanity is a tribute, it seems to me, to our hypocrisy rather than to our morality.

To be less aggressive about the matter and to put aside anthropomorphic allegations of hypocrisy, the special defense of insanity may properly be indicted as producing a morally unsatisfactory classification on the continuum between guilt and innocence. It applies in practice to only a few mentally ill criminals, thus omitting many others with guilt-reducing relationships between their mental illness and their crime; it excludes other powerful pressures on human behavior, thus giving excessive weight to the psychological over the social. It is a false classification in the sense that if a team of the world's most sensitive and trained psychiatrists and moralists were to select from all those found guilty of felonies and those found not guilty by reason of insanity any given number who should not be stigmatized as criminals, very few of those found not guilty by reason of insanity would be selected. How to offer proof of this? The only proof, I regret, is to be found by personal contact with a flow of felony cases through the courts and into the prisons. No one of serious perception will fail to recognize both the extent of mental illness and retardation among the prison population and the overwhelming weight of adverse social circumstances on criminal behavior. This is, of course, not an argument that social adversities should lead to acquittals; they should be taken into account in sentencing. And the same is true of the guilt and sentencing of those pressed by psychological adversities. The special defense is thus a morally false classification. And it is a false classification also in the sense that it does not select from the prison population those most in need of psychiatric treatment.

It may help to resolve these moral complexities to consider briefly how the law would work in practice were the special defense abolished, and then to offer an acceptable compromise position for those who strain at the simple solution of abolition.

Were the special defense abolished, mental illness would remain relevant and admissible on the question of the *actus reus* of crime. These questions are illustrated in chapter 3, "The Planter's Dream." They are rare situations but when they occur, acquittal is the proper verdict since the criminal law can seek to control only voluntary acts and not those achieved in fugue states. Manifestly, the epileptic in a *grand mal* whose clonic movements strike and injure another commits no crime; but we need no special defense of insanity to reach that result, well-established *actus reus* doctrines suffice.

The *mens rea* question is more complex though the principle is easy to state: evidence of mental illness is admissible to show that the accused lacked the prohibited *mens rea*. For states of mind defined as "purpose" or "intent" there is no analytic difficulty. For "recklessness," insofar as a definition of "recklessness" requires that it be shown that the accused in fact foresaw the risk of this type of harm, there is again no analytic difficulty; but when recklessness" may be achieved by "gross negligence," by failure to live up to an objective standard of care, then difficulties do come in the abolition position which will be addressed later in this chapter. But in the broad run of cases, certainly in those where the special defense is now pleaded, ordinary *mens rea* principles can well carry the freight.

One interesting aspect of the relationship between *mens rea* and mental illness was prescribed by the American Law Institute and widely copied by those states that have relied on the Model Penal Code in framing their criminal codes. For example, Illinois was in 1961 the first state to build its criminal law on the American Law Institute Model and in section 9-2-(b) of the Criminal Code provided:

> A person who intentionally or knowingly kills an individual
> commits voluntary manslaughter if at the time of the killing he
> believes the circumstances to be such that, if they existed,
> would justify or exonerate the killing under the principles stated
> in Article 7 of this Code, but his belief is unreasonable.[64]

64. Ill. Rev. Stat., ch. 38, §9-2(b).

Two

The relevance to mental illness is immediately obvious. Mental illness may well lead an accused person to believe he has justification for his conduct when objectively this is not the case. Unless that belief be disproved beyond reasonable doubt by the prosecution, one accused of murder having such a belief will be convicted of manslaughter and sentenced accordingly, taking into account his mental illness in sentencing.[65]

It must be admitted that the mental illness–*mens rea* relationship can be corrupted and confounded, as can most other legal doctrines, and that it has been corrupted and confounded in a line of California cases, *Wells-Gorshen-Conley-White*.[66] Sound principle, that mental illness may be relevant to disproving the presence of a state of mind necessary to first degree murder or necessary to the "malice aforethought" that is the distinguishing characteristic of murder in California, has been pushed to an unacceptable complexity and confusion in the law of homicide in that state. It is not necessary here to trace those developments; the largest part of the difficulty these cases present is to be found in the central role still accorded "malice aforethought" in the California doctrine of "diminished capacity" and in the elusive emphases given in *Gorshen* and *Conley* to the accused's capacity to identify to some degree with the suffering of his victim as a precondition to the full possession of a prohibited mental state. Structures of talmudic complexity have been built around the relationship between mental illness and "malice aforethought"; the problem is readily avoidable by the clear definitions of the *mens rea* of crime being followed throughout the common-law world by all law-reform commissions and legislatures acquainted with the work of the American Law Institute's Model Penal Code. This relationship between mental illness and *mens rea* has in various formulations been judicially

65. This relationship links closely to the alternative proposal of diminished responsibility discussed hereunder.

66. People v. Wells, 33 Cal.2d 330, 202 P.2d 53 (1949), *cert. denied*, 338 U.S. 863 (1949); People v. Gorshen, 51 Cal.2d 761, 336 P.2d 492 (1959); People v. Conley, 64 Cal.2d 310, 411 P.2d 911, 49 Cal. Rptr. 815 (1966); People v. White, 117 Cal. App. 2d 270, 172 Cal. Rptr. 612 (Cal. Ct. App. 1981).

recognized in twenty-one states, in the federal system, and in the District of Columbia.[67]

The California case law on this topic has, regrettably, often been confused with the doctrine of diminished responsibility offered as an alternative proposal in this chapter, although in fact that doctrine lies closer in practice to provisions like section 9-2-(b) of the Illinois Code earlier discussed.

No state has as yet accepted the central proposal in this chapter. Many commentators support it, many oppose it;[68] many federal and state legislative bills have been drafted incorporating its thesis. Its time will come. At present, unsatisfactory compromises like those in Michigan, Indiana, and Illinois of "guilty but mentally ill," considered hereunder, are in vogue, but they are unprincipled. The two commissions of inquiry—one in England and one in New York—have not accepted the abolitionist position in its entirety but they have moved far toward it.

The Butler Committee in 1975 recommended the substantial reduction of the reach of the special defense, placing their main reliance on diminished responsibility to solve the problems with which that defense was meant to grapple. To closely similar effect, but going further in the direction of complete abolition of the special defense than the Butler Committee did, a report entitled "The Insanity Defense in New York" made in 1978 by a distinguished committee and prepared under the direction of William A. Carnahan, deputy commissioner and counsel to the New York Department of Mental Hygiene (hereinafter the Carnahan Report), recommended the abolition of the special defense of insanity and the adoption of a rule of "diminished capacity under which evidence of abnormal mental condition would be admissible to affect the degree of crime for which an accused could be convicted."[69]

The Butler Committee recommended the retention of a special defense of insanity in a few very rare cases of "severe mental

67. See the Carnahan Report (text at n.69 *infra*), at 144 n.15.
68. For a summary statement of these views in 1968, see Morris, note 60 *supra*, the appendix by Gary Lowenthal, and see n.13 of that article.
69. *Op. cit.*, at 9.

illness" and "severe subnormality." They recommended, "a specific exemption from conviction of any defendant who, at the time of the act or omission charged, was suffering from severe mental illness or severe subnormality . . . notwithstanding technical proof of *mens rea*."[70] The Butler Committee definitions of "severe mental illness" and "severe subnormality" are extensive and difficult.[71] They certainly narrowly confine the defense. And part of the reason for the Butler Committee compromise here is the statistical reality of what has happened in England and Wales to the special defense of insanity pursuant to the legislative introduction of diminished responsibility in the Homicide Act of 1957. That Act provided in section 2(1):

> Where a person kills or is party to the killing of another, he shall not be convicted of murder if he was suffering from such abnormality of mind . . . as substantially impaired his mental responsibility for his acts and omissions in doing or being a party to the killing.

Prior to 1957, of all persons committed for trial for murder in England about 20 percent were found unfit to stand trial and diverted from criminal process and about 20 percent were found not guilty by reason of insanity (the terminology is adapted from English to American usage). As that Act has had its impact, by the late 1970s, about 2 percent are unfit and diverted, less than 1 percent are found not guilty by reason of insanity, and about 37 percent fall under the diminished responsibility provisions.[72]

The same thing would happen in this country. The Butler Committee's recommendation of a restricted retention of a special defense of insanity is thus almost a *de minimis* inconsequential recognition of an extremely severely mentally ill or retarded group who need not be brought within criminal processes.

---

70. *Supra* note 7, at 222.
71. *Id.* at 229 and app. 10.
72. These figures are adapted from app. 9 of the Butler Committee Report, itself relying on 1 Nigel Walker, *Crime and Insanity in England* 159 (1968).

There are three points to be made in favor of a legislatively introduced rule of "diminished responsibility" in this country of the type now well tested by English juries.

First, for some exceptional murder charges *mens rea* principles and even rules like the Illinois 9-2-(b) may not suffice to reduce murder to manslaughter in cases where such a reduction is desirable. I hypothesize an accused who is clearly psychotic and paranoiac believing he is commanded by God to kill, as Hadfield and some others have believed. He has heard voices to that effect and is in no doubt of his moral duty. He probably does not fall within any *mens rea* provisions which would reduce his crime from murder to manslaughter (unless one sets out on the unacceptable path of California case law) and does not fall within analogues of Illinois section 9-2-(b) since he does not believe he has a defense to a criminal charge. Yet such cases are, it is submitted, better treated and sentenced as manslaughter than as murder. A legislative provision modeled on the English Homicide Act of 1957 would achieve that result.

Secondly, where states impose mandatory sentences on those convicted of murder, some escape mechanisms from those sentences for the mentally ill (other than frustration by charge bargaining) is desirable. The evil to be remedied here lies in the mandatory sentence, not in the criminal law relating to mentally ill criminals; but the only politically acceptable remedy may be legislative enunciation of a doctrine of diminished responsibility.

Thirdly, diminished responsibility is, on close analysis, apart from the two special problems in the two previous paragraphs, a shift of sentencing discretion to a degree from judge to jury, the jury under diminished responsibility lowering the maximum (and sometimes the minimum) sentencing range within which the judge will impose sentence. In some states there may be advantages in such a limitation of judicial discretion.

I now try to draw the analysis to a close. For the reasons offered above I urge the legislative abolition of the special defense of insanity. For those who find persuasive the three reasons last offered for a special legislatively introduced doctrine of diminished responsibility to flush out ordinary *mens rea* doctrines I recommend a formula akin to that in the English Homicide Act of 1957 with the accused who falls within it being convicted of and sentenced for manslaughter, his sentence taking into account his mental illness at the time of the crime.

There remain for consideration three lines of criticism of these recommendations which have not been adequately presented or responded to so far in this chapter, namely, (a) mental illness and the lesser degrees of *mens rea;* (b) the trial as a public morality play; and (c) the constitutionality of abolition.

Mental illness and the lesser degrees of mens rea. When the criminal law embraces negligence liability and strict liability, the message to the accused is that he must fall for the common good. Clearly one cannot lapse into moral fault by failure to recognize the existence of a risk of injury to another or to property; the argument for conviction in these cases is opportunistic not moral: The processes of the law cannot stay to test the difficult question of whether the accused did or did not recognize the risk. The injury has occurred. In negligence liability the average person would have recognized the risk and that for us satisfies his liability; in strict liability the prohibited event has occurred, and that suffices for his liability if he indeed did it, whether he knew about it or not.

There are both a considerable literature and many cases supportive of negligence and strict liability in the criminal law. Problems of proof of higher degrees of criminal intent are often intractable, and when the circumstances of the prohibited event are peculiarly within the cognizance of the accused and the public injury is substantial, a case can be made for both these degrees of *mens rea* as sufficient to support criminal liability.

Does the mentally ill accused stand in any different situation in relation to his liability for crimes of negligence and of strict liability? Some have argued that *mens rea* doctrines can achieve justice for the mentally ill in crimes requiring purpose or intent, which involve proof of subjective prescription of the prohibited harm, but not for lesser degrees of *mens rea*. It is an awkward as distinct from a difficult argument to meet. That the mentally ill are in no worse situation than others who, because of stupidity or because of preoccupation with matrimonial conflict or because of a wide variety of distractions, have failed to live up to the assumed norm of perception and care is an accurate if curt reply and should suffice; there is equality in injustice.

The truth is that there should be neither negligence liability nor strict liability in the criminal law, whatever the social injury risked and whatever the modesty of the penalty imposed. A rational system, considerate of the need to use the great engine of criminal guilt and punishment parsimoniously and with moral sensitivity, would manipulate the onus and burden of proof in these cases to allow the accused who had fallen below statutorily imposed norms of care to explain that failure and the law would define what would be satisfactory explanations. But that is neither the rule nor the practice in a busy world and it is hard to see why a special rule to that effect should be made for the mentally ill if it is not available to other "innocents" convicted of crimes of negligence or strict liability.

One might argue that negligence and strict liability of the mentally ill are *de minimis* problems best solved by police and prosecutorial discretion. But that view is less confidently taken in relation to certain problems of reckless liability, in particular, reckless homicide. Whenever recklessness statutorily or by common law suffices for manslaughter and includes what has come to be called "gross negligence," that is to say, a substantial departure from an acceptable standard of care in which it is not necessary (as it is under those codes which follow the ALI's Model Penal Code definition of recklessness) to prove that the accused in fact recognized the risk and persisted in running it, the mentally ill are at risk for manslaughter convictions which many would think unjust.

The point was nicely made in a debate between Chief Justice Weintraub of New Jersey and Professor Herbert Wechsler in a conference of the Federal Second Circuit.[73] Chief Justice Weintraub had advanced an argument for the abolition of the special defense

73. 37 F.R.D. 365 at 381 (2d Cir. 1964).

of insanity; Professor Wechsler, the major architect of the Model Penal Code, took a contrary view. He sought to tear at the heartstrings of the assembled judges by asking them to suppose their arteriosclerotic father were in a hospital. The father experiences a delusion and in his anguish knocks over a lamp, causing a fire and killing an attendant. Are the judges really ready to accept that the father should in these circumstances be convicted of a homicide?

It was stimulating material for a conference, but surely consciously convoluted pleading by the leading American theoretician of the criminal law. Without reflection, it is clear that the offense is not murder. Can there be a manslaughter conviction? If the hypothetical events occurred in a state where manslaughter requires Model Penal Code recklessness as its minimum *mens rea*, then there can be no manslaughter conviction. If they occurred in a jurisdiction where gross negligence suffices, then there can be a conviction since there is considerable and compelling authority that abnormalities of mind cannot be included in weighing the negligence equation. In such a jurisdiction the elderly hypothetical father of the Second Circuit judges may be so convicted, his mental condition being taken into account in sentencing him. It is a grave injustice even though the accused is morally indistinguishable from others who would similarly be unjustly convicted though suffering deficiencies of intelligence, adversities of social circumstance which have led to overswift reactions, and a variety of other ills to which the flesh and life of man is prey. But the solution to this difficulty of mental illness and the lesser degrees of *mens rea* is, as I say, awkward rather than difficult, since it is clearly to be found in the general processes of reform of the substantive criminal law and of its supportive rules of evidence. Of course, in the interim, the problem is easily solved by a sensible use of prosecutorial discretion.

The trial as a public morality play. The whole argument for abolition of the insanity defense is misconceived, it might be argued. These trials have little to do with the accused; he is highly likely to be protractedly incarcerated whatever the outcome and it doesn't matter much where. The thesis is disingenuous, the criticism would continue; it fails to appreciate the larger function of the sensational trials of mad murderers and insane assassins. They

are the modern "Everyman"; they are public morality plays, spec-
tacles, moral circuses for the masses to educate them in virtue and
in moral sensitivity. For mass consumption they distinguish the
mad from the bad, even though on close analysis that is a philosophically impossible trick to perform.

It is not easy to respond to such high-flying rhetoric except
to reject it as a prescription. As a description it has truth but I
doubt strongly that community moral values are in any way
strengthened by the more publicized insanity defenses. At the time
of writing, John Hinckley, who shot President Reagan and most
seriously injured James Brady, is about to go to trial, the announced
defense being that of insanity. One wonders what social purposes
are to be served by what will indeed be a massively publicized
performance. The reputations of several psychiatrists and lawyers
will be made, their fee scales enhanced. Passionate and ill-informed
discussion will engulf dinner tables throughout the country. Hinckley will not be at large for many years. He clearly planned and
intended to shoot the President. His need for psychiatric assistance
may or may not be real and lasting; if it is, we should see that he
gets it. But the interstitial orgy of psychiatric moralizing seems of
no social utility.

Lurking within this rhetorically overblown argument may be
a more subtle and difficult point. It may be argued that, in addition
to deterrent purposes, criminal trials and convictions have another
important purpose, that of dramatically and formally affirming
minimum standards of moral conduct, of stigmatizing the wicked
and only the wicked. Seen thus, the criminal justice system is a
name-calling, stigmatizing, community-superego-reinforcing system—a system which should not be used against the mentally ill.
They are mad, not bad, sick not wicked; it is important that we
should not misclassify them.

Again, in my view, practice casts down theory. We fail in this
classificatory effort and are doomed to failure no matter how we
try since the distinction surpasses our moral and intellectual capacities. And, in any event, we do not stigmatize the insane killer
(who is at the heart of the argument about the special defense)
or other psychologically disturbed persons who commit serious

criminal acts as *either* bad or mad; in practice, we stigmatize them as *both* bad and mad.

This double stigmatization of the subjects of our inquiry can be seen by anyone who visits a prison containing mentally ill prisoners or a mental hospital holding the unfit to plead or those found not guilty by reason of insanity. Prison authorities regard their inmates in the facilities for the psychologically disturbed, no matter how they got there, as both criminal and insane, as bad and mad; mental hospital authorities regard their patients who have been arrested and charged with a crime as both insane and criminal, mad and bad. And it is a regrettable fact that conditions in both types of institutions are often adjusted adversely to the inmate to accommodate the larger political risks that would flow from his escape because of that double stigmatization.

And as a final sad point on this question: it is not only the public and those working in prisons and mental hospitals who doubly rather than alternatively stigmatize in these cases, the patient-inmates in my experience also see themselves as both bad and mad, though it is a tribute to divine mercy and the human spirit that processes of repentance and cognitive dissonance help them to fashion some sort of a life despite that miserable, doubly blemished self-image.

The constitutionality of abolition. In 1970, in *In re Winship*, the Supreme Court stressed that the due process clause of the Fourteenth Amendment "protects the accused against conviction except upon proof beyond a reasonable doubt of every fact necessary to constitute the crime with which he is charged";[74] it is my view that the abolition of the special defense of insanity would not conflict with that adjuration.

Predicting decisions of the Supreme Court of the United States is a popular though high risk occupation, a professional hazard of legal scholarship. To take the risks and to try to cut through a substantial body of case law and commentary, let me confidently affirm the constitutional validity of a statute abolishing the special defense of insanity, provided, of course, it left in place

74. 397 U.S. 358, 364 (1970).

basic common-law requirements of *actus reus* and *mens rea* for the conviction of a crime.

The several lines of authority supporting this conclusion are clear enough once it is appreciated that the *actus reus* would still need to be shown to be a "voluntary" act if the accused is to be convicted[75] and that mental illness would be admissible on the question of whether or not the accused had the prohibited *mens rea* at the time of the alleged crime.

Decisions of the Supreme Court on the burden of proof of the special defense of insanity and of an affirmative defense of "extreme emotional disturbance," in particular *Leland v. Oregon*[76] and *Patterson v. New York*[77] respectively, have made clear that these defenses do not go to the underlying facts necessary to be established by the prosecution for a constitutionally acceptable, due process conviction.

Another possible constitutional barrier is to be found in the Eighth Amendment. Would the abolition of the special defense of insanity lead to the infliction of constitutionally unacceptable cruel and unusual punishment? The decisions and much *dicta* in *Robinson v. California*[78] and *Powell v. Texas*[79] compel, it seems to me, an answer in the negative. Mr. Justice Black in *Powell* was express on the issue:

> A form of the insanity defense would be a constitutional requirement throughout the Nation, should the Court now hold it cruel and unusual to punish a person afflicted with any mental disease whenever his conduct was part of the pattern of his disease and occasioned by a compulsion symptomatic of the disease.[80]

The Court in *Powell* adopted the view that the statute did not violate the Eighth Amendment even if alcoholism was a disease,

75. See chap. 3, *infra*.
76. 343 U.S. 790 (1952).
77. 432 U.S. 197 (1977).
78. 370 U.S. 660 (1962).
79. 392 U.S. 514 (1968).
80. *Id*. at 545.

since it punished an act and not the mere status of being an alcoholic. By similar analysis, it would be cruel and unusual punishment to convict a criminal defendant of being mentally ill, but it would not be cruel and unusual punishment to convict a mentally ill person of a crime other than that of being mentally ill if the state proved beyond a reasonable doubt that he had possessed the *mens rea* of the crime of which he was charged.

Abolition of the defense of insanity would thus neither deprive a defendant of his Fourteenth Amendment right to due process nor impinge upon the Eighth Amendment proscription against cruel and unusual punishment.

IV. Incarcerating the "Not Innocent"

Halfway houses between guilt and innocence are being erected for the mentally ill charged with crime or "acquitted" of crime because of mental illness. Paradigmatic cases of innovative legislation in this area are the Illinois statutory provisions concerning the release of those found incompetent to stand trial and of those found not guilty by reason of insanity and the Michigan legislation relating to the "guilty but mentally ill." These legislative techniques of protractedly detaining those not convicted of crime, who are also often not civilly committable, are discussed under the following headings:

A. The Detained Incompetent
B. The Detained NGRI (Not Guilty by Reason of Insanity)
C. Guilty But Mentally Ill

A. *The Detained Incompetent*

Those found incompetent to stand trial may be held in a mental hospital for treatment until they are fit for trial, their constitutional protections of speedy trial and of bail being waived in the interim. But following *Jackson v. Indiana* those who do not make reasonable progress toward competence to stand trial or who are unlikely ever to become fit for trial may not be held indeterminately, since their continued detention must, under *Jackson*, bear "reasonable relation to the purpose for which" the state committed them, that is, to make them competent to stand trial. And hence we confront another of the testing overlaps between criminal law and the law relating to mental health.

The solution to this problem offered earlier in this chapter is to require the state to elect either to pursue the civil commitment or to take the incompetent accused to trial under rules of court designed to try to compensate so far as practicable for his incompetency. So far this recommendation has not attracted legislative support and its constitutionality remains in doubt. Other legislative paths have been followed to try to meet the *Jackson* problem.

Many states and the federal system[81] have passed legislation in the wake of *Jackson* to stretch out the period of detention of those few who are both unfit to stand trial and not seen as likely subjects for immediate civil commitment. The Illinois legislation is an ambitious scheme to this end.

The report of the Illinois Governor's Commission for Revision of the Mental Health Code of Illinois[82] dealt with the *Jackson* problem; its recommendations were accepted in the main but varied by extension by the Illinois legislature in 1979 in sections 104-10–19 of the Criminal Code.[83] Let me summarize the provisions of the statute which address the problem of those permanently or protractedly unfit to stand trial.

If the defendant is found unfit for trial, a determination must be made "whether there is substantial probability that the defendant, if provided with a course of treatment, will attain fitness within one year." If there is not such probability, a "discharge hearing" (on which, more later) must be ordered; otherwise a treatment plan must be made by the Department of Mental Health and Developmental Disabilities and reported on regularly to the court. If the latter course is followed, treatment may continue for up to one year. Thereafter the court must either determine that the defendant could be fit for trial if he were given special assistance at trial and set the matter down for trial, or order a civil commitment hearing, or proceed to a "discharge hearing."

81. 18 U.S.C., §§4244–48.
82. Report of the Governor's Commission for Revision of the Mental Health Code of Illinois (1976).
83. Ill. Rev. Stat., ch. 38, §§104-10–19 (1980).

The "discharge hearing" is the path to the *Jackson* problem; let us continue to follow it. At any time a defendant found unfit to stand trial can request such a hearing which can also flow from the legislative provisions summarized above. It is, in effect, an "innocent only" trial with somewhat relaxed rules of evidence. If the evidence does not prove the defendant guilty beyond a reasonable doubt (or if he is not found not guilty by reason of insanity), back to "treatment" he goes but this time for periods defined in relation to the crime of which he was charged and reaching a maximum of five years.

Draw a deep breath; we must continue. At the expiration of the time prescribed pursuant to the "discharge hearing" which did not discharge the defendant, the court must either order a civil commitment hearing or further extend the term of treatment detention again to the same maximum as was provided after the discharge hearing, but only if they also find that he is "reasonably expected to inflict serious harm upon himself . . . or others in the near future or constitutes a serious threat to the public safety." The total detention period—the year, the period after the "discharge hearing," and the period at the subsequent hearing—cannot exceed the term of sentence he could have served in prison had he been convicted of the crime with which he was charged but never convicted (setting aside capital punishment and any sentence of natural life).

It is a formidably complex scheme. The above paragraphs merely hint at its baroque encrustations. The periods of detention provided after the discharge hearing and the further periods after the continuing unfit and dangerous finding are of doubtful constitutional validity. But that is not the point I seek to extract from this legislative saga: the point is that a closet full of statutory language seeks to conceal the protracted detention of those who are neither convicted of a crime nor found to be civilly committable.

It can fairly be replied that the "discharge hearing," the innocent only trial, gives the accused as much as he would get at a trial even if the trial were modified to embrace and compensate for his incapacities as an accused person. And to a degree it can. Nevertheless one is left with the view that if this be merely a way around the constitutional prohibition of trying the unfit, it is a hypocritical path to follow, and, further, in practice the accused is unlikely to be as fairly judged as he would have been at trial.

What is in practice happening under these statutory provisions, and similar provisions in other states and in the federal system, is that sections of mental hospitals are being turned into prisons for those found unfit to stand trial for whom no treatment has over a substantial period been efficacious. The mental hospital in all these cases serves merely as a place of detention used because the patient was charged with a crime and not because he fits the criteria of civil commitment. The characteristic of a mental hospital that distinguishes it from a prison is that the patient leaves the former when he is "cured," when he is no longer mentally ill; the prisoner serves his term, the patient should not have to.

Let us turn to detention in mental hospitals under another area of overlap of the criminal law and the law relating to mental health, where mental hospitals again are being turned into prisons, this time for those found not guilty by reason of insanity.

B. *The Detained NGRI (Not Guilty by Reason of Insanity)*

It may be that, if the detention of those found not guilty by reason of insanity (hereinafter NGRI) lasts in practice for substantially the same period as it would if they had been convicted, public anxiety about this verdict will wane. After all, under such a practice, all the NGRI verdict avoids, from the public's perspective, is the capital punishment of those who may have been liable to that sanction, and few favor the execution of the insane. It matters no great deal to the public where they are held secure, provided they are held secure, and if the stigma is less for the NGRI than if he had been convicted and if his conditions of detention are somewhat better, those are hardly important disadvantages even to the punitively inclined.

This result may be achieved by legislative manipulation of the rules and procedures for releasing those found NGRI; in this area, Illinois has been a pathfinder.

In April 1981 there were 127 NGRI patients in the care of the Illinois Department of Mental Health and Developmental Disabilities. The number has been growing over the years: June 1978, 87; August 1979, 94; August 1980, 107; and it is likely to continue to grow under the pressure of the reintroduction of capital punishment in Illinois with the resulting increase in incentive for some accused persons to plead this defense.

Although a number of courts have required a hearing with some due process protections of the continuing mental illness and dangerousness of those found NGRI,[84] it is clear that the hearing may constitutionally differ in important respects from the ordinary civil commitment and release hearings the state provides. That difference allows ample room for legislative and judicial arrangements likely to prolong the detention in mental hospitals of those found NGRI to terms not dissimilar to those to which they would have been sentenced had they been convicted.

The Illinois legislation, Public Act 81-1497 of 1980, amending section 5-2-4 of the Unified Code of Corrections, is a paradigm of legislation designed to achieve that result.

In Illinois, as in other states, the power of discharging and conditionally discharging a civilly committed patient is given to the superintendent of the mental hospital where he is held.[85] The patient may, of course, independently petition a court for a discharge. The 1980 amendments make the situation of the NGRIs quite different.

On the finding of not guilty by reason of insanity, the trial court must within thirty days hold a hearing to determine if the NGRI is "subject to involuntary admission"[86] or in need of mental health services on an in-patient basis.[87] When the finding of not

84. See, e.g., Bolton v. Harris, 395 F.2d 642 (D.C. Cir. 1965); People v. McQuillan, 392 Mich. 511, 221 N.W.2d 569 (1974).

85. Ill. Rev. Stat., ch. 91½, §§4-700–708 (1979).

86. "Subject to involuntary admission" means a defendant who has been found not guilty by reason of insanity and (i) who is mentally ill and because of his mental illness is reasonably expected to inflict serious physical harm upon himself or another in the near future, or (ii) who is mentally ill and who because of his illness is unable to provide for his basic physical needs so as to guard himself from serious harm.

87. "In need of mental health services on an in-patient basis" means a defendant who has been found not guilty by reason of insanity who is not

guilty by reason of insanity is pursuant to a charge for a serious crime, particularly one involving violence or the threat of violence (and there are remarkably few others), such a finding is invariable. Socrates would, it seems clear to me, be so committed if he was found not guilty by reason of insanity of attempted suicide. The usual mental health law requirements of a continuing condition of mental illness or retardation as a continuing precondition for compulsory commitment are abrogated.

The commitment then ordered for the NGRI "acquitted of a felony" is for an indefinite period of time up to "the maximum length of time that the defendant would have been required to serve, less credit for good behavior, before becoming eligible for parole had he been convicted of and received the maximum sentence for the most serious crime for which he has been acquitted by reason of insanity."[88]

Conditional and temporary release as well as discharge are controlled by the court and not by the superintendent of the mental hospital. Likewise, the court controls off-grounds passes, home visits, and participation in work programs. The superintendent of the mental hospital may initiate discharge hearings, thirty days' notice being given to the state's attorney and to the defense attorney; but the court controls discharge, including the conditions of discharge, which will in all cases be conditional for five years.

As a final twist: these provisions for the release of the NGRI were given retroactive effect: "This amendatory Act shall apply to all persons who have been found not guilty by reason of insanity and who are presently committed to the Department of Mental Health and Developmental Disabilities."[89]

The facade of an acquittal is surely stripped away. In terms of the power exercised over their freedom by the state, the Illinois

---

subject to involuntary admission but who is reasonably expected to inflict physical harm upon himself or another and who would benefit from in-patient care or is in need of in-patient care. P.A. 1-1497, §(1)(a).

88. Ill. Rev. Stat., ch. 38, §1005-2-4 (1980).

89. P.A. 81-1497, §(1)(e).

NGRIs are prisoners "doing time" in a mental hospital. The conditions are better where they are held than in the prisons where they otherwise would be held. I do not begrudge them this advantage; I am merely making the point that they constitute an irrational classification. If one included them in the prison population of Illinois and then searched among that population for the 127 prisoners most needing and deserving psychiatric care in a mental hospital, these are certainly not the 127 one would select.

Confirmatory of this view is a letter to a Departmental Commission by the superintendent of the Manteno Mental Health Center, where 58 NGRIs were then held:

> ... The NGRI population, if mentally ill[,] are by and large very different in observable behaviors, proclivities, symptoms and care needs from the other patients treated in such psychiatric facilities as this. To the extent that one may with some measure of legitimacy generalize, NGRIs tend much more to have capacity and proclivity to conspire; they tend to engage more readily and frequently in antisocial, illegal activities; they tend to exploit and manipulate less "street-wise" patients and staff to the detriment of the latter; they tend to exercise more covert behaviors in accomplishing self-serving ends; they tend to retain and to utilize external resources of contraband. ...

> Care and treatment services for the category of mentally ill offenders now labeled "NGRI," I conclude, ideally should be provided for such time as is necessary in an appropriately secure psychiatric resource developed under the auspices of and directed by the Department of Corrections. ...[90]

This is not, I believe, merely an interdepartmental squabble; it represents a principled distinction.

In these techniques of protractedly detaining the unfit to plead and those found not guilty by reason of insanity (that is to say, in both

90. Letter of 28 May 1981 from Dr. Claude Roush, superintendent of Manteno Mental Hospital, to the Honorable Joseph Schneider, chairman of the "blue ribbon" panel, in response to a request by that panel for comments on their work by interested members of the public.

sections A and B above), it will be noted that the maximum period for such detention is the period the accused could have been held had he been convicted of the crime with which he was charged. This is a grossly unfair ceiling—as will be demonstrated in chapter 4, "Sentencing the Mentally Ill"; let me present the argument in capsule form here to make the point.

If the mentally ill were convicted and sentenced other than under these awkward legislative compromises, in all but an exceptional case—a rare case indeed—they would not receive the maximum sentence. All of them had powerful arguments in mitigation of sentence, the effect of mental illness on their behavior, which they were denied by these strained adjudicative processes. It is no answer to this to say that they need not have pleaded unfitness or insanity; there usually is indeed some quite florid psychopathology or substantial retardation among those for whom these pleas are made, and it is an exercise in legislative injustice to preclude entirely valid mitigation of punishment by reason of mental illness.

C. *Guilty But Mentally Ill*

Michigan is the leader in legislation designed to draw the weak old teeth of the special defense of insanity, to preserve its facade but drastically to change the realities behind it. Indiana and Illinois have already followed Michigan's lead and many other states are poised to do so, encouraged by the Attorney General's Task Force on Violent Crime,[91] which, charmingly enough, misstated the operation of the legislation it advocated.

In 1883[92] the form of the verdict in England and Wales pursuant to a successful defense of insanity was changed from "not guilty on account of insanity"[93] to "guilty but insane." This change was cosmetic rather than substantive, influencing neither the placement nor the duration of detention of persons so found.

91. Attorney General's Task Force on Violent Crime, Final Report, 17 August 1981, at 54.

92. The Criminal Lunatics Act of 1884, 47 & 48 Vict. 1 c.64.

93. Criminal Lunatics Act 1800.

In 1964, the Criminal Procedure (Insanity) Act restored the form of verdict in England and Wales to "not guilty by reason of insanity."

The Michigan legislation of 1976[94] is of a quite different order. Pursuant to a 1975 amendment to the Michigan Code of Criminal Procedure,[95] those found "guilty but mentally ill" may be sentenced as if they had been convicted of the offense charged and may be held either in the Department of Corrections or transferred to the custody of the Department of Mental Health. Wherever they are held, the duration of detention cannot exceed what could be imposed pursuant to a conviction without the mental illness rider unless, of course, they qualify for civil commitment at the expiration of the sentence.

Hence, if an accused person in Michigan pleads not guilty by reason of insanity, the result may be any one of the following: (a) not guilty, or (b) not guilty by reason of insanity, or (c) guilty but mentally ill, or (d) guilty. The Michigan special defense of insanity (b) is an American Law Institute test[96] providing that a person is "legally insane" if at the time of the alleged crime "as a result of mental illness . . . that person lacks substantial capacity either to appreciate the wrongfulness of his conduct or to conform his conduct to the requirements of the law."

By contrast—or *is* it contrast—"mental illness" for purposes of the new alternative verdict of guilty but mentally ill (c) is defined as "a substantial disorder of thought or mood which significantly impairs judgment, behavior, capacity to recognize reality, or ability to cope with the ordinary demands of life."[97]

"Significant impairment" must as a matter of logic occur at an earlier threshold of psychopathology than "substantial capacity" for a verdict of guilty but mentally ill ever to be reached. And juries are so instructed. The distinction cannot be unequivocally obvious to them, even if it is to lawyers and legislators. But in practice they probably find the alternative helpful. "Guilty but

94. Mich. Comp. Laws Ann., §768.21a(1) (Supp. 1976).
95. *Id.* §768-36 (Supp. 1981).
96. *Id.* §768-21a(l) (Supp. 1976).
97. *Id.* §330–400a (1975).

mentally ill" supplants "not guilty by reason of insanity." Juries must find *beyond reasonable doubt* that the accused had substantial capacity to appreciate the wrongfulness of his conduct and to conform to the law's demands but that he was suffering a substantial disorder of thought or mood which significantly impaired his judgment, behavior, capacity to recognize reality, or ability to cope with the ordinary demands of life. Forgive the repetition, but these are not easy distinctions—it is like trying to think of a very large gray animal with a trunk without thinking of an elephant. But, as I say, juries can do it—probably because they are informed as to the consequences of each verdict.

The maximum consequences in Michigan pursuant to each verdict are: not guilty, discharge; not guilty by reason of insanity, since *People v. McQuillan*[98] no automatic indefinite commitment but, in effect, civil standards for commitment and release; guilty but mentally ill, a sentence by the trial judge which will be served in prison or in a mental hospital for a period up to the maximum for the crime charged; guilty, commitment to prison up to the maximum period for the crime charged.

Since in Michigan any mentally ill prisoner may, with appropriate consent, be transferred to a mental hospital, the distinctions between "guilty" and "guilty but mentally ill" are not of translucent clarity. Both groups may be given psychiatric treatment in both types of institutions and for the same maximum periods. The punishment, setting aside capital punishment, may be the same; it is a matter for discussion whether the stigma of "guilty but mentally ill" is or is not any less than that of "guilty."

The argument grows burdensome. The Michigan statute has survived constitutional challenge before the Supreme Court of Michigan. Can it survive the challenge of analytic principle? I think not. It seems to me on its face and in its operation a means of drawing such acquitting and destigmatizing teeth as were left in the special defense of insanity—and they were not many—while pretending to preserve the moral values embedded in the ideas

98. 392 Mich. 511, 221 N.W.2d 569 (1974).

underlying that special defense. No one is deceived, certainly not the prisoner.

There are other useful insights into the operation of the special defense of insanity to be gained from considering the Michigan statute. First, as to the origin of this new "defense": In 1974 the Michigan Supreme Court decided *People v. McQuillan*,[99] holding unconstitutional Michigan's statute automatically committing those found not guilty by reason of insanity as a denial of both equal protection and due process.[100] Hearings on their present and continuing mental state were thus required. Within a year, sixty-four who had been found not guilty by reason of insanity were released from Michigan mental hospitals; within another year two of the sixty-four had committed violent crimes, Ronald Manlen raping two women, John McGee killing his wife—both Manlen and McGee had been found not insane in civil proceedings pursuant to *McQuillan*. Public clamor moved the Michigan legislature promptly to introduce the new verdict of guilty but mentally ill. Whenever the defendant pleads a defense of insanity, this alternative verdict, in substance avoiding the previously partly exculpatory effect of the special defense, will be available.

One advantage to the accused survives the new verdict if the Michigan pattern is followed in states that have reinstituted capital punishment; both those found not guilty by reason of insanity and those found guilty but mentally ill sidestep the executioner.

There are other consequences meriting mention. Some hold that a special defense of insanity is constitutionally required, a topic earlier discussed. If it is, Michigan has shown the way to an easy avoidance of the constitutional requirement: leave the special defense as it is but whenever it is invoked allow the jury to achieve the same result by this new verdict as they would with a conviction.

A final nicety about the Michigan statute is that it is triggered by the accused pleading not guilty by reason of insanity. It is not triggered and cannot be the verdict if the accused argues that his

---

99. *Ibid.*

100. See "Guilty But Mentally Ill: An Historical and Constitutional Analysis," 53 *J. Urban L.* 471 (1976).

mental illness at the time of the crime precluded his conviction on *mens rea* grounds but does not plead not guilty by reason of insanity, that is, in the structure of this chapter, by raising the *mens rea* issues he does not risk this new verdict.[101]

What then has happened in Michigan pursuant to this new initiative? During the seven years prior to the advent of the "guilty but mentally ill" verdict, 279 persons had been found not guilty by reason of insanity. During 1975, the year the new verdict was enacted, 33 persons were found not guilty by reason of insanity. The following year, 32 persons successfully asserted this defense. Between 1977 and 1980, approximately 57 persons were acquitted by reason of insanity each year. The "guilty but mentally ill" verdict was successfully asserted by approximately 80 persons a year in Michigan between 1979 and 1981. Of these 80 persons, half were found to be mentally ill at the time of their admission to prison. Only half of this group need any special mental health program.

Why should one who advocates the abolition of the special defense take such a carping line toward the Michigan venture, which appears to achieve a very similar result? One justification for the critical tone is doubt—given the overcrowded conditions of Michigan's prisons and the turmoil, brutality, and racial tensions which pervade them—that those found guilty but mentally ill under the new statutory provisions will be given minimum decent conditions and reasonably adequate treatment for their illness. While the statute suggests that these are to be part of the new verdict, I am skeptical that adequate psychiatric resources and minimally decent conditions will be given to these newly categorized offenders. If there is an argument of principle against the new verdict, it is not very powerful—merely the distaste of doing indirectly and clandestinely what should be done directly and openly. And to that there is the troublesome reply, What if the Constitution is interpreted to compel the indirection? If it is, we have then indeed entered a land of word magic, where form triumphs over substance.

101. People v. Fields, 64 Mich. App. 166, 235 N.W.2d 95 (1975), *rev. denied*, 397 Mich. 861 (1976).

THREE

The Planter's Dream

Dear Mr. Morris, Honoured Sir:

You will remember please I found for you some writings by Mr. Blair when you visited my country and that I accepted your very modest slight payment for them.

I hear you have since presented these writings and are posing in pride and making much profit from them. It is not surprising thus to be taken advantage of for unhappily such wicked things are common when Americans visit backward peoples like us. But my wife tells me strongly and often to hold not grudges and so I have another great favour I will do for you.

I have another writings by Mr. Blair which you will want certainly and which I will send you. Of course now that I know the value of Mr. Blair's writings I will not let you again cheat me. The price this time is two thousand (2,000) Swiss francs which is convenient for an honest trader in several countries. I have an account in a bank in Zurich so as legally properly and secretly to avoid the unfairness of exchange controls.

Send me the bank currency transfer and you will receive what you want.

Your very obedient servant
W. Jones

Three

I telephoned a friend in Burma, the Consul-General in Mandalay, who had read "The Brothel Boy." He made the trip to Moulmein, beat Jones down in price, and sent the manuscript to me. In form and script it matches "The Brothel Boy"; of identical provenance, according to Jones, and hence of equal validity as a major find.

It is less of a flowing story than "The Brothel Boy"—collected notes and sections of commentary rather than a rounded manuscript. Nevertheless, a reasonably clear picture emerges of an event in Blair's life in Burma, earlier than that narrated in "The Brothel Boy," since that hanging contributed to Blair's decision to leave Burma in 1927. The manuscript is not signed, nor is it sited or dated; my best guess: Eric Blair, Moulmein, 1925.

"The nightmare suddenly became real," Taylor later told me. "The noise of the gun was no dream, though the dream had seemed very real. I found myself standing there, shotgun in hand, close to the bed, her head and chest blasted, lumps scattered everywhere."

Dr. Veraswami had arrived before me, called by Taylor's boy, Aka Thon, who then came shouting on to my bungalow. Veraswami had bicycled up the hill at top speed through a pre-dawn rainstorm. When I got there, dawn was breaking. Taylor sat slumped forward in a chair on the verandah, Aka Thon squatting anxiously nearby, the details of the scene appearing like a developing daguerreotype as the light increased. They made no move as I hurried inside.

Dr. Veraswami was dressed in his usual crumpled white suit, but without shirt or socks, the suit probably pulled on over whatever he slept in and his feet pushed into his, also usual, black shoes. The effect was macabre, with blood now staining his sleeves and lapels.

I did not have to ask if she was dead. The stench was enough. And a shotgun fired at close quarters into a recumbent and plump female makes a gory mess. It was clear that there was nothing Veraswami could do as a doctor. But he busied himself energetically, cleaning the body and tidying the bed, to no purpose I could see except that somebody had to do it.

Veraswami was relieved to see me. "Terrible, terrible, it iss. You will know what to do, Mr. Blair."

I wished I did. They had not trained us sufficiently for such events. European planters were not expected to blow the top third off their Burmese mistresses. But the first thing to do seemed obvious: "Rest a bit, Dr. Veraswami. Have one of my cigarettes."

As we walked out to the verandah I asked Dr. Veraswami if he thought Taylor needed attention. "No. He iss best left sitting there, I think. He iss unhurt physically but, of course, most upset, though he wass able to speak sensibly enough to me when I arrived, to tell me what had happened. He called it an accident. Let us leave him with Aka Thon for the time being."

I rolled cigarettes for Veraswami and myself. We stood awhile silent at the other end of the verandah from Taylor and Aka Thon. "When does his wife return, do you know?" I asked Dr. Veraswami.

"Taylor came to see me the day before yesterday—a medical consultation, you see. But it iss not improper for me to tell you that Mrs. Taylor, Mary I believe iss her name, iss returning next week."

"Is that why he did it?" I asked. It was a stupid question, and Dr. Veraswami waved the hand that was not holding the cigarette about in a circular rejecting motion. He seemed bewildered and exhausted. I let the silence lie.

The morning sun was now strong on the verandah, steam rising from the surrounding vegetation. Dr. Veraswami peered at his clothes in distaste, fiddled with the buttons on his wet, stained, and wrinkled jacket and said he would go to his bungalow. He would, he added, send an ambulance for the body and would call on Taylor later in the day. "He may need a sedative, you see, or something to calm him, quite likely. He iss, after all, my patient. Where will you hold him?"

The question shook me to action. There was obviously much for me to do that day. I had best begin. I told Veraswami I would later advise him where Taylor was. I tried to thank Veraswami for what he had done, but that didn't make much sense either. We each had our duties.

I sent Aka Thon for tea for Taylor and me and pulled a chair up beside Taylor. I told him that from what I had seen, and what Aka Thon and Dr. Veraswami had told me, I would have to arrest him. He raised an anguished face: "Can it be done before she gets back?" The words were slurred and unclear, and at first I did not follow him. I thought he was talking of the dead girl.

"Can what be done?" I asked.

"Whatever you have to do." I understood—his wife's impending return was the capstone of his misery.

I had not thought what precisely had to be done and how long it would take. I told him I did not know the answer to his question and, as much for myself as for him, rehearsed what I thought should follow. "I will have to hold a preliminary enquiry and write up what are called depositions, signed statements, in effect, of what everyone who knows about her death can tell me about it. You can testify if you want to, but you don't have to. If I find she was killed, and not accidentally, then these depositions will be used at trial at Mandalay Quarter Sessions. You don't have to tell me anything now, but if you do it may be used as evidence. In the meantime I suppose I have to put you under arrest."

He seemed to understand but responded only by latching on to my mention of an accident. "Blair, it *was* an accident. I didn't mean to kill her. You must know that. Why would I want to kill her? I saw that filthy Black on her and shot at him. She wouldn't have been badly hurt. And then I woke and . . . and . . . bloody lumps were scattered everywhere." He slumped forward in his chair, gulping loudly in his reluctance to cry before me.

There seemed no point in pressing Taylor for details. Later would do. So I did my best to calm him, to get him to drink some of the tea Aka Thon had brought, and then to help him get dressed and gather a few clothes and toilet articles together.

We walked in silence the mile or so to the police barracks, where I had the sergeant give him a room. I told them both that Taylor must stay in the barracks, and I told the sergeant to have someone keep an eye on Taylor all the time. Taylor gave no hint of suicide, but I could not ignore the possibility. I told Taylor that Dr. Veraswami would come to see him later in the day and that he could send a message to anyone he wanted to call on him. I then went to the railway station to send a telegram reporting to headquarters at Mandalay.

It was mid-morning before I got back to my office. Aka Thon was waiting: "Mr. Blair, Sir, should I go to her village?" And sickeningly I realized the depth of my prejudice—the dead girl I had left to Dr. Veraswami. Taylor I had attended to myself with reasonable consideration, but I had entirely neglected the dead girl's family and her village community.

Aka Thon and I peddled in the heat the few miles to the girl's village. He knew where to go and whom to see. It was less painful than I had feared. Her father was dead; her mother had already been told—by whom I never discovered; the girl had no siblings. The mother was surrounded by weeping women and would not see me. There was little for me to do. Yes, Aka Thon assured me, it was understood that the mother should see Dr. Veraswami about the body and the funeral. And I pressed him to tell all who cared to listen that Taylor was under arrest and that there would be an enquiry into the death; but this seemed of no interest to anyone.

Intent on piecing together the story of the girl's death, I spent the later part of the afternoon at the barracks with Taylor. Police were about in the barracks, on and off duty; we could not conveniently talk in any of the public rooms. An office seemed too harshly official; so we talked in the white-painted, starkly furnished bedroom that had been allotted to Taylor. A policeman sat outside on the verandah, out of hearing, ensuring Taylor's safe custody as unobtrusively as he could.

Taylor needed prodding to talk. He said he wished to tell me about the killing and gave no hint of trying to conceal anything; but equally he volunteered nothing. He answered my questions and that was all. I had to keep at him and I disliked it. He needed rest, not interrogation; but there was no doubt of my duty, given his repeatedly expressed willingness to tell me all he knew about the girl's death. It was miserable work. The fan, rotating weakly, did little to move the humid air. It seemed unusually hot even for those pre-monsoonal days. By early evening we were both exhausted. As I left, Taylor said he would take a nap. I later learned that he slept until mid-morning of the next day—Veraswami's sedative was certainly not needed.

I went back to my bungalow, showered, and dined alone. After dinner I called on Dr. Veraswami. He saw me approaching and bustled his wife and child off the verandah, greeting me in his high-pitched, fussing way with solicitudes for my comfort, my need for a cold beer, my tiredness, the heat and humidity and their effects on me, and how upset I must be by the morning's tragedy. I made the point that he had got up before me, had a harder beginning to his day and probably harder work throughout; I didn't see why he should be offering sympathy to me. He chuckled as if my wit were profound and produced the nearly cold beer, settling his ample rump and a clean pair of baggy trousers onto the verandah rail beside the cane chair he had given me.

"Have you talked with Mr. Taylor yet?" Veraswami asked.

I told him of my visit to Taylor that afternoon and that from what Taylor and Aka Thon had told me I believed I knew what had happened—"not why it happened, Dr. Veraswami, but what happened."

"We are not likely, my friend, ever really to know the whys of such sad matters. Glimpses of such truths from the corner of the eye are all we can hope for. But tell me what your diligent police probings detected."

I disliked Veraswami's mocking description of what he knew I had had to do, but I did my best to summarize for him the facts as I saw them.

Only Aka Thon, the girl, and Taylor had been at Taylor's bungalow that night—it was not uncommon for him to let the other servants off, particularly when the girl visited him. Taylor had come home from the Club about ten-thirty, and Aka Thon and the girl were already at the bungalow. Taylor had had a few drinks but was not drunk. Aka Thon stayed in the servants' quarters. Taylor and the girl went straight to the bedroom. Aka Thon heard no sound of argument, indeed no sounds at all until the gun was fired. Taylor reported an argument between him and the girl about the return of his wife and how hard life was for the girl in the village, with so many knowing that she visited Taylor. Someone wished to marry her, but she must stop coming to Taylor's bungalow if she hoped to marry this man. Taylor had another whisky, and began to taunt the girl—and torture himself—by pressing her for details of her relationship with the man in the village. He told her to do what she liked—stay or leave, come back or not, he didn't care. She cried. He comforted her. They went to bed. Later he went to sleep. Then came the dream. Then the killing.

All this, I told Dr. Veraswami, seemed precise, clear, and likely to be true. Veraswami agreed, saying he knew it was.

"But how can you know, doctor, what happened? He reports a vivid dream. It matches his actions. He sticks to the details. Only he knows. There can be no confirmation or denial of the dream."

"Not so, dear friend. You forget he consulted me last week. Perhaps there is confirmation. But I am most troubled, most troubled indeed, by whether or not I can tell you. After all, you see, medical confidences, Hippocratic oath, the patient's interests, issn't it?" And Veraswami lapsed into gestures and head wavings, adding, "Would you tell me with your usual care and precision, if you will please, what he said about his dream? Perhaps I may be able to help you and him."

I did my best to summarize Taylor's story but made no effort to recapture his alternately halting and gushing words. Taylor had dreamt of the girl being fondled by a dark-skinned man of Northern Indian coloration and build, certainly not a Burmese. Taylor thought he was a Pathan, of a tribe now in revolt in the Northwest of India. Taylor laboured this matter of the man's origin; he could see the man plainly, well built, craggy features, turbaned, loose-robed. Taylor's anger and sense of helplessness grew—he could not move. Then the man and the girl were naked. He could see it all; the man rampant. And they were on his bed in his bungalow. On Mary's bed. The squalor and shame grew; rage and self-loathing overcame him. He struck at the figures on the bed, but his blows touched nothing and had no effect. The pair on the bed did not cease their wild copulation. The girl responded more than she ever had to Taylor. Taylor floated to the wardrobe; took his loaded shotgun from the top of the wardrobe; floated to the bedside and shot the filthy Black in the back of his head. The shot woke Taylor. Aka Thon came rushing in. We knew the rest.

"So, you see, Dr. Veraswami, it all makes sense if you believe him. And if you don't, it seems such a crazy story to make up, such an unlikely and unhelpful way of getting rid of a native mistress." I could have swallowed the word "native" as I said it, but I had forgotten that Veraswami seemed even more colour conscious, almost colour obsessed, than my fellow Europeans at the Club. Embarrassed, I pressed on: "At the Club, of course, they see it as a simple story: Taylor got drunk. Told the girl to leave since his wife was returning and he was suffering alcoholic remorse. She tried to blackmail him. Asked for too much money. He shot her. Damn fool act on his part. Others vary the story slightly by adding that the so-called girl wasn't all that young and was getting on the round and blowsy side even for a native mistress (that damn word would not go away) and that Taylor was tired of her, though they admit he chose an excessive way of dismissing her. All emphatically agree that you have to be careful when you take up too long with these village tarts. A few say that Taylor must be mad, bonkers, insane; but the only reason they give is that anyone who kills as he did must be mad and, so far as I can tell, Taylor seems clearly to understand what he did and, within his dream, why he did it."

Dr. Veraswami was uncharacteristically, almost ill-manneredly, silent. Even his head and hands were still. I waited, drinking my beer.

"Can you tell me, dear friend Blair, whether as a doctor I may tell you, a Police Magistrate, what my patient, Taylor, told me last week?"

"I don't know, doctor. Certainly if it would help to stop a serious crime in the future you may and should tell me—I believe the law is clear on that—but about matters of past guilt or innocence, which I suppose we have here, I don't know. But I have a telegram from Mandalay that a lawyer from the Imperial Police Service will be coming here tomorrow, and I suppose he will know. He may even ask you about it in court—I don't know."

Dr. Veraswami fell silent again for a time. Then he looked up at me with affection gleaming in the eyes behind his slightly askew glasses—a glance I had come to cherish: "Well, it iss to help Taylor. I will tell you. As you know, I trust you. If I have to forget it you will be able to forget it too—we will help one another to forget." And grinning at his own wit he launched into what was a considerable confirmation either of Taylor's story or of the depth of cunning of his plan to kill the girl.

Taylor had consulted Veraswami the week before, troubled by an event not unlike the killing. He had been sleeping badly, finding himself unable to concentrate on anything for very long during the day, dozing off unexpectedly, drinking too much. And the night before he had awakened—yes, the girl was with him, he had managed to tell Veraswami of her—to find himself brushing at the girl's face. Actually, she had wakened them both, startled by his pawing. He had dreamt that spiders had invaded his bungalow, many of them, large and loathsome, and they were on the girl's face. He fought them off.

Taylor had some memories of somnambulism in his youth—of being wakened by his parents as he apparently sleep-walked towards their bedroom. But nothing like this had occurred for over thirty years now. Could Dr. Veraswami help him? Did Dr. Veraswami think that a nervous breakdown threatened or mental illness?

Dr. Veraswami did his best to reassure Taylor that he was not suffering from any serious mental illness, that he was not losing his mind—he had rational reasons to be troubled and rational steps could be taken to minimize or eliminate his anxieties. Veraswami urged Taylor to try to regularize his life in a variety of ways and to take a few days' holiday with his wife when she returned from England; the doctor also prescribed and dispensed a sedative, and advised him to reduce his drinking. Veraswami now blamed himself vaguely for not having done more, but I couldn't imagine what more he should have done.

"You think, then, Dr. Veraswami, that Taylor told me the truth? It is not a story to cover up a simple murder?"

Veraswami nodded his head slowly, his eyes half-closed, in a manner indicating that he believed Taylor's story completely. He began to explain about "fugue states," in which people acted out their phantasies. Veraswami had studied these conditions, particularly one called "running amok," during his medical training in India and had then observed such a case after his hospital residency when he served for a short time on a freighter. A stoker, overcome by the heat in the boiler room while the ship was steaming through the Red Sea, had "run amok"—a well-known though rare form of behaviour in some Malayan villages. "To run amok" had become a popular phrase, its origin rarely understood. The stoker had come rushing up from the laddered purgatory of the boiler room onto an upper deck, wielding his shovel. With it he struck the head of an officer who chanced to be in his path, doing him no lasting injury, and then jumped overboard and drowned, still clutching the shovel. Dr. Veraswami thought that the stoker was not conscious of what he was doing. Those who run amok in this way rarely remember anything of what they have done when they come to their senses. Certainly, some actions of those under hypnosis may be completely repressed. The same is true for acts done by those in epileptic fits. By contrast, somnambulists who act out their dreams, about whom Dr. Veraswami had read when he was interested in the phenomenon of running amok, do remember their dreams when they wake from the somnambulist condition. So Taylor's story fit well with what is known about these conditions—he was unlikely to have made it up.

"If we believe Mr. Taylor," Dr. Veraswami asked, "what of his guilt? Did he murder the girl? Did he murder the dreamlike Pathan? Can you kill someone who issn't there? Or murder someone lying under someone who issn't there?"

"For the life of me, I don't know," I replied. "Do you think they worry about questions like that at the Burma Provincial Police Training School? Things there were simpler, not as complicated as fugue states, somnambulists, and running amok. So let me ask you the question they would have advised me to ask. Do you think Taylor would have killed her if he had not had a few drinks at the Club—I still don't know how many—and then a last whisky at his bungalow?"

Dr. Veraswami allowed that probably the girl would still be alive if Taylor had been, "ass you say it, 'on the water wagon.' But surely to be convicted of murder and, I suppose, executed, iss a considerable punishment, a very considerable punishment indeed, for not being entirely sober. Or even for having what you were pleased to call a 'native mistress' and not being always entirely sober. Few of your European colleagues would escape the hangman! That cannot be right. Iss Taylor any different from the rest?"

Nettled by Veraswami's deferred reference to my use of "native mistress," I responded brusquely. "Of course he's different, Veraswami: he killed her."

"Perhaps, dear friend, he did, but it iss hard to see how he can be responsible for his dreams. Are you? To be sure you don't act them out—I assume not, I hope not—but what iss he to do? He had no idea at all he would injure her that night. I am glad it iss your decision, not mine."

The telegram from Mandalay had advised that Arthur Grantham would arrive in Moulmein on the Wednesday evening train. Grantham was attached to the Legal Section of the Burma Police. Headquarters apparently did not trust me to run the preliminary hearing without legal advice. I did not resent this; I needed the help. Presumably he would interrogate the witnesses at the preliminary hearing, leaving me to preside and to see that the depositions were transcribed in a reasonably accurate manner. It certainly would make my task easier.

I set out to meet Grantham at the station some time before the train was due so that I could send a telegram to Mrs. Taylor, who was aboard ship somewhere en route to Rangoon, there to catch the train to Mandalay and on to Moulmein. Taylor had given, it seemed to me, more thought to softening the blow to his wife than to his own situation. He had talked to me more about this than about the killing, on which he seemed to think he had said all that he could say or indeed that anybody could say. The cable he asked me to send to her read: "SERVANT KILLED GUN ACCIDENT STOP IMPORTANT YOU STAY MANDALAY STOP WILL JOIN YOU THERE STOP DO NOT RETURN MOULMEIN STOP SEE YOU SOON LOVE PHILIP."

When he had asked me to send this cable I had commented that Mrs. Taylor could not believe the first word for long. He knew that, he said, but he could not stand the thought of how she would be received in Moulmein—the false sympathy, the cloying effusive comforting, the unqualified misery for her. He wanted to tell her about it himself, though he did not know how he would. He appreciated that in Mandalay, too, such is the capacity of scandal to spread, that his wife might be told more ample facts than were revealed in his cable, but he thought it worth the risk to try to lessen the hurt to her in this way. So I sent the cable.

The train, remarkably, was on time. Grantham was younger and of more junior rank than I had anticipated. Like me, he was an Assistant Police Magistrate. He was fresh from Gray's Inn, after a classics degree at Cambridge, with scant courtroom experience but some knowledge of legal theory, which I lacked entirely. I was glad to see him and told him so, going beyond the figure of speech to welcome him. He seemed pleased, but embarrassed.

He later told me that he had thought he was coming to Moulmein as a young interloper, wet behind the ears, to advise an experienced and sage police magistrate, in his phrase, "how to suck eggs." My obvious uncertainty and appreciation of his

assistance had cheered him greatly. But he had found it difficult—he always found it difficult—to express himself with any
warmth on such matters. He knew he was on the taciturn side,
and indeed he was, but there did not seem much he could do
about it. He always rehearsed inside himself what he wished to
say so that by the time he was sufficiently confident of whatever
it was, the moment had passed and there was no point in saying
it. He agreed that this did not make for an easy conversational
style and, daringly for him, allowed that I may suffer from a
mild form of the same malady—which is true.

There was a further odd embarrassment between us which
inhibited our first meeting. We looked rather alike. Of course
we were wearing the same uniforms and were of similar age,
but there was more to it: he was an ungainly figure, unusually
tall and of lean build, with feet and hands marginally but perceptibly over-sized, of slightly stooped posture, with straight
dark hair cut quite short—all physical qualities I shared without
any enthusiasm at all. We both looked awkward and probably
were. His features were more regular than mine but of the
same general balance or, rather, imbalance. He sprouted a thin
moustache while I was clean shaven; perhaps I should try a
moustache. Our similarity of appearance did not pass unnoticed
at the Club and provided the butt, I suspected, of many laboured jokes. Putting us together did not add to the presence
of each separately, and we both knew this immediately and well.

After a day or two, with these realities recognized between
us and circuitously discussed, our early embarrassments turned
to the beginnings of a bond of friendship which, however, has
not survived the Taylor case. It has been a disappointment to
me. As I think about it, I realize I came closer to forming a
lasting bond with Grantham than with anyone since the transient ties of childhood and adolescent friendships. Had we met
other than through the Taylor case perhaps it would have been
different. The fault must be mine; certainly Grantham has
friends, as do most others of my contemporaries, whereas I do
not. And this is not because I wish it so. Grantham did fail, it
still seems to me, in the Taylor case, but not in anything he did

or said to others. It was how he felt about it and talked to me about it that irked me and pulled me from him. But others would say he acted at least as effectively and honourably as I did. All that was in the future, however. On the evening of Grantham's arrival in Moulmein I had a horse-drawn personnel cart waiting at the railway station for him, and with few words passing between us I saw him to the Club, where I had reserved a room for him, and arranged to join him later for dinner.

Grantham listened determinedly, almost immobile, giving little help to my effort to tell him all I knew of Taylor, his wife, Aka Thon, and the dead girl. He interrupted me only to push me to confirm that neither Veraswami nor I thought Taylor was in any way mentally disordered, that Taylor impressed everyone as a sensible if somewhat stolid chap—no one saw any fires of mental illness below his dull exterior. Grantham seemed regretful of this: "It would," he said, "be such an easy way out."

Grantham was not forthcoming with information on how the law bore on the facts I had recounted. His ruminative style—he didn't actually move his jaws laterally as does a cow chewing the cud, but I kept expecting it—did not make for an easy extraction of information; and there was a good deal I wanted to know. What it amounted to, in sum, was this: Was Taylor guilty if his story was true?

Grantham said that there was some law on the matter, a few cases, but that they were not dispositive. He stressed that we didn't have to decide whether or not Taylor was guilty, which I knew. After some uncertain but determined prodding by me, he agreed that though we would not have to decide the matter, how he and I approached the preliminary hearing might help either to condemn or to spare Taylor, and that it did no harm for me, with his help, to try to form an opinion about Taylor's guilt even though my duties did not require me to do so.

There was no doubt that Grantham was exceedingly difficult to talk with at our early meetings—a hippopotamus would have been of lighter conversational foot. But I was able to wrench a few lines of cases and threads of legal analysis from him.

Apparently the law does not hold one responsible for an act of which one is unconscious. This is not a defense of insanity—there is simply no criminal guilt. As examples Grantham offered a blow by an epileptic given while in a *grand mal*, or a person fainting and falling on someone—neither would be criminal assaults, no matter what the injury.

Grantham could call to mind no case directly concerned with somnambulist acts and would not risk concluding that they were precisely like the acts of the epileptic or the person who fainted. There were differences, he thought, and after all, even if one completely believed his story, Taylor had a motive for what he had done—unlike the epileptic and the person who fainted, who did not even choose their victims. I pointed out that Taylor said he hadn't chosen his victim—the "victim" he chose was the energetic Pathan. Grantham's jaw moved but no words came.

Another difference Grantham suggested was that the epileptic and the person who fainted did not later remember what had happened, while in a way, a clouded sort of way, Taylor did. Grantham did not know, in his phrase, "which way this cut."

The case nearest to Taylor's that Grantham knew of concerned a Londoner who was working with his young son in a second-story room overlooking a river. The son was painting the windowsill, the father doing some carpentry work. Without warning the father struck the boy on the side of the head with a mallet. The boy fell in the river. Dazed but not seriously injured, he scrambled out and went to the police station for help, saying, "Come quickly, something has gone wrong with Dad." He was right. The father had a tumor developing on his brain. The father was acquitted of assault with intent to kill and of assault with intent to inflict grievous bodily harm—since he lacked those intents. The father was, however, convicted of simple assault. Grantham allowed himself the criticism, lengthy for him, that it was "an unimaginative, silly decision." Why this was so eluded me.

Grantham seemed to think it might be important to try to determine whether Taylor could have predicted any danger to the girl if he drank and had her share his bed. The general line of argument as I understood it was that Taylor, if his story were believed, might be guilty not of murder but of involuntary manslaughter—doing something which risked another's life and which killed, particularly if the something was illegal or immoral. And I suppose Taylor's acts could not be regarded as exemplars of chaste and sober virtue. Grantham gave as an example of this the manslaughter convictions of drunken mothers who unintentionally overlay and kill their infant children.

I latched onto this compromise. It seemed a wonderful way out. Grantham ceased his meditation long enough to urge me to be less confident about it; it would please no one except "uncertain chaps like you."

"Well then," I offered hesitatingly, "why not persuade Taylor to plead temporary insanity? Then, brief treatment in the mental hospital in Rangoon—if it's necessary to commit him at all. After all"—I said, struggling for a lighter touch in our burdensome dialogue—"he cured himself by killing her."

Grantham apparently found this distasteful, certainly unamusing; but he did abandon his taciturn mode long enough brusquely to squash my suggestion. "It is typical of you, Blair; another weak compromise. Dr. Veraswami saw Taylor before and after the killing. He diagnosed no mental illness, certainly no psychosis. In the language of the law which you must have studied in Mandalay, Taylor did not suffer from a defect of reason from disease of the mind. It won't wash."

Though relentlessly patronising of my ideas, Grantham neither exposed his own nor expressed what must have been his own uncertainties. I tired of this one-sided exchange. He made me feel a fool.

I arranged for Grantham to visit Taylor the next day and left him and his sparkling wit to the care of the few members of the Club who were still about. They would, I thought, like him about as much as they liked me. The thought cheered me.

Later in the week Grantham and I together interviewed Taylor at the police barracks. Taylor complained of nothing, asked for nothing, replied when spoken to but volunteered nothing. Grantham urged him to ask that the preliminary hearing be delayed until Taylor had a lawyer to defend him. Taylor refused. "I've told you both the truth. No lawyer can make it better. Can't we get this over and let me be taken to Mandalay?" Grantham stressed that though he would try to be as fair as possible at the hearing, there was much a lawyer could do for Taylor which might be important at trial in Mandalay if Taylor were committed for trial; but Taylor would pay no heed to this. "You know the facts. Whatever you decide my life is ruined. Just help me get away from here."

We arranged that the preliminary hearing would be held not at Taylor's bungalow—there seemed to be no need for this—but at the barracks. Grantham began to list those he would call to give evidence and to think about what he would ask them.

A message came to me from Veraswami inviting me and Grantham, "if he would be so very kind as to accompany you," to come to dinner that night. We accepted.

Veraswami had obviously gone to a great deal of trouble. I had never before dined at his home; we usually met after dinner. His wife and children were nowhere to be seen, but there seemed to be extra servants, and we were served an excessive and complicated Chinese dinner. Veraswami was garrulous, the overly considerate host, chattering about the food, what we might want, the heat, and a variety of painfully polite inconsequentialities. Grantham's taciturnity became Trappist under this treatment. I did my best to play the role of a graceful guest. But I was glad when dinner was over and we could go to the verandah to discuss what Veraswami obviously didn't want us to discuss at dinner, perhaps because of the servants, perhaps from a misguided sense of politeness—Taylor and the dead girl.

That day, Veraswami, accompanied by Aka Thon to help him as interpreter, had gone to the girl's village. He had talked to the girl's mother; there would be a cremation ceremony in the village tomorrow. Veraswami saw no reason not to release the body—the cause and time of death were obvious; there was no reason for an autopsy, "an exercise I have never greatly enjoyed."

Grantham enquired whether the mother would be likely to behave calmly at the preliminary hearing if he decided to take her deposition. Veraswami was unsure but doubted she would be a helpful witness, not because he thought her overcome by grief but because she might think she ought "to rant, to rave, to scream, to wail about her loss." His reasons for thinking this surprised me: "She does not worry at all what happens to Taylor. Like the rest of the village she does not believe he will be punished. But she hopes that she can get compensation from Taylor, or from the company he works for, or from the government. They took her daughter from her; she should be paid. She was, I am sure, getting some of the money Taylor gave the girl, and she hoped for much more; the loss of the money was grievous, quite grievous to her. She will scream loud and long for that, believe me, and keep wailing on and on whatever you say, Mr. Grantham."

We had dined early and it was pleasant on the verandah. Having told of his trip to the village, Veraswami seemed relaxed and delighted by our company, the compulsions of hospitality now apparently less heavy upon him. Grantham had relaxed perceptibly as the evening proceeded and now seemed almost at ease. With the bucket of beer and ice beside him, Veraswami beamed at us. "This iss a very delicate matter for you both. I hear it iss much discussed at the Club. Nothing else obtrudes, I am told. If I am not presumptuous, dear friends, what should happen?"

"He will be charged with murder, I suppose, and tried at Mandalay Quarter Sessions," Grantham offered, unhelpfully I thought.

"Oh, that I know, Mr. Grantham, but what do you think is the correct final result? If I am not again being presumptuous. . . ."

Grantham offered no reply. Opening both palms in an out-ward enquiring gesture, Veraswami turned to me. So I tried.

"Well, if we believe everything Taylor told us, and it does seem to hang together and to agree with what you said about fugue states, Dr. Veraswami, then I think Taylor is not a mur-derer. He, Taylor, awake Taylor, thinking Taylor, did not kill her. It is as if he were possessed, as if he were controlled by some-one else; but the someone else, the possessor, is sleeping Taylor. We can't hang Taylor for his dreams or even for acting them out. So I think a suggestion of yours, Grantham, is right: Taylor knew he was unwell, knew he should not drink, did so, and as a result killed the girl. He has been reckless. He should be con-victed of manslaughter and given a short prison punishment."

I rarely produced such rounded arguments, and Grantham and Veraswami both looked surprised. But with a smile to one another, a linkage I was pleased to see, they joined in attacking my conclusions, but from different directions. Grantham thought that on Taylor's story, drinking or not, he could hardly be expected to foresee any risk to the girl. He might see that he was getting himself into a psychologically depressed or dis-turbed condition, but surely not that this might injure the girl.

I reminded Grantham of Taylor's spider dream, which I had, with Veraswami's permission, previously passed on to him. Grantham said that was quite different. Taylor was protecting the girl then.

"So he was, in a way, on Sunday night. Protecting her from the Indian lover," I said.

Grantham thought that was farfetched; while he was awake Taylor could surely not foresee any risk to the girl from his protecting her in a dream he had not then had.

Veraswami had started pacing about on the verandah as our talk turned to the details of Taylor's dreams. He seemed agitated. With an odd gesture, a half-raised left hand like a hes-itant policeman stopping an oncoming car, he turned to Gran-tham and myself: "Perhaps that iss what this iss all about—racial prejudice. May we talk about it?" And, not stopping for our obvious assent, with little steps to and fro before us, the

107

sibilant words began bouncing from him in rapid flow. "Have you thought, dear friends" (it astonished me that he had so swiftly thus categorised Grantham), "what enormous trouble European ladies go to in order *not* to consult me? For minor and imagined medical ailments they make the fatiguing journey to Mandalay rather than come to me. They know I did an English residency, and they know that only the inexperienced or alcoholic European doctors will work in Mandalay. So why iss it? Of course, because I am black and am likely to leap on them in excessive venery if they reveal their flesh to me. It iss madness; they are mostly quite unattractive. You must understand how deep these feelings run."

"Now suppose it had been Mrs. Taylor that Taylor had killed. All else the same; the same dream; the same Pathan lover on top of her. And suppose Taylor's story were believed, as we now believe him. Would not everyone feel the deepest sympathy for him? Would you not hold the preliminary hearing with great circumspection and kindness to him and find that the death was accidental? Feel sorry for Taylor? I think you would. So they would at the Club. In the village they would not care—one less European to put up with." And Veraswami stopped, embarrassed after such an aggressive outburst.

Grantham was quite moved. "Perhaps you're right, Dr. Veraswami. Perhaps we are influenced by some sort of reverse racial sentiment. As I understand you, you are suggesting that we think Taylor should be punished, as a murderer or a manslaughterer, one or the other, because he had a native mistress, drank too much, couldn't behave with the gentlemanly confidentiality such things require, and has had the bad luck, entirely without malice, to kill someone as a part of this complexity of immoral acts."

"Yes, yes, exactly," Veraswami's hands flew up in agreement. "It must be so. Many Europeans here do not cleave unqualifiedly to their lady wives. Many drink. Many are fond of Burmese girls and vigorously and frequently express their affection. This is true, too," with a knowing glance at me, "even of the unmarried here. But they are at risk, deadly risk, that their

crossing the colour line does not become a public scandal—
even if the event which causes the scandal iss not their fault.
They are subject to being blackmailed, like poor Flory—you will
remember him, Mr. Blair—and if it becomes a public matter
they are lost. Taylor's dream made it a public matter; he iss lost;
neither of you can do anything for him. The law does not matter. What I told you, Mr. Blair, about running amok, fugue
states, and somnambulism does not matter. Taylor iss lost." And
Veraswami's right arm came down like a cleaver on a block,
severing head from shoulders.

"It iss strange indeed, dear friends, that the respective col-
ours of the penis and of its receptacle should be so important."

Later that week, again in the early evening on Dr. Veraswami's
verandah, but this time without Grantham, Dr. Veraswami was
struggling with the metal levers holding the rubber-ringed ce-
ramic stopper into the top of a bottle of Watney's Beer. It was
a tight fit, stubborn to move, so that he had to press both black
thumbs up and under the ring to release the levers that held
the top. I had watched him at minor surgery and remained perplexed how such deftness could be in the same hands that were
wrestling so clumsily with a beer bottle stopper. In the result,
the ring gave suddenly, and the bottle, being by now well
shaken, squirted foam onto his pants. Having apologized to me
and to himself—to me I don't know what for—and forgiven
himself on the ground that it didn't matter, we each got a
slightly flat, nearly cool beer.

The Taylor topic would not go away, and soon I was bur-
dening Veraswami with my doubts: "What in Heaven's name led
Taylor to make such a fool of himself with the girl? I don't
mean so much the shooting—I think I begin to understand
that—but the whole mess he was in with her, his wife returning, all the servants except Aka Thon sent away, the arguments,
all the squalor of an affair with someone he can hardly have
admired. I saw her—I suppose you did too—before he shot
her; she was no beauty. And this jealousy of the mysterious Pa-

than. Why didn't he just send her away and let Aka Thon bring him any other village girl, if that's what he wanted?"

Dr. Veraswami seemed in no hurry to reply to my convoluted questions. He mopped some more at his pants, turned to speak, thought better of it apparently, and then drifted off into comments on his own youth. "I was married when I was seventeen, before I even thought of becoming a doctor. An arranged marriage, I think you call it. I had no other woman until she died. Then I would patronise prostitutes occasionally but medical school cured me of them and then I married my present wife. And here I am, a child in love and in jealousy, though I am very fond of and grateful to my wife. But what your Shakespeare had Othello and Iago feel I don't feel. However, I watch others, particularly your English colleagues here in Moulmein, and I see that many of them get themselves involved beyond their wishes with one another's wives or with Burmese ladies. They surely know better than to ruin their careers, both in the government service or in a trading company, but a few do so anyways. So, I conclude, ass I told you before, that the gonads are very powerful."

I remonstrated with Veraswami. Though a quick flirtation or a passing affair may be risky, if it were kept light and transient everyone understood and there was no serious threat to anyone. So handled, tragedies like the dead girl and Taylor would not happen.

Dr. Veraswami seemed to be becoming—could it be?—annoyed with me. He paced about, settling his ample bottom here, then there, on the balustrade, glancing at me querulously. "Mr. Blair, my friend, you tell me important things about yourself which bind our friendship and I am glad of that, believe me, very glad, but then you talk ass if I didn't know them. You have told me some occurrence in your own life that should help you understand Taylor's folly, have you not?"

I was unsure of what he referred to. My thoughts pursued the line of any lasting affairs with Burmese girls, but I had enjoyed no such relationships. Indeed, I could not even remember discussing any such things with Dr. Veraswami and said so.

His petulance seemed to increase but he controlled it. He could never be direct with me though he was never, so far as I knew, withdrawn or secretive. But communication, as now, often had to be by indirection. "Do you remember the poem you showed me? I remember it. You let me write it down. I will get it now." And he bustled off the verandah towards his study.

I did recall a piece of doggerel I had played with. Dr. Veraswami had insisted it had promise. I doubted it. It was certainly meant in fun and seemed somewhat remote from the Taylor killing.

Waving a paper aloft like a winning race ticket, Dr. Veraswami returned. "Let me read it to you. You will see what I mean." He stopped, quite still, close to my chair, and read what a few months earlier I had facetiously called "Romance." In his Indian, sibilant, highly inflected voice it sounded a great deal better than I thought it would when I wrote it:

> When I was young and had no sense
> In far-off Mandalay
> I lost my heart to a Burmese girl
> As lovely as the day.
>
> Her skin was gold, her hair was jet,
> Her teeth were ivory;
> I said "For twenty silver pieces,
> Maiden, sleep with me."
>
> She looked at me, so pure, so sad,
> The loveliest thing alive,
> And in her lisping, virgin voice,
> Stood out for twenty-five.*

I knew the punch line, of course, but Veraswami had read it with such exaggerated inflection that I laughed out loud. He looked even more disapproving. "My friend, even though you

---

*EDITOR'S NOTE: In his *George Orwell: A Life* (London, 1980), at pages 92 and 93, Bernard Crick expresses uncertainty as to whether Blair wrote this poem while he was in Burma or shortly thereafter in England. The discovery of this manuscript puts that question to rest.

are an eminent police magistrate, do not think your servants are silent about your life. I know you occasionally have Burmese ladies brought to your bungalow." And suddenly I realized he was equating *me* with Taylor—and I resented it.

"Dr. Veraswami, occasionally to patronise Burmese prostitutes is one thing; to become involved to the point of murderous jealousy is quite another. Surely Taylor's situation is very far removed from what you say you know about me—and I confess to resenting being spied upon."

Dr. Veraswami did his Indian imitation of a blush, revealed more by jerky arm-waving than by much change in skin coloration. "My friend, I am not saying they are the same. Only that you know the delights of Burmese ladies and also that you have some experience of jealousy, do you not? Did you not tell me of Miss Buddicom and what you called your calf-love for her? Surely you must have been jealous of others if you loved her and she felt no more than friendship for you?"

Veraswami was right about the Burmese but wrong about Janice Buddicom. But he struck home nevertheless. In Mandalay there had been an affair with the wife of one of our training officers. I am sure I was neither her first extra-marital adventure nor her last, but that realization in no way diminished the hurt. A painful scene came back to me. A monsoon threatened. And there was I lurking beside the path to her bungalow, waiting for her husband to leave for the Club. Given the threatening weather, he might stay home. And he might already guess I—or someone—was hanging about outside his house. I did not fancy my jungle skills. One of his servants might well have seen me. And yet I stayed there. He held my career in his hands. So did chance. It was absurd. To turn and walk away firmly along the path meant complete safety. To stay to hide, perhaps to be discovered, could mean years of turbulence and many hidden obstacles in my career. And for what? I didn't even like her. She was open about sex, like the Burmese prostitutes, and no one else had ever wanted me in that way—or at least, I never knew if they did. And I hated him and probably her. But I stayed. And then he came out. He had seen me. He shouted at me to

come out of hiding. And angrily on the path he told me to
clear out and never to hang around his wife again—that he
would mistake me for a burglar and shoot me if I did. And I
cringed away, with nothing sensible to say. And yet he treated
me fairly in the training course. I hated him and feared him.
Even more ridiculously, I went back to her on several occasions
until she tired of my snivelling attitude to the whole affair and
told me it would be better for her and for me if we did not
again meet, except distantly when we had to be at official parties.

So, yes, Veraswami was right in his perception but wrong
on the occasion—I had indeed known what it was like to make
a fool of myself over someone I didn't really even like, to be
fiercely jealous of the sexual behavior of one I didn't love but
merely wanted. I had been where Taylor found himself, I suppose; I hated having been there; perhaps that was why I hated
the whole Taylor case.

When I reached my bungalow that night, a note awaited me
from Grantham. He had been directed to report to regional
headquarters at Mandalay on one aspect of the Taylor case and
thought I should see what he had written. He would send it off
the next morning, subject to any suggestions I might have.

His report combined overconfidence with simulated modesty of opinion, it seemed to me, but there was certainly nothing of substance in it to which I could or did take exception.
Grantham had presented it as a memorandum, with paragraphs
numbered as we had been taught at our respective police training schools; but I noted that he did not always bother, as he
had been instructed, to confine one paragraph to one topic.
Grantham liked to appear to conform; I increasingly noticed
that he often did not do so in fact.

> 1. You requested an immediate report on one aspect of the
> Taylor matter not mentioned in my earlier memoranda—the
> question of Taylor's mental state at the time of the killing and,
> in particular, "the likelihood of his pleading and being found not
> guilty by reason of insanity."

2. Here in Moulmein, the general comment is that "he must have been mad to kill the girl," and it seems likely to me that that will remain the popular opinion. I cannot assess its validity as a proposition of medical science, but I doubt that he was insane at the time of the killing as a matter of law.

3. There is no alienist in Moulmein. The Medical Superintendent of the local hospital, a Dr. Veraswami, has had some training in England as well as in India and also some experience in treating mental illness. He tells me, and it accords with everything Taylor tells me and everything I have learned about this killing, that Taylor suffers from no diagnosable mental illness. Apart from the killing, no one had ever thought such a thing of Taylor.

4. Some time before he killed the Burmese girl, Taylor had consulted Dr. Veraswami about being upset, troubled, and anxious and sleeping poorly; but Dr. Veraswami tells me that Taylor always had a clear and realistic grasp of his circumstances, and, by my own observation, he still does.

5. If mental illness is to be defined by being out of touch with reality, then only during the dream (if one believes his story), concerning which I earlier reported, was he so removed from clear understanding of the objective facts of his surroundings. Nor did he suffer any sense of persecution—no partial insanity, according to Dr. Veraswami; and he gives no hint of such now.

6. If mental illness is to be defined by a statistical abnormality of mind and behavior, then, of course if one believes his story, Taylor's somnambulist acting out of his dream is a gross abnormality; but that would make nonsense of any defense of insanity. Dr. Veraswami says that such a condition would not be regarded in medicine as "mental illness"; certainly it would be no ground for his compulsory detention in a mental asylum until the "disease" is "cured" under our law on civil commitment to asylums.

7. Despite paragraph 6, it may not be difficult for the defense to find a doctor in Burma who will give evidence at the trial that Taylor was mentally ill and that that is why he dreamed as he did and acted as he did. A jury, because of the popular belief that he would not have done it unless he was mad, may incline to believe such testimony, false though it is. I

appreciate that such a result may be extremely convenient, but it seems to me to be our duty to resist it.

8. Taylor resents and repudiates the suggestion that he was or is mad. He insists he has told me the whole truth; I believe him. He says it could happen to anyone who got himself into such a hopeless situation as he did. He rejects any suggestion that a defense of insanity may be advanced on his behalf—he prefers to see himself as wicked and stupid rather than mad. As you know, he has no defense counsel here and reiterates that he does not wish for such assistance; but when he has counsel in Mandalay these attitudes may change.

9. If one believes Taylor's story, then, in my view, as the law stands, he has no defense of insanity to a criminal charge. If he were thought of as responsible for his conduct in his sleep, then on his own statement he knew what he was doing—shooting the man above the Burmese girl. On his own story, that is a crime, "wrong" in law and in morality; at the least, taking his view, he would be guilty of manslaughter. And further, in my view, he was not at the time of the killing "suffering a defect of reason from disease of the mind" as that phrase has been interpreted and applied since its adumbration in the House of Lords in the case of *McNaughtan* and its adoption into the criminal law we apply in this country.

10. As I suggested in earlier written reports and will develop in detail when I report to you in Mandalay, my present opinion is that though Taylor has no valid defense of insanity in respect of his alleged crime, he cannot for other reasons be convicted. I see the disadvantage in this position. If found insane he could be held in an asylum until any public anxiety is assuaged, whereas if he is acquitted he must be released immediately, giving, perhaps, an appearance of the administration's excessive leniency towards crimes against natives by Europeans; but, with some hesitation, I think that is the law.

11. Please advise me if you wish me to expand on any of the points in this memorandum. I shall try to do so, although I suspect that my insecurity in these medico-legal problems is already all too apparent.

Grantham and I seemed equally to dislike the Club, so that for the few days he was in Moulmein we would, apart from the evening Dr. Veraswami invited us to dinner, tend to drift after dinner towards Dr. Veraswami's bungalow for our evening talks. In the small European community of Moulmein this was neither unnoticed nor uncriticized. But, since we were both seen as "stuck-up bores" our actions if resented were not regretted.

And we both *were* bores; that was another sad similarity between us. Not, of course, bores of the blustering, verbose, overbearing subspecies—which is the most deadly form—but of the hesitant, unsure, difficult-to-talk-to type. But undeniably bores. To drag an opinion from Grantham on the Taylor matter, which fascinated us both, was no sinecure, and I suspect he found me equally difficult. Like so many others of our class and training we were often paralyzed in word and deed by the fear that we might make fools of ourselves. But in Veraswami's presence, we could talk freely not only to him but also to one another—he unlocked the doors of our reticence.

One evening at Veraswami's bungalow the reason for our openness in his presence struck me—and I was ashamed. Colour prejudice, of course. No matter what we said or did, we were, it seems, sure of our superiority to Veraswami and had no need to protect our precious selves as we thought we did with others and even with each other. And when we were together at the bungalow we could talk and laugh with one another as well as with Dr. Veraswami, secure in our knowledge of our shared and unfailing inherent advantage. Yet in every way he was our superior—in education, skill, experience, character, and sensitivity—and we knew it.

So this was why I found so many reasons to visit his bungalow during my months in Moulmein. What a swinish motive! No, that is not fair; how weak, vacillating, and unsure of myself I must be—to be able to be open and direct only with one I see, for no possibly acceptable reason, as an inferior. Perhaps this is why the English lower middle class so relish India—it is not the servants or the comforts, but rather the pervading sense of their own greater worth vis-à-vis the lesser coloured breeds around them. At "home" the working class took less and less kindly to condescension, but the natives of the Raj at least pretended to accept it.

Grantham wrenched me back to civility. "Blair, you drift off. What troubles you? You look as if that beef at the Club sits heavily—it wasn't that bad."

I decided to risk my thoughts, even those on colour prejudice, with them both. "Dr. Veraswami, forgive me. I was thinking why Grantham and I can talk so easily to you about Taylor and that poor girl. You know, with others, even with each other, we mumble, are silent, and turn away from our ignorance. But with you . . . ," and I opened my palms in a poor imitation of his expansive Indian gesture.

Dr. Veraswami seemed pleased, and then the rounded smile left his face as understanding came. "Tell uss why, my young friend."

There seemed no avoidance. "Because you are coloured." I blushed fiercely, could feel it, and Grantham started making throat-clearing noises to signify a verbally crippling mixture of embarrassment and dissent. But it suddenly seemed important to me to press on. "I'm right, aren't I, Dr. Veraswami? You know more than we, you have proved your value to yourself and to others. If you were white we would not dare to talk so freely to you as we do. It would be 'Yes Sir; No Sir'. We might think you either an old fool or a wise and sound man of experience, but in either case we couldn't talk to you. But you are an educated Indian; we can talk openly with you on every topic except this one that I am gassing on about now, and, do forgive me, but I'm right, aren't I?"

Dr. Veraswami had begun his pacing about the verandah and jerky hand-waving, anxious either to interrupt me or certainly to get in on my first pause. Yet when I did stop he was silent and stood immobile for a moment. "Of course, Mr. Blair, you are right. It iss most unusual, most unusual indeed, for one of your age and background to see it. I do commend you, my friend. You would think they would let me into the Club to help their conversation by my pigmentation—if what you tell me about the talk there iss true. But I think there iss even more to this ease you and your lawyer friend feel in my company." And he beamed with unaffected joy on Grantham, who seemed to be overcoming the more acute pains of embarrassment he had suffered earlier. "Have you thought that that poor girl may have had the same effect on Taylor, issn't it? In another way, if you take my meaning, do you see?"

I didn't then understand what he was talking about, nor, apparently, did Grantham. But my earlier directness with Veraswami had allowed him to give us another view of Taylor which, the longer I thought about it, and later about myself, made more and more compelling but troubling sense.

I cannot recapture most of Dr. Veraswami's words, but his theme stayed with me quite clearly. And upsetting it was, since if he was right, my own chances of a happy marriage seemed to recede even further. I remembered poignantly my own vigour and confidence in the brothels of London and Rangoon as contrasted to those few graceless, wordless gropings with girls of my own age, class, and colour; perhaps it was not their relative inexperience that distinguished the encounters, but my own insecurity.

"What do you think Mr. and Mrs. Taylor talked about?" Dr. Veraswami said and launched into an almost clinical analysis of their sexual relationship which, if it were true, explained Taylor's preference for the teak estates over Moulmein, his cheerful acceptance of Mary's regular visits "home," and, like most of the other planters, his having "a bit on the side" both upriver on the estate and in Moulmein. The conclusion was that many Europeans could not feel easy, in or out of bed, with anyone "they could not either venerate or dominate"; that their vicious class structure had impeded sexual freedom between men and women, the alleged joys of the flesh also requiring for them dominance or subservience, and had severely complicated friendships between males, which were too often seen as dependent weaknesses unless they were of the sporting or hunting variety.

I must say he went on with some relish about what he called the well-known English weakness for ladies with whips and black leather, or for boys, most of which seemed a bit excessive to me.

"But, Dr. Veraswami, surely you in India have a very rigid caste system, more strict than ours. We don't have untouchables. Indeed, in England, the lower the class, the more touchable."

Veraswami allowed himself a smile at my turn of phrase but hurried to correct me. "No. No, Magistrate friend. You confuse class and caste. And in sexual matters we in India are much better instructed than you tell me you were in England, and also, from what you tell me about the girls on the ship coming out and the few young European ladies here, we are much better practised than you. The young ladies of your class have to sell themselves whole, you tell me, to marriage. Our young ladies have the bargains made for them. And they would be troubled indeed to think they were to marry a virgin. True, yes, I know, you will remind me that I have told you how I cannot discuss matters of my work or of the world with my wife—of these things she knows nothing it is true—but, believe me, on matters of our family, of this home, and of sex she is a torrent, a very torrent, word after word, and sensible and pleasing indeed they are to me."

Veraswami's view of the Taylor marriage was quite different. For Mrs. Taylor, resentful acceptance, with noble and resigned sacrifice the leitmotif. For him, a growing sense of the infliction of his desire on her, whisky at first helping to cloud the consequent sense of his own worthlessness and, as the years passed, whisky helping to prove that very worthlessness in impotence. Sex, for Taylor, Dr. Veraswami argued, was to be occasionally inflicted on a wife but only enjoyed with a Burmese girl or perhaps with a European prostitute.

Walking back to my bungalow from Dr. Veraswami's place that night, in the moonlit half-light, Grantham and I carried with us the ease of Veraswami's companionship. For the first time we talked without anxiety for ourselves about Taylor and the girl. Our difficulty was that though Veraswami was no doubt broadly right about the grim sex lives of the married Europeans in Moulmein, that really did not explain Taylor killing the girl. For nearly ten years he had adapted to life in Burma with Mary, as well as enjoying, according to Veraswami, enthusiastic copulation with more than one Burmese girl. He knew how to play these games; why the change? And such an extraordinary change. We had no very helpful ideas, but Grantham did produce the thought—probably improper for a potential prosecutor—that though Taylor was morally guilty for his treatment of the girl he was, it seemed to Grantham, in law entirely innocent of her death.

Although Grantham suggested as much before, I had never succeeded in seeing Taylor as innocent. The degree of his guilt had worried me, but that he was innocent, not guilty of any crime at all, had not really seemed likely to me. Grantham's argument was really very simple. "In the criminal law, Blair, you are responsible only for conscious, intended acts. There is also some learning on responsibility for certain failures to act, certain omissions, but that has nothing to do with Taylor's killing the girl. He is not responsible in criminal law for his dreams; he is not responsible for what he does in his dreams. Even if he just killed her in his dream—forget all that about the Pathan on top of her—he would not be guilty, even if he was in fact acting out his dream. Have you never dreamt that you were urinating and wakened to find it so? Or dreamt that you were copulating and wakened to a differently dampened bed? No. I think Taylor is innocent. But whether I will have the guts to say that in Mandalay and not to prosecute him is another matter."

"There must be more to it than that, Grantham, surely. Can he find another Burmese girl and have another murdering dream about her? And what if his wife forgives him, too, like you seem to, and returns to what Veraswami sees as their grim bed—he may dispose of her too."

Grantham did not respond to the probably alcoholic lightness of my analysis; that night I had made more than the usual dent in Veraswami's beer supply. He took me seriously. "Yes, of course, if he knew of any risk that he might injure her the matter would be very different. Certainly if he knew of any such risk if he drank a little or a lot before he went to bed with her. But there is no evidence at all of that in this case. So your idea about his next Burmese girl—I doubt there will be one—does not help here."

Grantham told me of one case where an attendant in a mental hospital, who was a diabetic, had drunk too much, had fallen into a fugue state, and was wrenched off the chest of a helpless patient he was beating cruelly but of whose existence he was not consciously aware. In situations like this, foresight of risk spelt criminal liability if the risk were consciously run. The diabetic hospital attendant knew that his blood sugar concentration went awry with alcohol and that he might—although, in effect, unconscious—act violently. He may not have known the chemistry, but he knew the risk. Taylor had no such advance warning; how could he be liable?

"They won't like this in Mandalay, Grantham."

"I know, I know," he replied, "but it's the truth. I shall tell them that the third eye is not farsighted; that will surely help." And on that unlikely note we parted, agreeing to meet for breakfast and a further talk with Taylor.

Taylor would not now talk to Dr. Veraswami about the events of the night when he killed the girl or what led up to them. "He thinks I failed him, when he came to me about the spiders. He cannot talk about matters of sexual jealousy to me, a Nigger as he sees me, and particularly of jealousy of another Indian, dreamlike though that man may be. Perhaps he can talk to you about it. He would certainly be helped if he could. You should try, my friend, to talk to him."

But how? How to move from policeman and magistrate to confidant and emotional supporter? And should I? I had no idea. Veraswami said it would not be hard if I were direct with Taylor. So I tried; Veraswami was, as usual, correct.

I told Taylor that I believed his story and, unless something he had not told me came up at the preliminary hearing, Grantham and I would likely send to Mandalay depositions supporting its truth. Taylor did not seem to care; he accepted it as obvious that we would believe his story, but that was not what worried him.

He seemed to need my absolution for his relationship with the girl rather than anything to do with her death. The killing was not his, so it seemed, but her sharing his bed was. I tried to tell him that I was unlikely to be of much use, but he kept repeating that he had no one else to turn to. And then I saw that it was not my absolution, or even Mary's, he needed, but that of everyone with whom he would in the future form any other than the most transient relationship—and that the forgiveness would not, could not, be given.

"Blair, I hated her, always hanging about. If I went upriver to the estates, there she would be. And always whining for money and getting it. If Mary went to Mandalay, the girl would wait until I came home from the Club and put me to bed. And if she didn't come I would send Aka Thon for her. It was awful. I once even went to her village and her miserable room. I hated her and yet kept her on." And in his misery he left unasked the obvious question of why, knowing, I suppose, the obvious answer. How appalling always to have to live with this.

Words came to me, and I heard myself saying them before I had thought through what a burden they would make for me: "If you want me to, I shall go with you to meet your wife in Mandalay."

My last evening with Dr. Veraswami before escorting Taylor to Mandalay—Grantham had gone ahead to arrange for Taylor's detention and trial—helped me to understand why I hated the Taylor case and the tension it was causing between Grantham and me.

Dr. Veraswami talked less than usual. An occasional question. But mainly he seemed intent on helping me to talk through what troubled me.

In the end, what it seemed to come to was this. Grantham saw the criminal law as a self-contained system, a pure and complete system—at any rate, that is what he thought it ought to be. Taylor was, therefore, innocent; that was all there was to it. He intended neither to kill the girl nor in any way to risk her life, except in a dream which didn't count. Oh yes, Grantham would admit the existence of other closely similar situations where if you are doing what is illegal or immoral and things go badly you may be convicted for the larger harm; but he saw them as errors in the law or at best rules of evidence that had been allowed to harden into rules of law—and should be changed.

By contrast, it seemed to me that the criminal law is a dependent system, very reliant on culture, moral values, custom, and the texture of all the interwoven rules of law. If you are vulnerable morally, and in relation to any of those rules, and the dice roll against you, then you may lose badly.

Grantham argued fairly, if often aridly, as if about a game long past. He gave me examples of existing rules of law which helped me make my argument for Taylor's guilt, but he also mocked them with what seemed to me distant arrogance. He reminded me of what I had been taught at the Burma Provincial Police Training Academy of the felony-murder and misdemeanor-manslaughter rules, by which acts that would normally attract no conviction for homicide did so if they were done in the course of a crime. He told me how "malice" in the criminal law originally meant a generalized illegal intent, intending evil, and how what he called the "growing maturity of our jurisprudence" had intended to shift its meaning to an intent to do the prohibited harm—or to risk it.

In the end I remained unconvinced. It was a strange inversion of roles between us. I sympathized with Taylor, thought I understood something of his torment, but thought he should be convicted of manslaughter. Grantham cordially disliked Taylor, had no patience with his self-indulgence and stupidity, yet thought he should be acquitted.

"It will be a miserable time in Mandalay, Dr. Veraswami. I do not look forward to being anywhere with both Taylor and his wife. And Grantham seems so above it all. Yet he is willing to risk his career, certainly to annoy his superiors, by taking what will be a very unpopular position. His superiors would much prefer him to stress the immorality and indeed the illegality of what Taylor did—adultery, after all, remains a legal and moral wrong—and the likely connection between his drinking and his killing the girl. That many of his superiors engage in all these acts, except the killing, will only heighten their sense of duty to be done. And they will expect Grantham to be skeptical of the dream and to say that even if you believe Taylor and his dream what he said he did in his dream was at least manslaughter.

"Certainly, Dr. Veraswami, it will not be an easy time for Grantham in Mandalay. Nor for me. Grantham will frustrate his superiors; I will annoy them even more. I will be on their side, in a sense, but they will even more dislike my view that Taylor should be punished for bad luck—for chance selecting him from many of us to help us all shape our moral and legal values."

Dr. Veraswami waved his head from side to side and patted his ample hips with pleasure in my analysis. "Eric (he had never before used my Christian name), you are right, I am sure, about Grantham and yourself. Whether you are right about what should happen to Taylor I do not know, and it doess not seem very important to me, I am most sorry to say. You are so much more important! You are right to be repulsed by the crime—if that iss what it wass—and also to glimpse Taylor's agony. Grantham may be right in law. He may even be right about how the law should be. He may be on the right side. But if you report him accurately, and I am sure you do, it will not be, ass you say, an easy time for you both in Mandalay."

To the distaste of the Europeans catching the mail train to Mandalay, Dr. Veraswami came to say farewell to his patient, Taylor, and, I suppose, to me.

Taylor loathed the increased attention Veraswami attracted. Veraswami understood and made his farewell brief and formal. But there was a fleeting chance for us to talk; he took it and managed to implant a parting barb. "Mr. Blair"—in public he was always punctiliously formal with me—"I have never heard

you use the dead girl's name in our discussion of the case. Do
you remember it?"

The name was, of course, spread all over the depositions;
some complex, sing song, Burmese name; but for the moment it
escaped me, and I said so.

"You should, may I most respectfully suggest, be careful to
use it often and precisely in Mandalay. After all, the tragedy
wass at least partly hers. You and I both seem a little insensitive
to her—you see, I too have been searching my conscience."
And he turned and, with light tread for his roly-poly shape, set
off to walk back from the railway station to the hospital.

A few months later the *Mandalay Times* reported the last I heard,
other than rumours, of Philip and Mary Taylor. Under the head-
ing "Moulmein Killing" it reported: "A spokesman for the Burmese Police announced yesterday that Philip Taylor was
acquitted of the murder of a Burmese girl in Moulmein. The
jury found that her death was accidental and that Mr. Taylor
was in no way criminally responsible."

Rumor in Moulmein had it that Mary had returned to England before the trial and that Taylor had drunk his way further
inland, doing odd jobs on rubber estates. I had heard nothing of
him since the trial. I knew Mary had left him. When it came to
the point, she did not care enough for him to run the gauntlet
of Mandalay, let alone to try to build a new life with him thereafter, possibly after a prison term.

In the end I didn't know if I felt sorry for Taylor or not. I
suppose I did, but it wasn't easy. I think I understand why he
kept the girl on—Veraswami had forced me to see that; but I
lack any abiding feeling for the tragedy of Taylor's life. Veraswami and I rarely mention the case nowadays. The last time
we spoke of it he compared Grantham's and my attitudes toward Taylor. Veraswami had not been to Mandalay while we
were all there, but I had told him something of the burdensome
weeks leading up to the trial and he guessed the rest. "The
trouble iss that Grantham wants men to be saints. You are too
sensible, perhaps too humanly weak for that, my friend. But I

have long thought that those who aspire to sainthood in themselves or others have not felt much temptation to be human—and you certainly have."

I think he was unfair to Grantham, but I am not sure. At all events, Grantham left the service soon after the trial and returned to a barrister's practice in England. When he and I were last together in Mandalay, before the trial, he had developed something like contempt for Taylor. Taylor's "innocence," on which Grantham kept insisting to the annoyance of his superiors in the Legal Section, didn't seem to have much to do with it. Grantham resented that Taylor's existence pushed him to those difficult and career-threatening intercessions. As Grantham said, "It was, after all, just bad luck. He should have taken it like a gentleman. He should have shot himself. He let the side down, really."

I never shared Grantham's view. We have lost touch with one another. He seems too proper for me. No doubt he will go far.*

*For those who wish to pursue the legal issues raised in this chapter, a guide to the case law and literature appears in the Appendix.

FOUR

Sentencing the Mentally Ill

This chapter traverses largely uncharted and sometimes treacherous terrain. Even the determined prospector is entitled to some hint of what awaits him if he makes the journey and of what the likely pay dirt will be. First, then, the conclusion, followed by a sketch of the journey to it.

Mental illness at the time of the crime is properly taken into account to *reduce* the severity or duration of punishment; mental illness continuing or likely to recur is also properly taken into account to *increase* the severity or prolong the duration of punishment. There is no contradiction in these opposing effects, no paradox. They may be reconciled and will coexist in every developed system of sentencing. This chapter provides that reconciliation, recommends that the criminal's mental illness should normally reduce the severity of the punishment imposed, and suggests the limits of that reduction. It further recommends that in exceptional cases the criminal's mental illness should increase or prolong punishment, and suggests the criteria for and the limits of that increase. In short, relative to the mentally ill, convicted criminal, principles are offered defining when to mitigate punishment, when to aggravate punishment, and the proper limits of both.[1]

This chapter is thus an effort to state the main jurisprudential themes in sentencing the mentally ill.[2] Perhaps a note of anxiety may be struck as one approaches this task: whereas gallons of ink and tons of printer's lead have been expended in considering the questions of the responsibility of the mentally ill for their criminal conduct and their fitness to be brought to trial, there is the merest trickle of commentary on the question of sentencing the mentally ill, that is, their fitness for punishment. This is surprising, since in practice the question of sentencing the mentally ill must be answered much more frequently than the others. The terrain is thus both uncharted and much frequented.

The common-law heritage, the historical background, need not long detain us. As a matter of legal theory, the insane were denied the release of capital punishment. Assuming sufficient sanity for trial and criminal responsibility but then supervening insanity, the felon would not be executed while he was insane. A jurisprudence sensitive to theological concerns allowed for repentance on the gallows or before execution, and the insane were in no position to repent. Modern capital punishment statutes, if such a phrase is not a contradiction in terms, also preclude the execution of the insane.[3] Problems of capital punishment are set aside in this

1. To write of "mitigating punishment" and "aggravating punishment" is common usage, though imprecise. More careful usage would refer to circumstances mitigating the gravity of the offense and hence properly decreasing punishment or to circumstances aggravating the offense and hence increasing punishment. The point being made, let lazy usage triumph.

2. In this chapter the phrases "the mentally ill" and "mental illness" will be used, without pretense to psychological precision, to include those who are psychotic, those who are substantially psychologically disturbed, and those who are substantially retarded or mentally disadvantaged. The intended precision of *DSM III*, the current *Diagnostic and Statistical Manual*, is unnecessary to our task. I am attempting to carve out for consideration the cases in which a psychiatrist would suggest a degree of illness or retardation that might be relevant to sentencing the convicted offender. The problems are jurisprudential; issues of psychiatric nosology are set aside.

3. See, e.g., Unified Code of Corrections, §5-2-3; Ill. Rev. Stat., ch. 38, §1005-2-3 (1979).

chapter; they are ornate and exceptional issues having little to do with the grist of the mill of punishment except to reveal the highly emotional context in which problems of punishing convicted offenders are to be found.

Here is the sequence of topics to be discussed:

I. Isolating the Issues
II. Legislation Concerning Sentencing the Mentally Ill
III. Sentencing Reforms and the Mentally Ill
IV. Mitigating the Punishment of the Mentally Ill
   —with an Aside on Justice, Mercy, Discretion, and Equality
V. Aggravating the Punishment of the Mentally Ill
VI. When to Mitigate? When to Aggravate?
VII. The Minnesota Sentencing Guidelines

I. Isolating the Issues

Observation of any busy criminal court of first instance, particularly any crowded court in an urban center, reveals an appreciable flow of psychologically disturbed and intellectually retarded convicted persons. This is so whatever rules and practices are applied to exclude the incompetents from trial or the mentally ill from criminal responsibility; the filtering mechanisms are insufficient to insulate many of the mentally ill from being convicted of crime.

In the more advanced systems of criminal jurisprudence, those offenders thought to be mentally ill are frequently remanded for psychiatric assessment as part of a pre-sentence report; but there is little information on what use should be made of such assessments when the sentence comes to be determined, particularly when the criminal is deemed mentally ill. Nor has it proved easy, from observing practice and drinking with judges, to perceive any general principles guiding the exercise of sentencing discretion in such cases. Sometimes the mentally ill are seen as morally less culpable and therefore to be less severely punished; in other cases, somewhat randomly, they are seen as likely to be more dangerous and therefore to require separation from the community, instead of the community-based sentence which would have been ordered were they not mentally ill. Despite these apparently contradictory tendencies, there is general agreement on one proposition: the mental illness of the convicted offender is relevant to just and efficient sentencing. Relevant, but how? To what purposes? By what measures? Does it mitigate punishment? Does it aggravate punishment? Both? How?

Scholarship requires artificial isolation of the issues to be addressed, and there is much in the relationship between the mentally ill and the criminal law which is excluded from this chapter. These exclusions do not indicate the unimportance of the excluded topics; though they are important we have enough to do without them and they are not essential to the analysis.

The following topics are excluded from analysis in this chapter:

"Diversions" to the mental health system of those who commit crimes, by victims, witnesses, police, prosecutors, those who run jails, and other functionaries of investigative processes and preliminary inquiries. This chapter is confined to judicial sentencing of convicted criminals.

Problems of the competency of the accused to stand trial; that is to say, "triability" is excluded.

The legal doctrines by which the mentally ill are to be found guilty or not guilty by reason of insanity; that is to say, "responsibility" is excluded.

The legal doctrine of provocation—which reduces murder to manslaughter, on the ground, in effect, of temporary insanity; this raises a complex of fascinating issues which are regretfully set aside.

"Diminished responsibility" and "diminished capacity"; this doctrine takes two forms: first, a judicially developed form which emerged most clearly in a series of decisions by the Supreme Court of California—the *Wells*,[4] *Gorshen*,[5] *Wolff*,[6]

4. People v. Wells, 33 Cal.2d 330, 202 P.2d 53 (1949), *cert. denied*, 338 U.S. 836 (1949).

5. People v. Gorshen, 51 Cal.2d 761, 336 P.2d 492 (1959).

6. People v. Wolff, 61 Cal.2d. 795, 394 P.2d 959, 40 Cal. Rptr. 271 (1964).

Conley,[7] *Wetmore*[8] line—but which is also to be found in other jurisdictions.[9] These cases go to issues of *mens rea* and the crime for which the mentally ill person is to be held responsible. They do not necessarily raise particular problems of sentencing for the judge, which is our central focus. And the same is true of the second form this doctrine assumes, the statutory form of "diminished responsibility." The English Homicide Act of 1957 provided that "where a person kills or is a party to the killing of another he shall not be convicted of murder if he was suffering from such abnormality of mind . . . as substantially impaired his mental responsibility."[10] Persons so found by the jury are then to be sentenced as if they had been convicted of manslaughter, not murder. The doctrine of diminished responsibility produces cases to be guided by sentencing principles considered in this chapter, indeed many such cases,[11] but the doctrine itself does not define problems in sentencing for the judge, and these are our concern.

7. People v. Conley, 64 Cal.2d 310, 411 P.2d 911, 49 Cal. Rptr. 815 (1966).

8. People v. Wetmore, 22 Cal.3d 318, 583 P.2d 1208, 149 Cal. Rptr. 265 (1978).

9. See, e.g., State v. Di Paolo, 34 N.J. 279, l68 A.2d 401 (1961), *cert. denied*, 368 U.S. 880 (1961). See generally Annot., 22 A.L.R.3d 1228 (1968 & Supp. 1980) (listing the following states as allowing the admission of evidence of an abnormal mental condition for the purpose of negativing specific intent: California, Colorado, Connecticut, Idaho, Indiana, Iowa, Kentucky, Michigan, Missouri, Nebraska, Nevada, New Jersey, New Mexico, New York, Ohio, Oregon, Rhode Island, Texas, Utah, Vermont, Virginia, Washington, Wisconsin, Wyoming).

10. The Homicide Act, 1957, 5 & 6 Eliz. 2, c.11, §2.

11. Of all persons committed for trial for murder in England and Wales in the decade before the Homicide Act, 1957, roughly 20 percent were found "insane on arraignment" (incompetent to stand trial) and another 20 percent were found "guilty but insane" (not guilty by reason of insanity). A decade after the Act these numbers have fallen precipitously. Less than 3 percent were found incompetent and less than 1 percent not guilty by reason of insanity, while more than 37 percent were found of "diminished responsibility." Nigel Walker, 1 *Crime and Insanity in England* 159 (1968); Report of the Committee on Mentally Abnormal Offenders, Cmnd. 6244, at 316 (1975). These figures are remarkable both for the constancy of the number (40 percent) of psychologically disturbed and for the engulfment of incompetency by diminished responsibility.

A final exclusion: because the focus is on adult mentally ill criminals, the problems of sentencing juvenile and youthful offenders are put aside by fiat.

What, then, is left within our terms of reference? I hope the answer is this: problems of sentencing those adults who have been convicted of crime and come to be sentenced, and who sufficiently depart from the prevailing norms of mental balance and rational competence as to be "mentally ill." Their condition may continue to affect their behavior and so be relevant to present problems of determining the sentence to be imposed on them for their crime, apart from its modulation of their degree of guilt.

II. Legislation Concerning Sentencing the Mentally Ill

If light is to be cast onto our topic, it is necessary to survey present legislative provisions for sentencing the mentally ill. This part of the chapter a reader more interested in theory than in practice might well skip over. What emerges is that some legislative and administrative rules and regulations provide for the reduction and some for the increase of punishment of the mentally ill, the former always justified by concepts of moral desert, the latter by predictions of dangerousness.[12] For the determined reader, however, the following scheme should assist toward a more detailed perspective:

A. Specific Provisions for Increase of Punishment
   —Sexual Psychopath Laws
   —Dangerous Offender Laws
B. Specific Provisions for Decrease of Punishment
   —Legislatively Defined Mitigating Circumstances

12. To decrease punishment mental illness operates through the medium of "desert": because the accused was psychologically disturbed at the time of the crime he deserves a lesser punishment than if he had been coldly calculating. To increase punishment, mental illness operates through the medium of "dangerousness": because the accused is now at time of sentencing psychologically disturbed it is appropriate to impose on him a greater punishment than if he were now not so disturbed.

A. *Specific Provisions for Increase of Punishment*

Sexual psychopath laws. Statutes on "sexual psychopaths" or "sexually dangerous persons" spread like a rash of injustice across the United States from 1938 onward, covering twenty-five states and the District of Columbia.[13] All aim to protect the public "through the proper disposition of persons with criminal propensities to the commission of sex offenses."[14] In their origin they claimed to be civil in form, not punitive, committing the mentally ill criminal with a propensity to sexual offenses to indeterminate treatment until "cured." The earlier statutes sought to intercept the "sexual psychopath" even before he was convicted of a crime, any crime, sexual or otherwise. But these unqualified preemptive strikes seemed so clearly unjust that later statutes have tended to require a conviction of some crime, usually a sexual crime (with great difficulties of definition) as a condition precedent to their invocation. The cloak of civil commitment, thin to begin with, became transparent with the decision of the United States Supreme Court in *Baxstrom v. Herold*,[15] and statutes passed subsequent to that case have tended to limit the duration of detention (and treatment, if any) to that which could have been ordered pursuant to the criminal conviction.

The cloak of civil commitment being removed, what remains? The mentally ill sexual offender must be seen as less morally guilty than an offender who is not mentally ill but is guilty of an offense

13. The literature on these Acts and their operation is extensive. The following will lead into it: Sutherland, "The Sexual Psychopath Laws," 40 *J. Crim. L.C. & P.S.* 547 (1950); Tappan, "Sentences for Sex Criminals," 42 *J. Crim. L.C. & P.S.* 332 (1951); Tappan, "Some Myths about the Sex Offender," 19 *Fed. Prob.* 7 (1955); Hacker & Frym, "The Sexual Psychopath Act in Practice: A Critical Discussion," 43 *Cal. L. Rev.* 766 (1955); Burick, "An Analysis of the Illinois Sexually Dangerous Persons Act," 59 *J. Crim. L.C. & P.S.* 254 (1968); Granucci, "Indiana's Sexual Psychopath Act in Operation," 44 *Ind. L. J.* 555 (1969). On this topic I have been greatly assisted by a seminar paper by Richard B. Friedman, "A Study of Sexual Psychopath Legislation in the United States" (27 February 1981).

14. Sutherland, *supra* note 13, at 547.

15. 383 U.S. 103, 110 (1966).

of identical severity and with an identical criminal record; hence the justification for an extension of state power over the mentally ill offender must rest on a belief in his increased dangerousness. Sexual psychopathy is an insufficiently precise diagnosis to sustain such far-reaching legislative intervention; psychiatrists disagree profoundly on its definition and all modern nosologies reject it as a diagnostic entity.

There is little of principle that can be said in defense of these sexual psychopath statutes. Most were immediate legislative reactions to sensational sexual crimes and illustrate a legislative capacity to conceal excessive punitiveness behind a veil of psychiatric treatment, independently of any knowledge evaluating the efficacy or provisions for the availability of such treatment. At base lies the false assumption of a connection between sexual offenses and mental illness, certainly mental illness subject to effective treatment within the constraints of human rights.

These statutes are also based on yet further false premises, in particular, that sexual offenders start with minor sexual offenses and move on to more serious ones—e.g., that exhibitionism or voyeurism proceeds to rape—and that serious sexual offenders have higher rates of recidivism than other criminals, which they do not.

The literature on these statutes is extensive and need not be expanded here. Let brief conclusions from that literature suffice: the best one can say in favor of these statutes is that they have been rarely and sporadically applied, except in California, Indiana, and Wisconsin, where mistaken enthusiasm has outrun both good sense and a sense of justice.[16] These three states apart, the judiciary elsewhere remains uneasy in applying sexual psychopath statutes.

16. Some illustrative numbers: Illinois, 1949–76, only 56 so sentenced; Oregon, 1963–72, 107. By contrast, the three states extensively applying this type of statute: Indiana, California, and Wisconsin. Indiana invoked its statute on 450 occasions during the 1960s. Granucci, *supra* note 13, at 557. Some California figures are, in 1964, 812; in 1966, 804; in 1968, 707. S. Brakel & R. Rock, *The Mentally Disabled and the Law* 348 n.59 (1971). In 1973 there were 675 offenders so sentenced in California institutions. Dix, "Differential Processing of Abnormal Sex Offenders: Utilization of California's Mentally Disordered Sex Offender Program," 67 *J. Crim. L.C. & P.S.* 233, 234 (1976). In Wisconsin, by

These statutes, where applied, have tended to sweep into their net minor sexual offenders, the inadequate repetitive voyeurs and exhibitionists, rather than those who commit serious crimes of sexual violence. They are exercises in retributive justice masquerading as "treatment"; they are one paradigm of injustice flowing from an unprincipled blending of powers under the criminal law and the mental health law.

My vituperations are, of course, not meant to deny that some sexual offenders are mentally ill, in need of treatment, and that the community is in need of protection from them. The indictment is different. It is, at base, that sexual criminality is a mistaken classification for these purposes, for the invocation of special powers by the state. A sexual offender may be mentally ill and properly civilly committed; a sexual offender may be likely to repeat his crime and properly punished for it; but no blending of sexual crime and mental illness can justify varying ordinary rules of civil commitment or of the criminal law. For these purposes, armed robbers and serious sexual offenders are jurisprudentially identical, though the former are more likely to repeat their crimes.

The vigor and cogency of the scholarly attack on sexual psychopath laws led to their rejection by the three main commissions which have contributed nationally in the past quarter-century to reform of the criminal law: the American Law Institute's Model Penal Code; the Model Sentencing Act of the Advisory Council of Judges of the National Council on Crime and Delinquency; and the National Commission on Reform of Federal Criminal Laws, the Brown Commission. All three reject "sexual psychopathy," "psychopathy," and the more recent "sociopathy" as acceptable referents for legislation; but all three, in rejecting that path of increasing punishment because of the mental illness of the accused, set out on another path we must now follow.

Dangerous offender laws. Criminal law, as a system of deterrent threats, aims to help the potential offender resist criminality by threatening punishment if he does not. Sexual psychopath laws are

---

1971 over 3,000 convicted sex offenders had been examined for sentencing under the sexual psychopath statute, and over half were recommended for institutional treatment. Brakel & Rock, *supra*.

based on the premise that such threats are not enough to deter certain psychologically disturbed sexual offenders. At best these laws rest on a view of such offenders as psychologically incapable, or less capable, of controlling their sexual instincts under the usual deterrent threat and therefore as properly requiring additional deterrence, more protracted detention, and special treatment to help them respond to normal controls for the sake of the community and, in a sense, for their own sake. Dangerous offender laws, the category to which we now turn, share with sexual psychopath laws a belief in the predictability of future criminality despite the deterrent threats of normal criminal law, but they apply this concept to wider groups of offenders. Again, provision is made for larger threats and longer incapacitation, the former to maximize deterrence, the latter because while the criminal is in prison he can commit crimes only against others in prison (prisoners and guards) and not against the community at large and because the passing of an extended term of years and with it the aging process will reduce the duration of the offender's life of crime in the community.

Three categories of serious offenders normally fall within the dangerous offender laws: habitual criminals, professional criminals, and psychologically disturbed criminals. Each category merits careful consideration and raises jurisprudential problems distinct from the other two; but in this chapter discussion will be confined to the third category, psychologically disturbed offenders, where again a link is forged between mental illness and crime leading to an increment of punishment.

The products of the three influential commissions referred to above—the Model Penal Code,[17] the Model Sentencing Act,[18] and the Final Report of the Brown Commission[19]—all recommended enactment of special and increased punishment provisions for psychologically disturbed dangerous offenders. These recom-

17. Model Penal Code, §7.03 (Proposed Final Draft No. 1, 1961).

18. Council of Judges of the National Council on Crime and Delinquency, Model Sentencing Act, §5 (2d ed. 1972).

19. National Commission on Reform of Federal Criminal Laws, Final Report, §3202 (1971).

mendations have been accepted in five states.[20] Early versions of the pending federal criminal code legislation contained a provision modeled on that of the Brown Commission report;[21] later versions deleted it, but with the clear understanding that guidelines for sentencing dangerous offenders would be included among the guidelines to be prepared by a National Sentencing Commission.[22] At least five states have special sentencing provisions permitting increased punishment for disturbed offenders thought likely to commit further crimes.[23]

The paradigm of these proposals for sentencing reform and of this legislative flurry is section 7.03(3) of the Model Penal Code, which authorized a court, when sentencing a person convicted of felony, to extend the term of imprisonment beyond the maximum provided for that category of felon when "the defendant is a dangerous, mentally abnormal person whose commitment for an extended period of time is necessary for protection of the public."[24] A precondition of such a sentence is a psychiatric examination

20. Hawaii, Hawaii Rev. Stat., §706-622 (1976); New Hampshire, N.H. Rev. Stat. Ann. §651:6(I)(b) (1974); North Dakota, N.D. Cent. Code, §12.1-32-09(1)(a) (Supp. 1979); Ohio, Ohio Rev. Code Ann., §§2929.01(B), 2929.12 (Page Supp. 1981); Oregon, Ore. Rev. Stat., §161.725(1) (1979).

21. See, e.g., S.1, 93d Cong., 1st Sess., §1-4B2 (1973), reprinted in Reform of the Federal Criminal Laws, pt. V: Hearings on S.1 before the Subcommittee on Criminal Laws and Procedures of the Senate Committee on the Judiciary, 93d Cong., 1st Sess., 4251 (1973).

22. See, e.g., S.1437, 95th Cong., 1st Sess. (1977), reprinted in Reform of the Federal Criminal Laws, pt. XIII: Hearings on S.1437 before the Subcommittee on Criminal Laws and Procedure of the Senate Committee on the Judiciary, 95th Cong., 1st Sess., 9485 (1977); S.1722, 96th Cong., 1st Sess. (1979), reprinted in Reform of the Federal Criminal Laws, pt. XV: Hearings on S.1722 and S.1723 before the Senate Committee on the Judiciary, 96th Cong., 1st Sess., 11090 (1979). See also Senate Committee on the Judiciary, Criminal Code Reform Act of 1979, S. Rep. No. 553, 96th Cong., 2d Sess., 928–83, 998 (1980).

23. Indiana, Ind. Code Ann., §35-50-1A-7 (Burns 1979); Louisiana, La. Code Crim. Proc. Ann., art. 894.1(A)(1) (West Supp. 1981); Montana, Mont. Rev. Codes Ann., §46-18-404(1)(b) (1979); New Jersey, N.J. Stat. Ann., §2C:43-12(e)(9) (West 1981); North Carolina, N.C. Gen. Stat., §15A-1340.3 (Supp. 1979).

24. Model Penal Code, §7.03(3) (Proposed Final Draft No. 1, 1961).

"resulting in the conclusion that his mental condition has been characterized by a pattern of repetitive or compulsive behavior or by persistent aggressive behavior with heedless indifference to consequences; and that such condition makes him a serious danger to others."[25] I have it on the best authority[26] that the mentally abnormal dangerous offender provisions of the Model Penal Code were the bargaining counter for the exclusion of any sexual psychopath provisions from the code.[27]

The Model Sentencing Act followed suit. Section 5 defines "dangerous offenders" as those who have committed or attempted certain violent crimes and who are found by the court to be "suffering from a severe mental or emotional disorder indicating a propensity toward continuing dangerous criminal activity."[28]

One marvels at the confidence reposed in the diagnostic and predictive capabilities of psychiatrists by these provisions despite the caution in the accompanying commentary. For example, the commentary to section 5 recognizes that the concept of danger-

25. *Ibid.*

26. Not references, not citations, just clear memory of the words of a scholar for whom I had the deepest respect and affection: Paul Tappan, who was the draftsman under the wise guidance of Herbert Wechsler of the sentencing and corrections provisions of the Model Penal Code. Prior to the promulgation of this code I assaulted him verbally and repeatedly about section 7.03(3); this was his best defense, a political confession and avoidance.

27. Comment 6 to §7.03(3) makes this point inferentially. It is there noted that the problem in drafting an extended term for "dangerous, mentally abnormal persons" is to "avoid the type of vagueness, if not quackery, involved in many current rubrics, such as 'psychopathic personality.' " Model Penal Code, §7.03(3), Comment 6 (Tentative Draft 2, 1954).

28. Council of Judges of the National Council on Crime and Delinquency, Model Sentencing Act, §5(1)(2d ed. 1972). There is here an interesting difference between the first and second editions. The first edition referred to "severe personality disorder"; the second edition to "severe mental or emotional disorder." The comment reports that the change was made because a "number of psychiatrists had pointed out that the term 'personality disorder' might be mistakenly construed as the classification of a specific type of disorder. Our intent, now clarified, was to refer to defendants who, in the terms of laymen, were suffering from some mental or emotional disorder and not to limit the disorder to any one specific diagnosis." *Id.* Comment on §5, at 11.

ousness is "difficult to accept," that "the behavioral sciences do not now have sufficient expertise to carry out this assignment adequately," but nevertheless claims to have provided a "legally and socially precise delineation of dangerous persons and a legally and clinically careful procedure for identifying them."[29]

To complete this trilogy of "model" legislation, the National Commission on Reform of Federal Criminal Laws recommended that extended terms of imprisonment be provided for "dangerous special offenders"[30] and included an offender whose "mental condition is abnormal and makes him a serious danger to the safety of others" and who committed the felony for which he is being sentenced "as an instance of aggressive behavior with heedless indifference to the consequences of such behavior."[31] As usual with such recommendations, a comprehensive psychiatric examination and report are required as a precondition to the imposition of such an extended term.[32]

As we have seen,[33] in a variety of ways ten states have followed these recommendations. Other states, of course, can and do reach similar results, without express legislative direction, extending the duration of imprisonment of the mentally ill beyond the term that would have been imposed had they not been so diagnosed. That result may be achieved, as a matter of judicial discretion, whenever likely future criminality is a ground authorized expressly or implicitly for aggravation of sentence and when the mental illness of a convicted person is relied on as indicative of likely future criminality. Of course, when extended terms are legislatively provided, the stakes are higher.

One can thus draw the conclusion that in the prevailing jurisprudence of the past twenty years, in legislation, theory, and practice, in the legislative commissions, legislatures, and courts, the mental illness of the convicted criminal when it leads to pre-

29. *Id.* at 10.
30. National Commission on Reform of Federal Criminal Laws, Final Report, §3202(1) (1971).
31. *Id.* §3202(2)(c).
32. *Ibid.*
33. *Supra* notes 20 and 23.

dictions of his increased "dangerousness" is a ground for increasing the severity or the duration of his sentence. His mental illness may lead either to his imprisonment, when he would not have been imprisoned for what he did had he not been mentally ill, or to the extension of the term of his imprisonment. In parts V and VI of this chapter, the justice and wisdom of such increments of punishment of the mentally ill will be considered.

There is, of course, a pervasive theme running at cross purposes to the punitive direction we have been considering. Mental illness is widely seen and frequently legislatively prescribed as a ground for ameliorating punishment, for avoiding imprisonment, or for reducing its term. We turn now to legislative provisions for such mitigation of sentences imposed on the mentally ill.

B. *Specific Provisions for Decrease of Punishment*

So pervasive is this theme of lesser punishment being appropriate because of the lesser degree of moral guilt of the mentally ill convicted criminal that a few examples should suffice to lay the factual basis for its later analysis.

A convenient opening example is the ALI's Model Penal Code, which provided that in determining whether it is necessary to imprison a convicted offender, the fact that "there were substantial grounds tending to excuse or justify the defendant's criminal conduct, though failing to establish a defense," should "be accorded weight in favor of withholding sentence of imprisonment."[34] This is often the situation where a defense of insanity fails or where the crime committed is not of sufficient gravity to attract such a defense though the offender is mentally ill—one does not plead this defense to minor charges.

Twenty years later, in the declining days of the Ninety-sixth Congress, House Bill 6915 provided that the first purpose of sentencing is to "assure that the severity of the sentence is proportionate and directly related to the culpability of the defendant and

34. Model Penal Code, §7.01(2)(d) (Proposed Final Draft 1, 1961).

the harm done."[35] In this bill and in the independent Senate Bill 1722, sentencing courts are directed "in determining the particular sentence to be imposed" to consider "the history and characteristics of the defendant."[36] In addition, S.1722 directs the sentencing commission, in producing sentencing guidelines, to consider the relevance of a defendant's "mental and emotional condition to the extent that such condition mitigates the defendant's culpability or to the extent that such condition is otherwise plainly relevant."[37]

The Model Sentencing and Corrections Act is also express on the matter of mental illness as a mitigating factor: "[M]itigating factors may include . . . [the fact that] the defendant was suffering from a mental or physical condition that significantly reduced his culpability for the offense."[38] This provision directs the sentencing commission to include this factor in guidelines for the sentencing judges, and also directs those judges to include it in their assessment of the sentence to be imposed in an individual case.

Another clear example of the relevance of mental illness to the reduction of punishments comes from the emerging jurisprudence on the constitutionality of capital punishment. A series of decisions[39] of the United States Supreme Court in the wake of *Furman v. Georgia*[40] has made clear that a capital punishment statute, to be in accord with the fundamental respect for individual dignity underlying the Eighth Amendment, must require the sentencing court to consider the character of the individual offender. And those statutes which have been drafted seeking to distinguish cap-

35. H.R. 6915, 96th Cong., 2d Sess., §3101 (1980).

36. *Id.* §3102; S.1722, 96th Cong., 1st Sess., Title 1, §2003 (1979), *reprinted in* Reform of the Federal Criminal Laws, pt. XV, *supra* note 22, at 11243.

37. S.1722, 96th Cong., 1st Sess., Title III, Ch. 58, §994(d)(4), *reprinted in* Reform of the Federal Criminal Laws, pt. XV, *supra* note 22, at 11386.

38. National Conference of Commissioners on Uniform State Laws, Uniform Law Commissioner's Model Sentencing and Corrections Act, §3-108 (1979).

39. Gregg v. Georgia, 428 U.S. 153 (1976); Proffitt v. Florida, 428 U.S. 242 (1976); Jurek v. Texas, 428 U.S. 262 (1976); Woodson v. North Carolina, 428 U.S. 280 (1976); Roberts v. Louisiana, 428 U.S. 238 (1976).

40. 408 U.S. 238 (1972).

itally punishable criminals from those not so punishable provide for the convicted offender's mental illness to be considered a mitigating factor in determining his punishment.

But all this is belaboring the obvious. Pre-sentence psychiatric and psychological assessments are often drafted and applied to give the court understanding of the psychopathology of the convicted offender. The express and latent effects of such pre-sentence reports are frequently to lessen the offender's moral culpability in the eyes of the sentencing judge and hence, in practice, to mitigate the sentence.

Any acquaintance with sentencing practice will reveal the importance of the judge's view of the degree of guilt of the accused in determining punishment. The mental illness of the accused at the time of the crime will weigh with the judge to reduce his assessment of the moral depravity of the criminal (just as, for example, it weighed with those legislatures that have established statutory diminished responsibility, reducing murder to manslaughter). In parts IV and VI of this chapter, the justice and wisdom of such reductions of punishment of the mentally ill will be considered.

III. Sentencing Reforms and the Mentally Ill

A flurry of sentencing reform, federal and state, over the past twenty years and in particular since the mid-1970s, has largely neglected the particular problems of sentencing the mentally ill.

Of the major commentaries which fueled this reform movement—*Struggle for Justice* by the American Friends Service Committee,[41] *Fair and Certain Punishment* by the Twentieth Century Fund Task Force on Criminal Sentencing,[42] and books by Marvin Frankel,[43] Nigel Walker,[44] Andrew von Hirsch,[45] David Fogel,[46] Ernest

41. American Friends Service Committee, *Struggle For Justice* (1971).
42. Twentieth Century Fund Task Force on Criminal Sentencing, *Fair and Certain Punishment* (1976).
43. M. Frankel, *Criminal Sentences: Law without Order* (1973).
44. N. Walker, *Sentencing in a Rational Society* (1969).
45. A. von Hirsch, *Doing Justice: The Choice of Punishments* (1976).
46. D. Fogel, *We Are the Living Proof: The Justice Model for Corrections* (1975).

van den Haag,[47] and myself[48]—most make no mention of the problems addressed in this chapter, and such comments as are offered are scant.[49]

This neglect is not surprising. Sentencing reform has been influenced intellectually and theoretically by an effort to minimize unjust disparity in sentencing, to move away from indeterminate sentences and the hypocrisy of adjusting prison terms to supposed indicia of rehabilitation demonstrated in prison, and by a trend toward models of guided discretion in judicial sentencing.[50] That one modulating contingency in sentencing, important in practice though it may be, is lost in the larger turmoil is to be expected. Nevertheless, under all emerging patterns of sentencing reform there is room for the twin effects of mental illness on the sentence—reductive because of lesser culpability, additive because of increased "dangerousness."

Modern sentencing reforms are distinguishable by how they allocate sentencing discretion. The California pattern gives less discretion to the judge, but even there in most cases the judge has a margin of fine-tuning of sentencing which may sometimes influence the "in-out" decision, imprisonment or an alternative sanction, and may usually influence the duration of the prison term imposed, allowing him to add or subtract up to defined limits when aggravating or mitigating circumstances are found.

At the other extreme, moving from the mischievous sentenc-

47. E. van den Haag, *Punishing Criminals: Concerning a Very Old and Painful Question* (1975).

48. N. Morris, *The Future of Imprisonment* (1974).

49. Frankel, *supra* note 43, at 100–101, offers a brief commentary on mental illness and the dangerous offender; Walker, *supra* note 44, at 97–100 discusses the use of the pre-sentence psychiatric investigation, at 159–62 the role of a sentencing authority for those appearing to be mentally ill, and at 167–73 the mentally disordered offender as an example of mitigation of sentence. *Fair and Certain Punishment*, *supra* note 42, includes, at 44–45, mental disorder as one factor in a list of mitigating factors in an "illustrative presumptive sentencing statute for armed robbery."

50. F. Zimring and M. Tonry, *Reform and Punish: Essays on Criminal Sentencing* (forthcoming, 1983).

ing "reforms" of California[51] to the intelligently and maturely contrived Minnesota reforms,[52] the trial judge is given some latitude within the sentencing guidelines (both as to the in-out decision and the duration decision) and, equally important, may decide not to impose the sentence prescribed by the guidelines provided he gives reasons for not doing so, which reasons may be examined on appeal. The mental illness of the convicted offender may well thus often lead to judicial fine-tuning and variation from sentencing guidelines.

To conclude this chapter, there follows some consideration of the relationship between the Minnesota Sentencing Guidelines and the mentally ill offender. All that need be established to press on with our analysis is this: recent sentencing statutes allow some room for judicial discretion in their application, and the mental illness of the convicted offender may be relevant to the exercise of that discretion.

IV. Mitigating the Punishment of the Mentally Ill—with an Aside on Justice, Mercy, Discretion, and Equality

I have argued elsewhere[53] that it dignifies rather than debases the mentally ill to hold them responsible for criminal harms which they have committed with the same intent, recklessness, negligence, or other state of mind as to the consequences of their actions as is required for the conviction of those who are not or do not claim to be mentally ill. The thesis was both prudential and, I hope, principled. Does this insistence on the responsibility of the mentally ill preclude recognition of their sometimes lesser degree of moral fault? Surely not. Surely responsibility for a proscribed harm, defined as to conduct, consequence, and mental state of the actors,

51. One is reminded of Anon's excellent exclamation: "Reform, Sir, Reform. Don't talk to me of Reform. Things are bad enough as they are."

52. Minnesota Sentencing Guidelines Commission, *Minnesota Sentencing Guidelines and Commentary* (1980).

53. Morris, "Psychiatry and the Dangerous Criminal," 41 *S. Cal. L. Rev.* 514 (1968); Burt & Morris, "A Proposal for the Abolition of the Incompetency Plea," 40 *U. Chi. L. Rev.* 66 (1972).

may be an all or nothing matter, guilty or not guilty, whereas the punishment may properly be a matter of degree.

Not even the most perfervid proponents of capital punishment argue that mental illness at the time of the crime should not sometimes be a ground for waiving execution, and I doubt that their reasons turn on preserving the killer's hope of repentance and redemption. The reality is that at every level of the criminal justice system, as well as of human intercourse, we take cognizance of mental illness in attributing blame and, no doubt imprecisely, trying to estimate degrees of fault. We do this often on insufficient data and, if we have any sense, recognizing our own inadequacy to the task, but it is unthinkable that we should entirely reject such sentiments.

It seems to me, preserving the analogy that I have developed in relation to punishing those whose behavior is influenced substantially by adverse social circumstances,[54] that there is here too a parallel with criminogenic social pressures. We do not blame the slum-dwelling, impoverished thief as much as the privileged, prosperous thief.

The problem is not whether degrees of culpability influenced by considerations of mental illness should be taken into account in sentencing; the problem is how to do so.

Does such an ameliorating function for mental illness in the fine-tuning of sentencing diminish the force of the earlier argument that where socially necessary the mentally ill should be tried for their alleged crimes, and if they were indeed guilty under ordinary principles of criminal liability, should be convicted? I think not. There is a clear distinction between being held responsible as an adult citizen for the commission of a crime and the amount of punishment which, for a complexity of reasons, should be imposed. Nevertheless, it may be useful at this point to offer a brief statement of the jurisprudential theory behind this distinction, which will be more fully developed after we have considered reasons for both the mitigation and the aggravation of punishment because of the

54. See pp. 62–63 above, and also Morris, "Psychiatry and the Dangerous Criminal," *supra* note 53, at 520.

mental illness of the convicted offender. To do so, let me make use of H. L. A. Hart's distinction between those principles which may justify punishment itself, the justifying aims of the punitive system, and those principles which should control the distribution of punishment.[55] The latter may determine non-liability or eligibility for punishment and also the amount of punishment to be imposed.

In considering the justification of punishment or concepts of desert, ideas which are at base nonutilitarian govern eligibility for punishment. There is no sound utilitarian reason why it may not be sensible in a variety of circumstances to reject the proposition that it is better that nine guilty men be acquitted rather than one innocent person be convicted. As a utilitarian proposal, that balance is unpersuasive. The imposition of the punishment on the innocent tenth may well save the suffering of a considerable number of victims who are protected by the deterrent sanction now imposable on all ten (the nine guilty and the one innocent) rather than rendered vulnerable by the acquittal of all ten. Nevertheless, we adhere to that proposition, and it seems to me good that we do so, but not for reasons of utility. We prefer a world with official condemnation and punishment confined to those who qualify by fact-finding processes minimizing errors of condemnation and punishment. We are prepared to pay substantial costs in increased criminality for this independently valuable sense of individual protection from state authority. If this is to be seen as a utilitarian analysis, as it certainly can be, it is a utilitarianism that looks far beyond the much more confined values normally sought to be balanced in jurisprudential analysis.[56]

If we turn from the question of the justification of punishment to its distribution, the amount of punishment to be imposed on the eligible, concepts of desert remain, but they operate differently. It is rarely possible to say with precision, "that is the deserved punishment." All one can properly say, I submit, is "that is not an undeserved punishment."[57] Desert defines a range of punish-

---

55. H. L. A. Hart, *Responsibility and Punishment*, ch. 1, §2 (1968).

56. For a criticism of this kind of analysis, see *id.* at 22–24.

57. For a parallel argument, see E. Cahn, *The Sense of Injustice* (1949).

ments. One can say that this punishment is too severe, that too lenient, but within the range desert will not define to a precise point the socially necessary, wise, or desirable punishment. Now utilitarian values also become of determinative importance far exceeding their earlier role in relation to the justification of punishment.[58]

Desert justifies and limits eligibility for punishment; desert and utility combine to distribute punishments. The fine-tuning of sentencing, its distribution, is the result of a balance between social protection by deterrent and incapacitative (or social control) punishment, on one side of the scales, against the minimization of suffering by a parsimonious application of punishment on the other.

If this be acceptable analysis, there is no contradiction between advocating the conviction and punishment of some of those whose crime was in part attributable to their mental illness and yet insisting that their mental illness should be taken into account in fixing this punishment, within the deserved range set by the interrelationship between such concepts as general deterrence, the prevention of repetition of crime by the criminal, mercy, parsimony in punishment, and the perceived degree of moral fault and social harm in the crime.

Desert cannot precisely define like-kind punishments except in rare cases, and even these are doubtful. For example, capital punishment for killing may be thought of as an equivalent retributively prescribed punishment, but even here few adhere to that equivalence when pressed. Is the life for a life to be with or without prior torture (if the victim was killed in a savagely cruel way)? Is it to be a life for a life for all murders, loving but criminal euthanasia

58. In exceptional circumstances the talionic equivalences seem acceptable, life for life, eye for eye; but that analysis soon breaks down. What is the equivalent punishment for attempted murder? And in fact the talionic law was itself a limiting and not a defining principle. Historically and psychologically it is to be understood as "only a life for a life," not breaking on the wheel, quartering, and then execution; "only an eye for an eye," not capital punishment for assault occasioning grievous bodily harm. The question of punishment equivalent in the sense of its lying on a hierarchy of proportional harm will be later considered.

as well as murder for hire? Even the most dedicated and impassioned opponents of abortion do not call for capital punishment for abortionists. And even if we confine ourselves to the punishment of those who have intentionally taken human life after its fetal stage, are we really going to take that equivalence seriously to the point of, say, twenty thousand executions each year in the United States, not including manslaughter and motor manslaughter (which also are criminal homicides)? Surely the automatic equivalence breaks down here as it does in relation to most crimes against both person and property. If, in practice, we avoid like-kind punishments, there is no possible abstract equivalence between imprisonment (which is, in practice, the contemporary residual punishment) and the harm, physical and economic, the criminal has inflicted on his victim.

Finally, to destroy any lingering view that desert can of itself define punishment, consider a crime such as attempted murder where the victim was ignorant of the impending but never occurring impact, or a crime such as conspiracy to corrupt a public officer. How would one recreate, as a punishment, equivalent lack of suffering in the convicted criminal as in the victim?

Hence, a deserved punishment must mean a not undeserved punishment which bears a proportional relationship in the hierarchy of punishments to the harm for which the criminal has been convicted. Such proportionality will be partly arbitrary, shifting between cultures and over time.[59]

59. The United States Supreme Court seems to have adopted this view of proportionality and desert. Thus, Weems v. United States, 217 U.S. 349, 366–67 (1910): "[I]t is a precept of justice that punishment for crime should be graduated and proportioned to offense." Or, even earlier, Mr. Justice Field in O'Neil v. Vermont, 144 U.S. 323, 340 (1892): The "cruel and unusual punishment" clause is directed "against all punishments which by their excessive length or severity are greatly disproportionate to the offense charged." Similar negative, or limiting rather than defining, formulations percolate through the Supreme Court's statements on this problem. For example, Mr. Justice White in Coker v. Georgia, 433 U.S. 584, 592 (1977), stated that a punishment is unconstitutionally excessive if it "is grossly out of proportion to the severity of the crime." Though the Court divided 5–4 in Rummel v. Estelle, 445 U. S. 263 (1980), its latest consideration of this issue, the plurality and the dissenting opinions agreed on this "limiting" retributivist approach. Thus Mr. Justice

As well as being arbitrary, in any developed jurisprudence of criminal law the hierarchy of deserved punishments will be in the form of a range of proportionately acceptable punishments, as distinct from a fixed or set list of punishments. Even well-fashioned definitions of crime cover a diversity of behaviors, a diversity that in some cases must be reflected in the amount of punishment. So the hierarchy of deserved punishments will in practice prove to be a hierarchy of deserved ranges of punishment. Even the most determinate of recent fixed-sentence schemes, that of California, assigns to each felon a range of three possible prison terms, the choice to be fixed by balancing factors in aggravation and mitigation.[60] And, in relation to capital punishment for murder, such a range is constitutionally required, though it may consist of only two choices: life imprisonment or death.[61]

A final point about this proportional range of deserved punishments: the range often has to be quite wide, and that applicable to some crimes will overlap that applicable to others. Some manslaughters deserve more punishment than some murders; the hierarchy of deserved punishment categories must allow for this. Some rapes are less serious than some aggravated batteries which are not rapes.

Hence, it is not a quibble we are pursuing, not a nicety about retribution, but a central principle. A deserved punishment is rarely fixed by the offense; it is, in all but a very few cases,[62] a punishment within the limits set by a retributive calculus of overlapping and quite broad ranges of not undeserved punishments. Moral fault

---

Rehnquist for the majority somewhat grudgingly conceded that a proportionality principle would preclude life imprisonment for overtime parking, while Mr. Justice Powell's opinion, joined by Brennan, Marshall, and Stevens, spelled out at length the function of desert as a nonutilitarian limitation on punishment. "The inquiry focuses on whether a person deserves such punishment, not simply on whether punishment would serve a utilitarian goal." *Id.* at 288. He then analyzes a "principle of disproportionality . . . rooted deeply in English constitutional law." *Ibid.*

60. Cal. Penal Code, §1170(b) (West Compact Ed. 1980).

61. Woodson v. North Carolina, 428 U.S. 280 (1976).

62. Minor offenses, such as traffic and parking offenses, are often properly fined independent of circumstances.

and many other circumstances of the offense and the offender will then define punishment within that range. If this analysis is correct, if moral fault both limits and helps to define a just punishment, there is jurisprudential validity in the common acceptance of mental illness as reducing the degree of culpability of an offender in many instances. Indeed, if one accepts the psychodynamic view of the integrated personality of man, *all* of his actions—including his criminal actions—will be in part related to any mental illness or abnormality that he may have. Mental illness may not determine that conduct but at least it will influence it. Though precise scaling of moral guilt is far beyond our capacities, a gross and generous weighing of fault is not. The paranoid who lashes out at another, moved in part by his exaggerated and sick fears, merits clemency in punishment. It may be both fair and desirable to hold him responsible in law for assault or murder, but it is surely appropriate within limits of desert and the demands of deterrence to reduce the sanction imposed on him. The bottom limit of that reduction will be the ongoing concept of a minimum deserved punishment for that offense by that offender, including his mental illness, which the rough sentiment of the community expressed through its agencies of punishment thinks minimally appropriate. Punishment will be reduced by reason of mental illness to the degree to which those imposing that punishment regard the offender's moral culpability as lessened by his mental illness. That these concepts are not precisely quantifiable does not lessen their analytic value. In time, with an emerging common law of sentencing, defined and quantifiable gradations of fair sentencing in relationship to moral fault and mental illness will indeed develop.

In the above discussion I have had in mind major crimes against both persons and property, where mental illness is more frequently pleaded either to excuse guilt or to mitigate punishment. Does this analysis apply equally to crimes of negligence, to crimes of strict liability and that range of regulatory offenses where the criminal law has already moved to exclude the requirement of personal guilt as a precondition to punishment? It is an oddly convoluted inquiry. If there be crimes of negligence as distinct from recklessness (as those terms are defined in the ALI's Model

Penal Code)[63] and crimes where there may be a conviction independently of establishing any knowledge of wrongdoing, or the
risk of wrongdoing, by the accused person (strict liability as modified by the Supreme Court's decision in *Park*),[64] then there would
seem no particular reason why the mentally ill should be treated
any differently in relation to those crimes than the sane. In all
these situations those who may be morally innocent are to be
punished; personal fault does not have to be proved. Is there any
ground on which any special indulgence should be extended to
the mentally ill? I join many scholars of the criminal law in arguing
that in all these situations there should at the very least be a
possibility of allowing no fault and, if that could be established,
of acquitting them.[65] If such were the rule, one basis upon which
such a burden of proof could be carried would, of course, be
by submitting evidence of mental illness. But that is not the
rule and we face a situation in which punishment is imposed
within our present jurisprudence absent proof of moral fault. Even

63. "A person acts recklessly with respect to a material element of an
offense when he consciously disregards a substantial and unjustifiable risk that
the material element exists or will result from his conduct. The risk must be
of such a nature and degree that, considering the nature and purpose of the
actor's conduct and the circumstances known to him, its disregard involves a
gross deviation from the standard of conduct that a law-abiding person would
observe in the actor's situation." Model Penal Code, §2.02(2)(c) (Proposed
Official Draft, 1962).

"A person acts negligently with respect to a material element of an offense
when he should be aware of a substantial and unjustifiable risk that the material
element exists or will result from his conduct. The risk must be of such a nature
and degree that the actor's failure to perceive it, considering the nature and
purpose of his conduct and the circumstances known to him, involves a gross
deviation from the standard of care that a reasonable person would observe in
the actor's situation." *Id.* §2.02(2)(d).

64. United States v. Park, 421 U.S. 658 (1975) (holding that a corporate
officer may be held criminally liable, regardless of ignorance or care, for his
company's violation of the Federal Food, Drug, and Cosmetic Act, if in virtue
of the responsibility and authority of his position he had a duty to prevent such
violation).

65. N. Morris & C. Howard, "Strict Responsibility," in *Studies in Criminal
Law* 197 (1964).

so, in sentencing for crimes of negligence or of strict liability, evidence in mitigation of punishment is certainly admissible under current law. The corporate executive who can show that though he was within the hierarchy of control in the company and thus "responsible" for the failure which led to the strict liability conviction may offer evidence that at the time of the breach he was in the hospital having suffered a heart attack totally unconnected with these criminal processes. And if this evidence is accepted as true, it is properly and presently relevant and influential in determining the sentence that will be imposed on him. In exactly the same way it seems to me clear that evidence of mental illness may be admitted in relation to the punishment of any crime of negligence or strict liability.[66]

There remain, I submit, two obstacles to the simple proposition that mental illness may properly have a reductive effect on the appropriate punishment for any crime—the demands of general deterrence may be thought sometimes to cut against any reduction of punishment, and there is the further discomforting fact that some mental illness may increase the dangerousness of the convicted offender and thus press not for any reduction of punishment but for its increase or extension. The latter problem, that of increased dangerousness, will be considered in the last section of this essay; let us now try to assess whether the utilitarian requirements of general deterrence preclude a reduction of sentence on the mentally ill offender.

Can the mentally ill be deterred by the threat of punishment? Some can, some cannot; some will be deterred, some will not. The equations are probably very similar to those applicable to the mentally healthy. But that is not the question. The issue is different. Will reduction of the severity of threatened sanction because of mental illness reduce the marginal deterrent efficacy of the threat to all—sane and insane together, however defined? And here spec-

66. Of course, under a more just system of criminal law moral fault would be relevant to liability, to eligibility for punishment, in relation to crimes of negligence and *a fortiori* strict liability, and some of the mentally ill would then have defenses to criminal liability.

ulation swamps empirical knowledge. The general view seems to be that if such an effect exists it is indeed very marginal. And certainly, at the level we are considering the question—the amount of punishment after detection, trial, and conviction—it is hard to see how general deterrence can be thought to provide any impediment to the mitigation of punishment imposed on mentally ill criminals. It is most unlikely that potential offenders calculate, consciously or subconsciously, at that level of contingency.

Subject then to later consideration of the question of the dangerousness of the convicted offender as a reason for increasing the sanction upon him even though he is mentally ill, and the complex relationship between these two effects of mental illness on punishment—mitigating or aggravating punishment—we reach a situation where on grounds of a rational distribution of punishment it is appropriate sometimes to reduce the severity of sanctions because of the mental illness of the accused. This raises a general issue on the relationship between justice, mercy, discretion, and equality.

Justice, mercy, discretion, and equality. It is the cardinal defect of those who see desert as defining punishment, as distinct from defining its proper outer limits, that in their understandable anxiety to preclude the exercise of discretion in punishment—which has so frequently in the past been exercised on an unjust racial or class discriminatory basis—they create systems of justice insufficiently responsive to the compelling need for mercy in all human relationships, but most particularly in the relationship where the social collectivity is imposing punishment on the wrongdoer. If we all get our deserts, who escapes the rack? A system of criminal justice that is not infused with parsimony in punishment and such clemency as punitive societies can summon creates an intolerable engine of tyranny. Discretion in quantifying punishment may well be highly susceptible to abuse, but it cannot be exorcised.

Nor, oddly enough, is it within our competence to exercise it with completely even-handed justice. I am advised that St. Peter can do so, but we cannot; we lack both the moral subtlety and sufficiently precise instruments of inquiry. The mind of man cannot thus simply be laid bare, even to the actor himself; such is the immediate overlay of rationalization and misperception that clouds our every understanding even of our own motivations, let alone those of another. Gray matter is much less cognizable than other matter and, for practical purposes, so it will remain. All we can do is to take cautious account of our growing through very imperfect understandings of how the pride and passions of man relate to his mechanisms of understanding and self-control to produce conduct.

As the papal encyclical of 2 December 1980, *Dives in Misericordia*, argues, "Mercy differs from justice, but is not in opposition to it." And later:

> The experience of the past and of our own time demonstrates that justice alone is not enough, that it can even lead to the negation and destruction of itself, if that deeper power, which is love, is not allowed to shape human life in its various dimensions. It has been precisely historical experience that, among other things, has led to the formulation of the saying: *summum ius, summa iniuria*. This statement does not detract from the value of justice and does not minimize the significance of the order that is based upon it; it only indicates another aspect, the need to draw from the powers of the spirit which condition the very order of justice, powers which are still more profound.

It is a not inconsiderable burden; we must extend mercy to the mentally ill whose crime is causally related to their mental illness, but we know we can do so only with imperfect and most hesitant understanding. It is beyond our power to treat morally like cases alike; all we can do is to develop a rough gradation of clemency which will permit us to take some gross account of moral imperatives. This relationship between justice, mercy and discretion, particularly in relation to sentencing principles and practice, has been a source of concern to liberal and conservative reformers and commentators in the United States. The problem is, of course, wider than that of sentencing under the aegis of the criminal law; it percolates through all law and in particular, in recent American commentary, the control of discretion exercised by regulatory agencies. But it is in the criminal law of sentencing that these problems present, it seems to me, the most wrenching difficulties. Our history and our culture create a context in which sentencing discretions tend to be exercised adversely to the interests of the less privileged groups. The tradition of equality which energizes American constitutional law has thus pressed for the elimination of the most rigid control of racial and class-biased exercises of the sentencing discretion. Hence the efforts of the Quakers in *Struggle for Justice*[67] and of subsequent commentators and legislative reformers moving toward fixed or presumptive sentencing either to eliminate or rigidly to control sentencing discretion in the individual case.

If sentences are known in advance, adjusted to the severity of the offense and the criminal record of the accused, and modulated not at all by the individual personal psychological or social circumstances of the accused, then there is no room for mercy, clemency, or parsimony in sentencing in the particular case; those qualities can only be expressed in the definition of the sentence appropriate to the category of offenders convicted of the crime of given severity. One could thus have a merciful system, but not the expression of mercy in the individual case. One could have a parsimonious system, but not the parsimonious allocation of a punishment. A clement system, but not clemency.

The difficulty in accepting such a development with any equanimity is that it reflects precisely the historical experience to which the papal encyclical refers: it produces and will produce if followed in this country the situation of *summum ius, summa iniuria*. Given the incidence of serious crime in this country, given the numbers of people and the proportion of the population who commit serious crimes at one time or another in their lives, and even assuming a continuance of our present relatively low levels of efficiency in detecting and convicting for crime, a system of deserved punishments not modulated by substantial discretion to allow clemency in the individual case would be incomparably more severe than the one we now have. Nor would it lie within our power, as a legislative reality, to modulate the entire system toward

67. *Supra* note 41.

lesser severity, so as to achieve a merciful system without relying on mercy in the individual case. Legislators inevitably tend to define punishment in terms of the upper limits of deserved punishment for any offense-offender relationship; the political pressures on them to do this are great and will not decline.

What happens in practice is that sentencing discretion cannot be confined in this way; if it is restricted at the judicial level it will be expressed at the prosecutorial level; if it is restricted at those levels it will be expressed at the police or complaining witness level. The total amount of discretion may well not change. It is very much better to create a system which allows room for mercy and parsimony of punishment in the individual case than to deceive oneself that there is a possibility of creating a just punishment system lacking such discretion.

This conclusion is, of course, no great consolation to the member of the racial group or economic class who finds that the sentencing discretion toward clemency is exercised less rarely in his favor than it is for others in the community. Can one respond to his complaint? I believe so, though the questioner may not be entirely satisfied by the response. One can say that though his group may be less well off than other groups in the community, in terms of the severity of the punishment imposed, those who make up his group will be absolutely very much better off than if there was not room for the exercise of mercy in the individual case in the system itself. The data we now have would seem to support the proposition that the black street criminal is slightly more severely treated than the otherwise identical white street criminal, crime for crime and offender for offender. There is increasing perception of this reality among observers of the criminal justice system, and steady and reasonably successful efforts are being pursued to reduce this type of discrimination. But if we are to move to a system of fixed sentences, without room for mercy in the individual case, it is certainly true that even if one could achieve relative balance between black and white criminals, black offenders would be treated very much more severely than they now are.

It is a poignant commentary on the unanticipated consequences of benevolent efforts that the struggle for even-handed
justice, unless it be infused with a broad sensitivity to the demands
of mercy and to the frailties of human judgment, is quite likely
to lead to "reforms" which simply increase the levels of punishments for all offenders without any evidence that society is better
protected.

It is important not to overstate this argument. There are
situations in which the misapplication of discretion in sentencing
can be so gross as to be unacceptable, a denial and not a modulation
of justice. This was obviously so in Germany in relation to Jewish
criminals in the years immediately preceding the Second World
War, and it may well be so in a few of the urban areas of South
Africa today. But these do not represent the general pattern, or
the situation in the United States today. If we are to put any
reasonable limit on the number of our citizens whom we hold in
prisons and jails, if we are to bring needed increments of both
decency and efficiency to our criminal justice system, we will have
to create sentencing systems in which there is room for mercy in
the individual case and parsimony in the exercise of punishment
generally. This implies judicial discretion in sentencing since, I
submit, only the judge can provide the fine-tuning of sentencing
essential to a just system. That such discretion may be exercised
with racial or class bias is a fact with which we must continue to
wrestle. And we know how to wrestle with it: an open system,
reasons being given in advance for the exercise of the sentencing
discretion; if possible principles enunciated in advance to guide
the exercise of that discretion, and critical observation of the
operation of the criminal justice system guided by a sensitivity to
the pervasive risk of racial or class bias. Throwing the baby out
with the bath water is a minor mishap compared with the effects
of throwing mercy in sentencing in the individual case out of the
criminal justice system.

If the analysis so far is correct, one is pushed to a most
difficult thesis. If a just and merciful system of sentencing (as
distinct from a just system allowing for mercy in the individual
case) cannot be created, if it is impossible to define in the reality

of social and political attitudes toward crime a sentencing system in which *categories* of offenders may be treated identically and also mercifully, then one has to set up a system in which the categories define the upper limits of sentencing authority, which are equal in their processes and procedures for considering each individual case, but which allow room for merciful individualization of punishment. I believe this to be a correct analysis. I believe that categories of offense-offender relationships can define only the upper and lower limits of just punishment and that within those limits it is essential to allow room for mercy to modulate justice in the individual case. I thus find myself forced to argue against the widely accepted precept that treating like cases alike is a governing rule of justice. I think it has been much overstated and that there is ample room within an entirely just system of guilt and punishment not to treat like cases alike and indeed that any humanely and decently structured system of criminal justice should not do so.

I defer this argument to the next chapter. What it comes to, however, is that the principle of equality in punishment is an important factor in fine-tuning the sentence within the range set by concepts of desert, but it is by no means a categorical imperative. In the next chapter I will argue that there can be just sentences in which like criminals are not treated alike as to either who goes to prison or for how long. But I need neither to stipulate that view now nor to ask you to accept it. It strengthens the analysis in this chapter but is not essential to it.

Whether or not it is an essential principle of justice to treat like mentally ill criminals alike, the present stage of our analysis is this: within a range of punishment guided by concepts of desert it is both principled and desirable to take into account the degree of the offender's moral fault—and hence, in some cases, his mental illness at the time of the crime—in setting the sentence to be imposed.

V. Aggravating the Punishment of the Mentally Ill

Having relied on the papacy in the previous part of this chapter, let me take as launching text for this part the American secular equivalent of infallibility, the Supreme Court of the United States:

> [A]ny sentencing authority must predict a convicted person's probable future conduct when it engages in the process of determining what punishment to impose.[68]

The Court offered this proposition in the course of deciding the constitutionality of statutes imposing capital punishment on more dangerous killers and approved it in considering constitutionally acceptable processes of making that classification. But though future dangerousness is fairly obviously relevant to sentencing, closer analysis is necessary of why that is so and how "dangerousness" might be defined and measured for sentencing purposes. For present purposes, this can be done in the context of why mental illness may press toward increasing punishment.

There are two ways in which mental illness aggravates punishment. First, desert itself may be conditioned by fear, and the mentally ill may properly or improperly be more feared in relation to criminal behavior than those who are not mentally ill. Secondly, the likelihood that the convicted person will repeat his criminal conduct, his "dangerousness," also real or imagined, will influence the sentence imposed on him. Each process merits discussion.

The perspective of this chapter on questions of desert is that of a "limiting retributivist" as distinct from a "defining retributivist." To the limiting retributivist, desert sets the outer limits, upper and lower, of punishment. It is the reflection of society's official view of what the criminal deserves; it is not finely tuned; it makes few subtle distinctions. The limiting retributivist recognizes, however, that within that range more subtle, finely tuned moral distinctions of desert relevant to punishment can and should be made. Desert thus has a societal face and an individual face; both are difficult to quantify but clearly they often differ.

The societal face of a deserved punishment expresses fear of the criminal among other sentiments. Irrational behavior that is

---

68. Jurek v. Texas, 428 U.S. 262, 275 (1976). Approved (or to be more precise "while in no sense disapproving") in Estelle v. Smith, 451 U.S. 454 (1981).

not easily explained or is seen as out of control tends to be more feared than similar behavior that is thought to be planned and rationally controlled. And that those fears help to define the deserved punishment in the view of the legislator, judge, and counsel requires no analysis; brief introspection in which one empathizes with the victim suffices. Of course, the more we understand conduct the more these irrational fears (to the extent they are irrational) can be reduced. But clearly, being generative of irrational fear, the criminal's mental illness tends sometimes toward increasing his punishment.

This process by which the criminal's mental illness increases society's fear of him and hence his punishment is, of course, closely linked to the next ground for such an increase, the reality of his increased dangerousness, but the distinction between these two processes is worth preserving. For example, we saw that the sexual psychopath laws of this country swept within their purview a large number of exhibitionists and voyeurs, known in the trade as "flashers" and "peepers." The bizarre nature of their behavior leads the uninstructed to assume that such behavior indicates a lack of control of the sexual impulses and constitutes an immediate threat of serious harm to the woman made victim of such behavior and also of serious harm to other women. In fact neither she nor other women are in peril; she is fearful, and she and the community express this fear in assessing substantial sanctions as justly deserved. One can rationalize this assessment as a misperception of dangerousness in which sexual inadequacy is misinterpreted as incipient aggression; but it seems to me that it is functioning at a different level, at the level of an intuitive link between fear and desert.

Now, what of the more direct impact of the perceived or real dangerousness of the mentally ill offender on the sentence that should be imposed on him?

The second most significant factor in defining the amount of punishment in all existing systems of criminal punishment, is the existence or nonexistence of past conviction and past punishments; the first is, of course, the gravity of the offense. The criminal record is of such great significance for two reasons: First, each succeeding conviction and punishment increases the likelihood of a future conviction and punishment until the intersection of the line of increasing age works its biological reduction on criminality. The best predictor of future criminality is past criminality; so far as I can discover every existing and proposed criminal justice system takes cognizance of this and increases punishment accordingly. There may, however, be a second justification for this pervasive increase of punishment, a justification akin to that of contempt of court or contempt of the state. He has been punished once and here he comes again for punishment—will he never leave us alone? Will he never learn to be a law-abiding citizen? The message of punishment has been given to him and willfully he has closed his eyes to it. But the more one reflects on this particular analysis the less persuasive it seems, unless it be related to an understandable clemency extended to a first offender which is withdrawn after the first offense; but the force of this analysis as the criminal career grows in frequency becomes more attenuated.

Indeed, it seems somewhat strange to have to argue that dangerousness figures in the definition of criminal punishment; the fact of that relationship is so frequently apparent when particular sentences are being discussed. Hence, let us focus on the particular question of the propriety of increasing sentences on the mentally ill when it is suggested, or when it is true, that their mental illness increases the likelihood of their involvement in crime.

The jurisprudential proposition that I would offer is this: punishment should not be imposed nor the term of punishment extended by virtue of a prediction of dangerousness (no matter how valid) beyond that which would be justified as a deserved punishment independently of that prediction. Powers under mental health laws may well be appropriately exercised on the basis of certain high predictions of dangerousness beyond those justified as criminal-law sanctions, but they cannot be justified as criminal-law sanctions. To stipulate, for the time being, the validity of this limitation, how would it be applied to the mentally ill?

There is a considerable literature on this question which I can incorporate here by reference and move through it to the conclusions I would offer.

When I first came to this country in the mid-1950s the answer that the informed scholar would give to the question of whether the mentally ill were more dangerous than those not so classified would be that the mentally ill had lower crime rates than the sane of similar age and socioeconomic circumstances. That answer was supported by studies showing that those released from mental hospitals had lower crime rates than comparable groups in the community who had not been hospitalized.

If the question were posed now, a different answer would be given. More recent studies tend to the conclusion that the mentally ill have somewhat higher crime rates, in relation to several types of crime, than those not so classified. Why the change? It appears not to be substantially a product of any improved methodology in our investigative technique, though this has made a small contribution. The changed perception and indeed the changed reality seems more likely to reflect differences in social attitudes toward the mentally ill and improved techniques of treating them. We are in the process of emptying the back wards of our mental hospitals. Lifetime detention of the mentally ill is much less common than it used to be. The geriatric wards are largely closed. We have increased the frequency of hospitalization of the mentally ill but dramatically reduced the duration of such hospitalization. As a result, a large proportion of the mentally ill population is at risk at earlier ages for the commission of crime, and it would appear that they are more frequently involved in crime than we had previously judged.

Two streams of research lead to this conclusion. First, there are studies that measure the frequency with which those who have been classified as mentally ill or retarded are arrested or convicted of crime. Secondly, there are studies that measure the frequency with which those who have been arrested or convicted of crime have been classified as mentally ill or retarded. These two disparate lines of inquiry come together in the cautious conclusion that there are certain categories of mental illness that increase the base expectancy rate for certain categories of crime. And this is surely not an unexpected conclusion. It merely confirms the obvious proposition that problems flowing from mental illness sometimes

make it more difficult to live a law-abiding life. It does not oppose—rather it blends well with—the perspective underlying this
chapter that the causes of crime must be sought in the most
complex and varying interrelationships between social and psychological pressures.

Let us consider, then, the extent of our present capacity to
predict dangerousness in relation to the mentally ill and, given that
capacity, its proper bearing on criminal sentences. If one defines
"dangerousness" as the likelihood of the commission of a crime
of personal violence or of a crime threatening personal violence
and if one selects those to be predicted as dangerous or as not
dangerous only from a group who have already committed such
a crime (since it is only from such a group that even marginally
useful predictions can be made), then the present outer limit of
our knowledge is that, when we bring to the selection of the
highest risk group all the skills of the sociologist, the statistician,
the psychologist, and the psychiatrist, this group has a base expectancy rate of about 33 percent. That is to say, if we use every
resource of knowledge we now have to define groups to whom
predictive criteria can be applied with the highest confidence, we
find that in the group judged most dangerous only one out of three
actually goes on to commit a violent crime. There will be two false
positive predictions of dangerousness for every one true positive
prediction.[69]

In a recent and important book by John Monahan, *The Clinical
Prediction of Violent Behavior*,[70] the present state of the art is carefully
and exhaustively considered. Monahan reaches the conclusion immediately relevant to sentencing the mentally ill, that "the best"
clinical research currently in existence indicates that psychiatrists
and psychologists are accurate in no more than one out of three
predictions of violent behavior over a several-year period among
institutionalized populations who had committed violence in the

69. It is important to stress that this assessment of a one in three positive
prediction base expectancy rate is a most generous assessment, tending to
exaggerate present knowledge.
70. J. Monahan, *The Clinical Prediction of Violent Behavior* (1981).

past (and thus had high base rates for it) and who were also diagnosed as mentally ill.[71]

Given this limitation on our present predictive capacities, what are the consequences for sentencing policy that flow from the fact that for every three we predict as dangerous only one commits a crime of violence? Such a prediction would be no justification at all for imposing a sanction in excess of the "deserved" punishment, but, to apply the philosophy of sentencing I am offering, it could be a ground for increasing punishment up to the deserved maximum. This increment of punishment is to be justified on utilitarian grounds with the maximum not so justified.

The view of the proper role of predictions of dangerousness on sentencing offered in this chapter may be more sharply presented by contrasting and then reconciling the following two propositions:

> *Proposition A*: It is better that nine guilty men shall be acquitted than one innocent man convicted even if the acquittal of all ten leads to three crimes of personal violence which the conviction of all ten would have avoided.

> *Proposition B*: Among those convicted, it is better that seven "false positives" be imprisoned together with three "true positives" up to the maximum period deserved for their crimes if the thus extended imprisonment of all ten prevents three crimes of personal violence.[72]

Let me first comment on these two propositions. Proposition A is the usual Law Day boast of the common law. It expresses an important truth about the degree of certainty that we strive for as a condition precedent to a conviction of crime. I think if we were to put ourselves in Rawls's "original position," ignorant of whether we would be law-abiding or criminal, victims of crime or untouched by crime, we would vote for Proposition A. But it

71. *Id.* at 48–49.

72. I choose these numbers for Proposition B as reflecting our likely highest operating base expectancy rate—over two false positives for every one true positive prediction of "dangerousness" as earlier defined.

is a "human rights" rather than a utilitarian proposition. The suffering flowing from the three crimes that occur as a result of our adherence to Proposition A may well exceed the suffering involved in the incarceration of the one innocent together with the nine guilty. This may be true whatever one's hedonistic calculus, unless one gives an extraordinarily high hedonistic value to the avoidance of the conviction of the innocent, which, of course, would finesse the issue.

It may be proper to note that sometimes, under the pressure of emergency, most legal systems depart from Proposition A. For example, in times of war most countries under emergency powers round up and incarcerate resident enemy aliens. No great effort is extended to distinguish the loyal from the disloyal, even though it may be well known that the vast majority of the enemy aliens so segregated are loyal to the country of their residence. What are seen as utilitarian values, in these emergency situations, seem swiftly to overcome the value of protecting individual freedom. One can imagine a situation of rampant crime in a setting of social calamity where Proposition A might be temporarily abandoned; but happily it is only in the most extreme circumstances that there is a temptation in any reasonably developed jurisprudential system to depart from its controlling force.

How then can one support the apparently contrary result reached by Proposition B? Again some "innocent" (in this case seven as distinct from only one in Proposition A) suffer unnecessarily extended imprisonment to prevent three crimes of personal violence. The distinction is, of course, obvious. In the fine-tuning of punishment between the upper and lower limits of retributively deserved punishment there is powerful reason why utilitarian values should apply. None of the ten is "innocent" in the sense that he does not deserve the punishment imposed upon him. The "false positive" is excessively punished only in the sense that his sentence of imprisonment would not be so long if we had the power to predict violent criminal behavior with completeness and accuracy.

This argument does not mean that we have warrant to be lax or cavalier in our application of these utilitarian values. It is of the first importance that the expectancy rates upon which such predictions of violence are based and the prolongation of detention sought to be justified should be meticulously and precisely carried out. Injustice can indeed flow from a methodologically unsound and superficial indulgence of our fears of repetition of violent crime by categories of offenders, as distinct from careful validation of their base expectancy crime rates. In practice, at present levels of knowledge it will be rare indeed that we can apply Proposition B,[73] but when it can be applied, it is my submission that it states a proposition of justice. And I think it states a proposition of "justice as fairness" and that all of us in the Rawlsian original position, ignorant of whether we would be a false positive or a true positive, and ignorant of whether we would be one of the three victims saved or not, would vote for the acceptance of Proposition B.

So we are left with the conclusion that predictive criteria of mental illness may properly lead to the imposition of a punishment, say, imprisonment, which otherwise would not have been imposed, or to the prolongation of that punishment beyond what would have been imposed had the desirability of incapacitating the dangerous not been taken into account. Mental illness may thus both reduce culpability and increase punishability. In the next section we treat this apparent paradox.

VI. When to Mitigate? When to Aggravate?

Some tidying up of the apparent paradox between the mitigating and aggravating effects of mental illness on punishment is required. The essential reconciliation is no doubt all too obvious but some frayed ends merit attention.

Within retributive limitations on punishment, the finer-tuning of moral fault allows for mercy, clemency, and parsimony in punishment of the mentally ill. It is not a sentimental but rather a judicious use of the heavy weapons of punishment to lighten its impact on the less morally guilty to the extent that decent community sentiment allows. Psychological and social adversities may

---

73. See part VII of this chapter for some examples of its consideration and rejection as current practice.

both properly have this influence on punishment, and we risk little by recognizing their sometimes undue criminogenic pressure and by mitigating punishment accordingly. Since parsimony in the use of punishment is desirable in itself, mitigation of punishment on grounds of mental illness is both justified and socially desirable unless it increases the risk to the community beyond that which the community bears from the ordinary limitations on the operation of the criminal justice system generally.[74] This increased risk may flow from reduced general deterrence from the sentence known to be imposed or from the larger danger of the mentally ill criminal leniently sentenced.

As to general deterrence and the punishment of the mentally ill: earlier it was submitted that the marginal general deterrence lost by mitigating the punishment of the mentally ill does not preclude that mitigation. There is no evidence at all to support the proposition that those criminals who plan their crimes calculate the cost in likely punishment with a precision that includes a possible mitigation of punishment if they are mentally ill or can simulate mental illness. And it is an inherently unlikely proposition. If there is a marginal deterrence sacrificed here to clemency, it is a very small sacrifice indeed.

As to the increased risk to the community flowing from the suggested larger dangerousness of the mentally ill criminal, I submit that though in jurisprudential analysis aggravation of punishment up to a deserved maximum may properly supplant any argument for mitigation on grounds of lesser moral fault, the empirical preconditions of such aggravation are restrictive and will in practice rarely be encountered.

All predictions of "dangerousness" have the following paradigmatic form: of the last 1,000 cases studied there were 100 like the present offender who were predicted as "dangerous," 900 were

74. Reductions of punishment which lead to community placement as distinct from imprisonment or which reduce the period of detention probably have *some* effect on increased crime, but we bear that adversity for other valid reasons. The issue is whether a different balance should be applied to mentally ill criminals; locking them all up for the term of their natural lives would probably measurably reduce crime but ordinary principles prohibit it.

predicted as "safe." (By "dangerous" I mean likely to commit one of a list of serious crimes within two years; by "safe" I mean not likely to do so.) When these predictions were checked on—and we have checking techniques that are infallible—the following was the result: Of the 100 predicted as dangerous, 34 were arrested for crime, 66 were not arrested; of the 900 predicted safe, 100 were arrested for crime, 800 were not arrested. To agree on language: the predictions produced 66 false positives for 34 true positives, and 100 false negatives for 800 true negatives.

To set aside one validation question: in fact, such figures exaggerate both false positives, since some of the crime by the 66 goes undetected, and true negatives, for the same reason. But if we are relying on empirical proof of criminality to justify increments of punishment, we can hardly rely on our lack of empirical proof.

To set aside another validation question: I am assuming repeated testing of the prediction on a series of groups using identical predictive criteria and our usual infallible follow-up techniques. I want to argue in principle in relation to practice, the discussion not being avoided by our present unsatisfactory predictive techniques.

The base expectancy rate of the above figures, were the prediction that of arrest for a crime of personal violence (or threatening personal violence),[75] would be as high as clinical predictive knowledge has achieved.

Of course, for a different prediction a higher rate could be achieved. Suppose the prediction is that a defined group of adult alcoholic owners of motor vehicles will drive a car within the next two years under the influence of alcohol; I hazard the guess that instead of the one in three base expectancy rate in the above figures, a rate of two in three could easily be achieved. Hence, as a departure point of some obviousness: the moral issues in using such base expectancy rates turn in part on the severity of the harm

75. Arrest, of course, does not establish commission of the crime but for purposes of structuring the argument against my conclusion I would make the concession that it does establish crime for present purposes.

risked in relation to the severity of the harm imposed in order to minimize that risk. To expand this: car drivers convicted of driving under the influence of alcohol who have a base expectancy rate of 66 percent of repeating their crime should be denied a driving license for the maximum period justified by their offense even though, lacking such a base expectancy rate, their license would not be revoked for what they did. Transpose that to predictions of a crime of violence and a base expectancy rate of 33 percent and assume a five-year increase of imprisonment as defining the maximum addition for what the offender did. It is certainly a different calculation; how is one to address it?

At this point the literature on prediction of dangerousness falls silent; it is unlikely that I can answer the question. But some suggestions might be made tending toward an answer and also meeting our control question: when should mental illness be treated as so increasing the dangerousness of the convicted offender as to justify punishing him on the high side of the range of deserved punishments for what a criminal with his record of crime has done?

The key is this: his base expectancy rate must be shown by reliable evidence to be substantially higher than the base expectancy rate of another criminal with an identical record and convicted of a closely similar crime of violence but who is not mentally ill. The likely recidivism of the mentally ill offender must substantially exceed the likely recidivism of the sane offender. If that cannot be shown, then he should be sentenced on the low side of the deserved range if his criminality is causally related to his mental illness.

It is my submission that this principle governs both main sentence fine-tuning decisions: the in-out decision and, if in, the duration decision.

It is important to insist on clear and compelling evidence of a higher base expectancy rate attributable to mental illness before it can, in justice, increase punishment. This is not the occasion to affirm skepticism in psychiatric clinical predictions generally; the literature on this is compelling. And even when sociological predictors are added and sophisticated statistical techniques and research methodologies applied there will be very few cases indeed where the principle I have enunciated will justify such an increase of punishment. But that does not invalidate the principle; to the contrary, it tends to affirm its importance and to stress the need for more reliable data than we now have as a precondition to any increase of punishment of the mentally ill relying on the mediating concept of their unestablished heightened dangerousness.

Hence the conclusion: the range of deserved punishment being otherwise determined, the judge should sentence the mentally ill offender toward the bottom of that range to the extent that his mental illness was causally related to his crime (or to his earlier crimes), unless reliable evidence is adduced that because of his mental illness this offender is substantially more likely than others in that range to be involved in similar or more serious crimes in the future.

This conclusion should not be seen as supporting the current tendency to misuse "dangerousness" to increase punishment. I very much oppose this tendency, because I consider it based on uncritical acceptance of specious predictions claiming reliability grossly in excess of truth. But if and when base expectancy predictions of future criminality meet the criteria I have suggested, these predictions should properly infuse a just sentencing system.

VII. The Minnesota Sentencing Guidelines

The above is an effort at a principled theoretical statement of when to reduce punishment and when to increase punishment because of the mental illness or retardation of the convicted offender. It may add to clarity to test these principles in relation to the best practice.

There is at present general agreement among scholars of sentencing—though you can be sure it will change; it always does—that the guidelines set forth by the Minnesota Sentencing Guidelines Commission[76] are a most sophisticated attempt to bring predictability and order to sentencing practice. They provide a grid with one axis based on gravity of crime and the other on criminal record to guide the judge in determining both whether the offender should go to prison and, if he does, the period he should serve. The grid gives the judge a "presumptive sentence";

76. *Supra* note 52.

but this "presumptive sentence" is not the last word on the matter. The guidelines provide:

> The sentences provided in the Sentencing Guidelines Grid are presumed to be appropriate for every case. The judge shall utilize the presumptive sentence provided in the Sentencing Guidelines Grid unless the individual case involves substantial and compelling circumstances. When such circumstances are present, the judge may depart from the presumptive sentence and stay or impose any sentence authorized by law. When departing from the presumptive sentence, a judge must provide written reasons which specify the substantial and compelling nature of the circumstances, and which demonstrate why the sentence selected in the departure is more appropriate, reasonable, or equitable than the presumptive sentence.

The statute further provides a list of factors in the offender's person and history that should not be used as reasons for the departure from the guidelines and a nonexclusive list of factors that may be used for that purpose. Among those usable expressly as "mitigating factors" is:

> The offender, because of physical or mental impairment, lacked substantial capacity for judgment when the offense was committed. The voluntary use of intoxicants (drugs or alcohol) does not fall within the purview of this factor.

The Supreme Court of Minnesota, over the more than a year that the sentencing guidelines have been in operation, has in several cases considered this structure of presumptive sentences and the proper grounds and appropriate ranges of "departures" from such sentences by trial judges. Departures on grounds of mental illness have several times been approved.

Let us turn, then, to the practice of trial judges in Minnesota applying the guidelines, and departing from them, in the first year of operation of the guidelines. In respect of offenses committed between May 1980 and 30 April 1981 there were 5,500 presumptive sentences imposed on those charged and convicted of felonies. Of these, 4,792 were within the guidelines both as to the dispositional decision (imprisonment or not) and the duration decision.

Of the 708 "departures," 222 (31.4 percent) were departures to
a more severe sanction (either crossing the in-out dispositional line
to imprisonment or increasing the term of imprisonment); 423
(59.7 percent) were departures to leniency; and 63 (8.9 percent)
were double departures in which the sanction imposed was more
severe with respect to one aspect, e.g., disposition, and less severe
with respect to the other, e.g., duration.

In these 5,500 felony cases, the factor of "mental impairment"
causing "lack of substantial capacity for judgment when the offense
was committed" or the factor of "psychological problem" was
given as the reason by the sentencing judge either for not im-
prisoning offenders whose presumptive sentences recommended
imprisonment or for reducing imprisonment below the presumptive term in 29 cases, that is, in 6.9 percent of all mitigations. The
reasons for departures offered by trial judges were often boilerplate
(and there is no necessary harm in using boilerplate; it is often the
wisest course) such as the "diminished mental capacity of the
defendant at the time of the commission of the acts" (Offender,
Parole; Report date 11–3–81), but more ample exegesis was often
offered. Here are an illustrative few (followed by departure report
date):[77]

> "[L]acked substantial capacity for judgment when the offense
> was committed. He was also, at the time of the commission of
> the offense, suicidal and in a highly emotional state" (10-3-81).

> "[H]is 'emotional age' was significantly younger. He grew up in
> a pathological family with elements of physical abuse, mental ill-
> ness, and sexual abnormality which combined to retard his emo-
> tional and interpersonal development" (l0-20-81).

> "It appears to me that although the crime obviously is terribly
> serious, it is clearly the product of a mental disorder. There's no

77. The Minnesota Sentencing Guidelines Commission keeps a running
list of all such appeals to the Supreme Court. Those seeking to pursue this topic
further should contact the Minnesota Sentencing Guidelines Commission, 284
Metro Square Building, 7th and Robert Streets, St. Paul, Minnesota 35101. I
am grateful to the director and the research director of that commission for
their generous assistance with the concluding section of this chapter.

question in my mind but that we have a mental illness. I believe that the facts surrounding this entire episode and the medical evidence . . . constitute compelling and substantial reasons for departing from the Sentencing Guideline, and I do depart from the Sentencing Guidelines" (6-19-81).

"[D]efendant was in such an emotional state as to impair his capacity for judgment. He had cut his wrists in a suicide attempt. While his emotional state was not such as to constitute a defense, it should be considered in mitigation" (12-88-80).

"[D]efendant suffered from a number of worsening psychological and emotional problems at the time of the offense . . . in view of those factors . . . the Court feels that a gross misdemeanor sentence of one year is warranted in this case" (11-6-80; effect misdemeanor record only and no time to be served).

In accepting a plea bargain below the presumptive guideline: "The probation officer concluded that the offender 'presents a very complex social and psychiatric background'" (3-3-81).

There is much similar language in "departures" and appeals justifying, in my view, these proper reductions of punishment because of the mental illness of the accused, a wise use of parsimony in punishment. To that extent, the Minnesota experience in the early months of applying its system of presumptive sentences blends well with the principles offered in this chapter. Nor is there much tension between Minnesota practice in relation to mental illness increasing punishment and the views I have advanced, but there is some, and it merits attention.

Those who fashioned the legislation in Minnesota and those who serve on the Minnesota Sentencing Guidelines Commission are well aware of the weak empirical base of predictions of "dangerousness" as a ground for an increase of sentence. Hence, such predictions are not specified among the list of aggravating factors, nor, of course, are they specifically excluded. The judge would thus be free to order a "departure" by reason of such a prediction provided he set out the basis for the prediction.

The Minnesota experience in its early months gives no example of the type of increment of punishment by reason of increased dangerousness from mental illness discussed earlier in this chapter. This is not surprising. A sound basis for such a prediction is very rare. The Minnesota experience so far thus neither supports nor controverts the theoretical analysis here offered.

There is, however, one type of case which causes difficulty. Of the first 222 felony "departures" to increased severity in Minnesota, 7 were of the following nature: the imposition of a term of imprisonment on an offender whose crime and criminal record gave him a nonimprisonment presumptive sentence but who was an addict, in need of detoxification or treatment for his addiction, who had several times failed in such treatments when they were offered while he was at large in the community or as a condition of a probation order.

A difficulty emerges. Whereas the analysis I have offered of dangerousness and mental illness as a one-step basis for increasing the severity of a sentence stands up well to Minnesota experience, it fails to incorporate a two-step process of the following nature: because of his addictive condition which may be related to his mental illness, this convicted offender requires specialized medical-psychological treatment in the community. So far we are within or below the guidelines. The treatment is ordered as a matter of sentencing or parole release—the tendency is still toward lesser severity. But a substantial proportion of those ordered to attend such out-patient treatment units or halfway house treatment-placement facilities either do not attend or soon abscond. The result is then often imprisonment in excess of the presumptive sentence.

There is room for abuse here. On the other hand, a few such cases may well reflect situations where as knowledge increases mental illness may be used along lines presented in this chapter as a just ground for increasing the severity or certainly the duration of a penal sanction. Much depends on the quality and sensitivity of the drug treatment offered and on the degree to which any half-way house treatment facility restricts the accused's life in the community.

FIVE

Anisonomy, or Treating Like Cases Unlike

An Angelo for Claudio, death for death!
Haste still pays haste, and leisure answers leisure;
Like doth quit like, and Measure still for Measure.

Measure for Measure (5.1.412–14)

As usual, Shakespeare was both plagiarizing and modifying the source: Matthew 7:1–2: "Judge not, that ye be not judged; and with what measure ye mete it shall be measured to you again." Both texts suggest a heavenly-terrestial equation which would impose a massively punitive burden on earthly justice. But the issue phrased by Matthew and by Shakespeare remains central to sentencing policy.

In the previous chapter I argued that "a deserved punishment" when carefully analyzed does not mean the infliction on the criminal offender of a pain precisely equivalent to that which he has inflicted on his victim; it means rather a "not undeserved punishment which bears a proportional relationship in a hierarchy of punishments to the harm for which the criminal has been convicted." I argued further that this "hierarchy of deserved punishments will in practice prove to be a hierarchy of deserved ranges of punishment." I then finessed until this chapter the question of whether within

179

each range of deserved punishments it is a necessary condition of justice to treat like cases alike, to impose identical sentences on the equally undeserving. I affirmed that justice does not require such precise equality. The present task is to move from affirmation to argument and, one hopes, to persuasion.

To try to make a case against equality is, on its face, offensive to the American ethic. Hence, I solicit your tolerance—let your leisure in condemnation answer your leisure in analysis. To that end let me put the thesis in less offensive terms: justice and mercy both have roles in the criminal justice system; mercy cannot be precisely quantified and institutionalized or it ceases to be mercy and becomes leniency; mercy is the trump that can capture equality's ace and allow punishment at the bottom range of a deserved punishment.

It is courageous, probably foolhardy, to quibble with Aristotle, but given the opinions advanced in this and the preceding chapter the conflict cannot be avoided. I find unacceptable his thesis on rectificatory justice (what most now call "retributive justice"), in book five of *The Nichomachean Ethics*, by which the leading principle of justice is equality in punishment according to proportionality in guilt. Justice demands, he tells us, that like cases must be treated alike and unlike cases must not. And powerful cohorts of philosophers march through subsequent generations proclaiming the truth of this Janus-faced principle and discussing the criteria of "likeness" for its application—defining those criteria that are properly relevant to punishment and distinguishing those that are not.

It was refreshing and liberating for me to find H. L. A. Hart writing of "the somewhat hazy requirement of justice that like cases be treated alike."[1] It is no doubt crass to admit it, but I prefer to consider the theoretical by observing tensions in practice, rather than by analyzing tensions in theory, and here was a leading jurisprude expressing a similar uncertainty to that which I found in practice. This is my dilemma. I find cases I would judge to be

1. H. L. A. Hart, *Punishment and Responsibility: Essays in the Philosophy of Law* 24 (1968).

equally morally deserving of punishment treated differently; theory tells me this is injustice; but I think about the observations rather than the analyses and come to the view that quite often, within limits, like cases *ought* to be treated differently. An approach from a stance of observing operating systems of punishment thus leads me to the view that Aristotle's precept of justice and Hart's "somewhat hazy requirement" of justice are neither precepts nor requirements; justice does not require identity or equality of punishment of the equally undeserving; it requires only that they be punished within a just range of punishments fitted to their desert. This is not a minor quibble; it strikes to the heart of current punishment policy. It is relevant to punishing not only the mentally ill criminal but all criminals. The excuse for its inclusion here is, however, that it was implicit in much of chapter 4 and requires clarification here if my thesis on sentencing mentally ill criminals is to be analytically acceptable.

Let me be cautious in the thrust of the present argument: the proposition is that there are many cases in which those who have inflicted equal harm and are of identical moral guilt should not be punished equally; that the principle of punishing like cases alike has been overstated and, if seriously followed, would in the current state of knowledge about crime and its control and in the context of current political attitudes create an excessively severe criminal justice system. To develop this thesis I shall consider and defend selective enforcement and prosecution and divergent sentencing of cases identical in terms of harm and moral fault. I am anxious in this chapter not to argue the "likeness" of cases. When I aver that two cases are alike, the reader controls the facts (they can be monozygotic twins with identical records, equal temptations, killing monozygotic twins) and should make them identical in all those qualities the reader regards as properly relevant to sentencing. There will be some qualification to this invitation, but not much.

The sequence of topics in this chapter is:

I. Definitions—Defining, Limiting, and Guiding Principles
II. Desert as a Defining Principle

I. Definitions—Defining, Limiting, and Guiding Principles

I wish to distinguish between three types of principles of justice: those that define, those that limit, and those that guide.

By a *defining* principle of punishment I mean a principle which if adopted as the purpose to be served by punishment would give the exact sanction to be imposed. If we knew enough about a particular offender, special deterrence could be a principle defining his punishment, the exact pain and no more that would inhibit him from future criminality (or future criminality of this type). Similarly, if we knew enough about general deterrence, it too might be a defining principle of punishment. It may be possible in the future to graph the precisely appropriate general deterrent punishment for a given crime committed by a given type of criminal. We would have to know a great deal more than we do now, but if we did, the graph could be drawn and the hedonistic utilitarian precise punishment found. We would have to know for each community all about the relationships between certainty, celerity, and severity of punishments and the incidence of the crime we are to punish. We would have to make value judgments relating the criminal's pain to the pain of future victims, say, fifteen hedonistic units to one. But if we knew all this, and more besides, the precise point on the graph of punishment could be determined where any additional punishment of the criminal was not worth the margin of increased crime prevention it would produce.[2]

2. I set aside possible questions of the disutility of increased sanctions achieving lesser enforceability. I assume, for this argument, that the co-rela-

Thus, given sufficient knowledge, on utilitarian grounds we could determine the precisely appropriate special and general deterrent punishments. There may be other reasons why we would not wish to impose the punishments so defined; for example, they may exceed what we think is just, but nevertheless deterrent utilitarian values could precisely determine the punishment. Deterrence could be a defining principle of punishment, achieving the fine-tuning of punishment to its precise utilitarian purpose.

It is suggested by many commentators that both desert and equality should be defining principles, the going rate of desert fixing the punishment of all like cases. This chapter argues that this is an error.

By a *limiting* principle of punishment I mean a principle that, though it would rarely tell us the exact sanction to be imposed, as deterrence might, would nevertheless give us the outer limits of leniency and severity which should not be exceeded. Desert, I submit, is such a limiting principle.

By a *guiding* principle I mean a general value to be respected unless other values sufficiently strongly justify its rejection in any given case. Equality, I submit, is such a guiding principle.

II. Desert as a Defining Principle

With the decline of "the rehabilitative ideal" as a purpose of punishment,[3] desert has come to be seen as a central purpose of punishment. In the previous chapter I sketched the movement and listed the main commentaries by which "desert justifies and limits eligibility for punishment."[4] Where I part from most of those commentators and much recent sentencing reform is that I see desert and social utility as properly combining to distribute punishments while they claim to reject utilitarian considerations and to confine themselves to considerations of desert in that distribution.

---

tionship between increased punishment and reduced incidence of crime is linear; the contrary assumption would, of course, not weaken the analysis.

3. See Francis A. Allen, *The Decline of the Rehabilitative Ideal* (1981).

4. *Supra* pp. 148–50.

Again, it may help to rest first on practice before reflecting on theory. The formulation of sentencing guidelines, of presumptive sentences, to guide the judge or parole officer in determining the actual punishment usually can be illustrated as a grid. Along one axis will be the crime or series of crimes last committed by the offender—this is the pure "desert" axis. On the other axis will be the offender's criminal record. Outside the grid, there will be other criteria of aggravation and mitigation of punishment allowing or advising movement within the ranges of punishment prescribed by the grid. Such is the pattern for the Federal Parole Guidelines and for the guidelines of California, Illinois, Indiana, Minnesota, and others.

Is "desert" a defining principle within such a structure? The answer is affirmative, I assume, if prior criminal record is seen as forming a part of a larger concept of "desert." There is much conflict on this point, and I wish to avoid it here on the ground that I already have enough to contend with. Let me rather ask you to assume for present purposes that those states and those commentators who see their sentencing systems as based on concepts of desert and who include prior record as relevant to determining desert are to be believed. When you have a record of conviction for crime and of punishment for it, the slate is not really clean; further crime by you is a larger moral obloquy than an identical crime by your unconvicted and previously unpunished brother and therefore deserving of larger punishment, and not, as commentators like Fogel and von Hirsch[5] would have it, because you are more dangerous than your unconvicted brother.

The distinction between a pure desert model of punishment (punishment justly deserved for the crime or series of crimes for which you are now being sentenced) and an expanded or modified desert model merits further attention.

Contemporary commentators are vigorous in their affirmation that an increase in the justly deserved punishment based on prior record is *not* a utilitarian addition based on the larger dangerousness

5. See David Fogel, *We Are the Living Proof: The Justice Model for Corrections* (1975); and Andrew von Hirsch, *Doing Justice: The Choice of Punishments* (1976).

of the offender. If they are wrong in this, their whole argument for excluding concepts of dangerousness from the assessment of punishments is undermined to the point of being fatally flawed. If they are right, the deserved punishment must incorporate prior record for, it seems to me, either one or more of the following reasons: (1) the prior record manifests greater wickedness, larger moral fault, than does the last crime absent a prior record—thus it is proper to assess this larger moral fault in establishing the hierarchy of deserved punishments; (2) there is a quality of contempt of law in coming yet again to punishment—and again it is proper to consider this contempt in establishing the hierarchy of deserved punishment; (3) prior offenses were dealt with leniently— there is, in effect, a deserved punishment yet to be endured which should properly be added to that deserved for the last crime or series of crimes. (First offenders have had a leniency discount which is now reclaimed. This analysis becomes somewhat awkward as the criminal record grows.)

One of these reasons must explain the structure of recent legislative and administrative sentencing guidelines initiatives unless they are merely the affirmation of arbitrary decisions that, from the complexity of our sentencing purposes, the gravity of the crime and prior record should be selected from a host of other moral and utilitarian considerations in order to reduce existing sentencing disparities. Certainly more than this is claimed; concepts of justice and equality of deserved punishment are invoked. The analysis here pursued accepts that invocation of desert and equality as accurate; if it is not, the requirement that like cases must be treated alike becomes very hazy indeed, because so very much would have to be included in "likeness" for sentencing purposes.

It is perhaps appropriate to note that the Supreme Court of the United States in *Rummel v. Estelle*[6] held as constitutionally acceptable Texas habitual criminal legislation which imposed a life sentence on a third-time offender whose three larcenies added up in value to $229.11. As a limitation to criminal punishments, in terms of desert, the Eighth Amendment as presently construed

6. Rummel v. Estelle, 445 U.S. 263 (1980).

allows a formidably important role to prior convictions. The Supreme Court would thus seem to argue with *Struggle for Justice*,[7] *Fair and Certain Punishment*,[8] and the writings of von Hirsch,[9] Fogel,[10] and van den Haag[11] that prior criminal record is relevant to determining a justly deserved punishment.

If we give "desert" this expanded meaning accorded it by contemporary commentators, it is important to see what is excluded. Some would see the fact that the convicted offender was married and had a dependent family as relevant to sentencing him. Those who advocate a desert-based sentencing system would reject such a fact as relevant to sentencing unless, of course, the existence of the family increased the criminal's temptation to commit the crime. (At the outer limit, if the family were starving, some might acquit the accused of larceny or certainly greatly reduce his punishment if convicted.)

Hence, for purposes of this chapter, I accept a view of desert as a basis for sentencing which goes to the moral desert of the offender. This includes his criminal record and excludes such considerations as, for example, the level of crime in the community, the fact that others depend on him, and the fact that he is gainfully employed, all of which are extrinsic to the social harm and moral quality of his crime or series of crimes.

This distinction is obviously important to my argument about treating like cases alike. The issue is joined only if a clear role is given to desert in setting punishment. To underline this point, compare the following propositions:

A. Cases that are alike in all respects relevant to the moral desert of the offender should be treated alike.

---

7. American Friends Service Committee, *Struggle for Justice* (1971).

8. Twentieth Century Fund Task Force on Criminal Sentencing, *Fair and Certain Punishment* (1976).

9. *Supra* note 5.

10. *Supra* note 5.

11. E. van den Haag, *Punishing Criminals: Concerning a Very Old and Painful Question* (1975).

B. Cases that are alike in all respects relevant to the choice of sentence should be treated alike.

It is my purpose to argue that proposition A states a limiting and not a defining principle of justice and that equality too is but a guiding and not a defining principle. The second proposition entirely subverts the argument. It shifts the focus to all and everything that may be properly relevant to sentencing and, in practice it seems to me, leaves one with no two like cases, producing at its best only equality of procedure and not equality of outcome. Hence, to take on the harder and more important argument, I address myself to problems of equality as defined in proposition A not those avoided by the width of proposition B.

III. Exceptions to the Desert-Equality Principle as a Defining Principle

All contemporary sentencing reforms, in their effort to avoid excessive disparity in sentencing, favor systems of sentencing which are primarily retributive, which do not pretend to benevolent or curative effects on the criminal, and in which the sentence to be imposed is strongly influenced if not determined by what the criminal has done. Concepts of just desert are of overwhelming importance and for some they define the sentence and require the equally undeserving to be equally punished. Let me start my attack on that view by offering some examples where departures from that view are pervasively accepted. Their consideration will, I submit, lead to a modification of the "just desert—treat like cases alike" position (hereinafter "the desert-equality principle").

A. *Exemplary Punishments*

Exemplary punishments are, so far as I can tell, a uniformly accepted departure from the "desert-equality" principle. As Professor Nigel Walker put it, judges will sometimes "impose sentences which are markedly more severe than the norm for the express purpose of increasing their deterrent effect."[12] He gives as an

12. N. Walker, *Sentencing in a Rational Society* 69 (1969).

example the imposition of a sentence of four years' imprisonment on each of nine young white men who were involved in attacks on blacks in the Nottinghill district of London in 1958. This sentence was at least double the sentence normally imposed for their offenses, and the sentencing judge held it to be in excess of his normal sentence for such offenses; but it was within the legislatively prescribed maximum for those offenses. It was imposed expressly as an exemplary punishment, to capture public attention and, as a dramatic punishment to deter future such behavior. It needs no refined analysis to demonstrate that these nine offenders were selected for *unequal* treatment before the law. Please do not misunderstand me; I am not opposing such sentences, quite the contrary. Rather, I am arguing that if the increased penalty is within the legislatively prescribed range, then any supposed principle of equality does not prevent such a sentence from being in the appropriate case a just punishment. Many such examples occur in all countries and are generally accepted. Let me give you just one more example. Annually, in Chicago, there is what is called a "crackdown on drunken driving." Occurring in the latter weeks of November and the early weeks of December, it is designed expressly to reduce the carnage from drunken driving in Chicago over the Christmas period. Often, those selected for punishment during this crackdown have committed their offenses in the summer or autumnal months, when thoughts of the allegedly jolly penury of Christmas is far from their minds; but such are the delays in the courts that an opportunity to serve their country as recipients of exemplary punishment is vouchsafed them—in this instance, a jail term for what would at other times be punished by lesser sanctions. My excellent colleague Franklin Zimring has done a close study of this practice and has concluded, cautious fellow that he is and addicted as he is to methodological niceties, that it has not been disproved that the "crackdown" may have reduced the Yuletide devastation in Chicago resulting from the combination of the ingestion of alcohol and the activation of the internal combustion engine.

Exemplary punishments are surely discordant to the desert-equality principle, if that principle is seen as a defining principle of just punishment.

B. *Pardon and Amnesty*

At the other end of the punishment process another example is to be found of generally accepted practices irreconcilable with the desert-equality principle. The pardon and amnesty power is exercised in dramatically different ways in different jurisdictions, but it exists in all of them, at home and abroad. Pressures entirely extrinsic to the prisoner and his crime, plainly irrelevant to the deserved punishment, plainly unequal as between equally undeserving prisoners, the birth of a prince, the inauguration of a new government, the cessation of a foreign war, the political links of a prisoner's counsel soliciting exercise of the governor's or president's pardon power, and other political processes far removed from whatever makes criminal cases alike, except differences in the date the crime was committed or the sentence imposed, will lead to clemency to one prisoner which is denied to another.

A current similar widespread exercise of the pardon power, splitting like cases however defined, is early release to minimize overcrowding in several state prisons. Prisoner A came in with a cohort which in due course occupies unconstitutionally overcrowded prisons, or prisons which are on the border of unconstitutional overcrowding; he may be released thirty or more days earlier than Prisoner B, who came into prison for the identical crime with the identical record but with a different cohort of prisoners. The release may come by order of a court or by direction of a governor or prison administrator, but it has nothing to do with the deserved punishment.

These developments of block early releases to cure overcrowding and the exercise of the pardon and amnesty powers generally are impossible to reconcile with the desert-equality principle.

C. *Selective Enforcement*

If the view of punishment policy pervading this book is correct, the concept of desert justifies punishment but does not require its imposition. Punishment is a scarce resource to be used for social advancement, not for its own sake, since it involves suffering and cost which are both to be minimized if they can be.

This principle of parsimony in punishment conditions the distribution of punishments so that in all cases the least afflictive (punitive) sanction necessary to achieve defined social purposes should be imposed.[13]

We operate an overloaded criminal justice system in the United States so that the flow of cases at the police, prosecutorial, and judicial levels compels us to select which cases we shall pursue and which, in one way or another, by plea bargains or exclusionary discretion, we shall neglect. In this overload, the desert-equality principle must frequently yield to the exigencies of selective enforcement. But I am anxious not to argue this case on such pragmatic grounds; the case for selective enforcement and for the rejection of the desert-equality principle at the police, prosecutorial, and judicial levels can be made even assuming a criminal justice system not pressed by shortage of personnel and facilities but capable of meeting all proper punitive and treatment demands.

Let me select an area of current enforcement practice that is not overloaded and demonstrate that selective enforcement is currently contravening the desert-equality principle—and argue that it is right to do so. Let me present a law teacher's hypothetical which I shall later submit is realistic and provide some data to support that claim.

Let us suppose that six medical practitioners in Denver are discovered to have a preference for patients who pay them in cash and who do not require receipts. Let us suppose that on full investigation we discover that all six doctors have understated their income last year by, say, $20,000 each. For some time we have been doubtful of the precision of tax returns by medical practitioners in this city and, as advisers to the Internal Revenue Service, we discuss what should be done about the six doctors. Well, to start with, it is quite clear that all six must pay tax on the income they have failed to declare, interest at appropriately high rates on that tax, and substantial financial penalties for their criminality. All this can, of course, be arranged without the need for their prosecution before a federal district court. Most of the six and their

13. N. Morris, *The Future of Imprisonment* 60–62 (1974).

tax advisers will be happy indeed to arrange such settlements with
IRS agents or, if necessary in relation to disputed issues of fact,
through the tax court. Do we need to prosecute all six in the
federal district court and do we need to send all six to prison? We
have no lack of prosecutorial, judicial, and federal prison resources
to do so if we decide such a course is wise—the IRS and the U.S.
attorneys do not make up a particularly overloaded system. Nevertheless, I submit we will not and should not send all six doctors
to prison. Our purposes are utilitarian, deterrent. We wish, as
Voltaire said of the English practice of killing an occasional admiral
to encourage the others to bravery, publicly to punish by sending
to prison an occasional medical practitioner "to encourage the
others" to observe integrity in their tax returns. We do not need
to send all six to prison. The extra increment of deterrence would
be bought at too high a cost. It would be wasteful of our own
resources, wasteful of the court's time, and, what is perhaps also
relevant, it would inflict unnecessary suffering on those doctors
whose punishment did not substantially increase the deterrent
impact we would gain by the imprisonment of, say, two of their
number. The principle of parsimony overcomes the principle of
equality.

How should we select those to be imprisoned? Perhaps we
should struggle for some distinguishing characteristic of deserved
severity or some opportunity of extra deterrent utility in the
punishment of some among the six, but what is important to
recognize is that we are involved in a conscious breach of a principle
that like cases should be equally punished. It may be that we would
select those doctors whose lives had achieved the larger contribution to social welfare and who, as a consequence, were the better
known of the six; their punishment would thus achieve the larger
deterrent impact. *That* can hardly be a reason of equality for
selecting them for the larger punishment.

This principle of parsimony in the imposition of punishment
is, I think, of great importance, and is too often neglected. Let
me offer some figures to demonstrate the frugality with which the
Internal Revenue Service in practice applies its massive punitive
powers. In fiscal year 1981 throughout this vast country, only 1,436

defendants were indicted for federal income tax violations, of whom 1,241 were convicted and sentenced, and of whom only 457 were sent to prison or jail.[14] This is an astonishingly selective and cautious use of the sanction of imprisonment for deterrent purposes. Is it unjust? It cannot be treating like cases alike if any reasonable concepts of the quality of guilt and deserved suffering are to be applied. In my view, on the data that have been published about the implication of the prison term in federal district courts, the system is both unequal and just, and it is precisely that apparent paradox I am seeking to defend.

When I put this type of case to many people, academic and civilian (if the distinction will be accepted), they tend to reply that this discriminatory selective invocation of the prison sentence by prosecutorial agencies, by administrators, is to be approved, provided it is properly controlled by K. C. Davis–like criteria that can be announced and tested as to their validity, but that it would be grossly unjust for a judge to act in this fashion in exercising his sentencing discretion. This distinction puzzles me. You will note that it is not made about exemplary punishment, where there seems to be general acceptance of the judge as the selector of the individual for the exemplary punishment. Why should the judge not be equally capable of being the selector of the four of my six doctors not to receive the more severe punishment? It can hardly be that the sentence of two of the six to prison, if only two are taken by the prosecutor to trial and four are handled administratively, is a just sentence but that it would not be a just sentence if the selection were made by a judge. Equality in that case would serve only to protect the judicial role, to protect the oracle, the black robe—although that too is an important value which cannot be dismissed out of hand.

D. *Sentencing Guidelines*

"Your Denver doctors are a mildly interesting problem," you reply, "but after all, selective enforcement by prosecutors is now

14. Letter of 26 February 1982 from Statistical Analysis and Reports Division, Administrative Office of the United States Courts.

old hat, part of the accepted machinery of low visibility decisions by police and all other administrators of the criminal justice system, tolerable though not desirable, necessary to run a system but hardly a principle of justice or acceptable practice by a judge. Your six doctors need not fall equally before the IRS; procedural equality rather than substantive equality will do there; but once prosecution is launched and conviction reached, such uneven treatment is unacceptable; it offends that great and lasting desert-equality principle."

Well, let us test it further. Let us move to a problem facing a sentencing commission designing sentencing guidelines to assist the judge in imposing punishment of convicted criminals.

There are two broad paths to designing such guidelines, both reaching apparently very similar results. By one path the members of the commission consult their collective views of just punishment and social purposes to be achieved by punishment, construct a table or tables of recommended sentences controlling both the in-out decision (prison or not and a variety of sanctions not involving incarceration) and the decision regarding duration of detention, see how those tables match present practice and available resources, and modify them accordingly. By the other path the commission first searches out what is currently done, how sentences are imposed, both as to prison or not and as to the duration of imprisonment, and then uses this current practice as a guide to what ought to be, but then modifies it in framing the recommended sentencing guidelines to reduce disparity and to achieve other purposes sought by members of the sentencing commission.

Let us suppose that the commission we are studying followed the latter path. They found in their jurisdiction over the years studied that seriousness of the offense and criminal record dominated sentencing decisions (a common discovery) and they decided to structure the guideline grid accordingly, adding to it a nonexclusive list of aggravating and mitigating factors to vary the presumptive sentences. As in Minnesota, the judiciary must by statute impose a sentence within the guidelines (both as to prison or not and as to time to be served if imprisonment is ordered) or give reasons subject to appellate review for any departure from the guideline sentence.

Here is the problem and it is a common problem. Male purse snatchers who had not used or threatened violence beyond the snatch of the purse were sentenced in recent years as follows: overwhelmingly, on first conviction to probation; on second conviction sentences were scattered between probation and six months in jail. This is a highly simplified presentation of the hypothetical data but in no way unreal or misleading. For first offense purse snatchers there is no difficulty: probation. Let us confine our attention to such of those who snatched again. The actual distribution of the last 99 such cases was, setting aside a few outlying unusually severe and unusually lenient sentences, 33 to six months in jail and 66 to a variety of probation and other community-based supervision orders. Restitution was ordered where appropriate in all 99 cases and fines were also imposed where appropriate. How should the commission guide the jail or probation sentence for such second-time purse snatchers in future?

Assume that the ranking of severity for the new guideline grid at this point roughly matches both past practice and the values expressed in the sentencing system—something between probation and six months in jail seems right to all members of the commission and can be fitted into the hierarchy of other punishments. The first suggestion for a presumptive sentence for these offenders in the future would be two months in jail for all of them. Equality would thus be served and idiosyncratic cases requiring increased severity or leniency could be handled by the aggravating and mitigating circumstances provided for such cases.

Let us put aside these aggravating and mitigating circumstances and continue to consider the proper presumptive sentence for the rest, assuming the next 99 are identical to the past 99 in all criteria the commission regards as morally relevant to their crime. Is two months' jail time the right presumptive sentence?

It is pointed out in response to the two-month recommendation that this will achieve more suffering than the present unequal system of six months for 33 and probation for 66. From probation to six months in jail is not a continuum of punishment. The jail threshold is consequential. The difference in punishment between probation and two months in jail is certainly greater than between two months and four months—it is probably greater than between two months and six months.

But the equality-desert principle must govern, it is said. Why? Unless there is some other value to be served, an unsupported plea for automatic equality does not seem compelling. Those other values may be deterrent or incapacitative—they can hardly be anything else. In incapacitative terms, on present knowledge, the two months for all will achieve no reduction in the incidence of purse snatching with this group (except for two months, with a likely compensating bulge thereafter). In terms of deterrence, again on present knowledge and given our current or likely future detection and conviction rates, there is nothing to suggest that the two months for all holds more general deterrence than the previous distribution of punishments—probably less. There is no empirical evidence to choose in terms of social utility between two months for all and the earlier distribution (and the former certainly offends the principle of parsimony in the distribution of punishment; it is more punitive). Of course, if we allot the six-month sentences to the likely more dangerous (presuming we can pick them) and probation to the others, we may maximize the utilities of punishment—but that would deny the assumption on which this both hypothetical and desert-equality sentencing rests.

Hence, why not a box in our sentencing grid offering us a presumptive range anywhere from probation to six months in jail for such second-time purse snatchers? This will reduce existing disparity of sentences without negating equality, which may be the best the commission can achieve within present or likely future knowledge. Sentencing purposes are to our best knowledge not frustrated, unless desert-equality is treated as a categorical imperative; probation is not seen as unjustly lenient nor six months in jail as unjustly severe; and this result favors the value of parsimony in punishment.

If that is what is happening—and it is, not only in this hypothetical but in practice—the burden of proof lies heavy on those who wish for no reason other than equality itself to increase the punishment of the 66.

Let me, before abandoning this hypothetical, give it one more twist. You are now a judge applying the presumptive guidelines the sentencing commission drafted for two-time purse snatchers. As chance will have it, you must sentence one such on Monday, one on Tuesday, one on Wednesday; none falls within any of the listed aggravating or mitigating circumstances. Each may or may not find out about the sentences imposed on the other two. If you wish you may give your reasons for sentence, but unless you depart from the presumptive guidelines, the statute does not so compel you. I add this fact: All three seem of equal moral guilt to you, but one is married and does help to support his wife and child. Will you not sentence him to probation? I would. Will you say why? I would not.

To conclude this long hypothetical: The task proved to be to reduce disparity in sentencing, not to achieve equality—and by disparity in sentencing I mean the imposition of sentences randomly or deliberately outside a range agreed, expressly or implicitly, to be justly deserved and socially necessary punishments. The range from six months in jail to probation meets both criteria with the knowledge we have of the consequences of such a distribution of justified punishments.

IV. Desert as a Limiting Principle

It is argued in opposition to the thesis here presented that to treat desert as a limiting rather than a defining principle of punishment unjustly reduces the central importance of that concept. Let me therefore restate and develop the argument and urge the continuing importance of concepts of desert and of equality to just sentencing.

It needs no argument; affirmation will suffice: if desert is a limiting principle of punishment, and not a defining principle, desert will allow for the differential treatment of morally like cases. Desert as a limiting principle is irreconcilable with the desert-equality principle.

Our entire present criminal justice system is infested with discretion in the exercise of the punishment power, and much of this discretion must continue to be exercised, guided but not determined by principles of equality in punishment. At present, the shortage of police, prosecutorial, defense, judicial, and punishment resources compels the discretionary selection of cases to be prosecuted; but the constraint that the principle of parsimony in punishment properly imposes on the principle of equality in just punishment would remain were such resources unlimited. Equality would still remain only a guiding principle; even with adequate resources in the criminal justice system, equality would neither define nor limit just punishment. By contrast, the principle of a deserved punishment is and should remain a limiting principle of just punishment.

Let me propose that the death penalty be the mandatory sentence for anyone convicted of abortion. I am not talking only about abortion in which the mother dies but the run-of-the-mill, legally unjustified abortion in which the life of the well-grown third-trimester fetus is terminated. Well, why do you not leap to accept such a proposition? Why does no one, so far as I know, advocate *that* punishment? Not even the most perfervid advocates of the right-to-life position seem to take themselves that seriously in equating abortion with murder. On deterrent utilitarian grounds there would be a great deal to be said for such a penalty if you were a true believer in the right to life. It would certainly push the price of the backyard abortion up to a very high figure; it would greatly reduce the number of fetuses whose existence was terminated; it would greatly increase the number of tickets that were purchased on international airlines and I would, for my own part, immediately reinvest in TWA. Well, why not? The answer must surely be that no one would see such a punishment as an appropriately *deserved* punishment, even those who are both in favor of protecting the fetus and in favor of capital punishment for convicted murderers. The limiting principle is the principle of desert. As elsewhere, it is hard to quantify this principle, but it clearly operates in this case to hold that such a punishment would be undeserved.

Desert thus operates categorically to limit the maximum of punishment. Sometimes it operates to limit the minimum, as when it is argued that a too lenient punishment would unduly depreciate the seriousness of the offense that the accused has committed. An example of this was the sentencing of Spiro Agnew which, in my view, was entirely correct, for utilitarian and governmental practical reasons, but which certainly strained at the lower level of the deserved punishment.

By contrast, I am suggesting that the principle of equality—that like cases should be treated alike—is not a limiting principle at all, but is only a guiding principle which will enjoin equality of punishment unless there are other substantial utilitarian reasons to the contrary, such as those that favor exemplary punishment or the parsimonious punishment of some of my six doctors, or in situations where there are inadequate resources for or high costs attached to the application of equal punishment. The equality principle neither restricts nor limits; it merely guides. The principle of desert is not much of a guide, but it does restrict and limit.

When we say a punishment is deserved, we rarely mean that it is precisely appropriate in the sense that a deterrent punishment could in principle be. Rather we mean that it is not undeserved; that it is neither too lenient nor too severe; that it neither sentimentally understates the wickedness or harmfulness of the crime nor inflicts excessive pain or deprivation on the criminal in relation to the wickedness or harmfulness of his crime. It is not part of a utilitarian calculus, in the properly restricted Rawlsian sense of utilitarianism. The concept of desert defines relationships between crimes and punishments on a continuum between the unduly lenient and the excessively punitive within which the just sentence may be determined on other grounds.

It is not my concern in this chapter to try to explain how complexities of social relationships and the dialectic of human thoughts and actions determine over time the values that set these minimums and maximums of deserved punishments for diverse crimes. What is determinative is that these values exist and underlie concepts of "just desert" which set the limits of acceptable intervals on a spectrum of just punishment.

To summarize: Desert is not a defining principle; it is a limiting principle. The concept of "just desert" sets the maximum and minimum of the sentence that may be imposed for any offense and helps to define the punishment relationships between offenses; it does not give any more fine-tuning to the appropriate sentence than that. The fine-tuning is to be done on utilitarian principles.[15]

These arguments have a long heritage in the literature of philosophy.

In the *Protagoras*, Plato suggests:

> He who undertakes to punish with reason does not avenge himself for past offense, since he cannot make what was done as though it had not come to pass; he looks rather to the future and aims at preventing that particular person and others who see him punished from doing wrong again. . . . He punishes to deter.[16]

Seneca puts it more curtly, "Nemo prudens punit quia peccatum est, sed ne peccetur" (No reasonable man punishes because there has been a wrongdoing, but in order that there should be no wrongdoing). That is the purely utilitarian statement, the extreme contrast to which is that of Kant:

> The Law concerning punishment is a categorical imperative, and woe to him who rummages around in the winding paths of a theory of happiness looking for some advantage to be gained by releasing the criminal from punishment or by reducing the amount of it—in keeping with the Pharisaic motto: "It is better that one man should die than that the whole people should per-

15. The argument presented in this chapter has asked the reader to accept that there are "defining" principles of punishment as well as those that are "limiting" and "guiding"; special and general deterrence were cited as possible candidates. This may be error. There may be no "defining" principles of punishment; all relevant principles of punishment may be either "limiting" or "guiding" as I have defined those terms. If this is so, the argument in this chapter that desert is a limiting principle is strengthened and the desirability for room for inequality in the application of these principles is reinforced.

16. Trans. W. R. M. Lamb, 139 (1952).

ish." If legal justice perishes, then it is no longer worthwhile for men to remain alive on this earth.[17]

Thus the issue has been drawn in philosophic discourse between relativist, utilitarian guides to punishment and categoric, nonutilitarian absolutist principles. The argument survives the centuries but has been rendered of immediate importance by the modern pervasive suspicion of uncontrolled discretion in punishment masquerading or self-deceiving as benevolence. All commentators now see categorical concepts of desert as at least limiting discretionary punishments; many, of course, go further.

The genius of H. L. A. Hart has moved the philosophic discourse into contemporary reality. His distinction between those values which justify punishment and those which should guide the distribution of punishments is of first importance, and his view on treating like cases alike merits repetition. He describes the "somewhat hazy requirement"[18] of justice that like cases be treated alike and suggests that "there is, for modern minds, something obscure and difficult in the idea that we should think in choosing punishment of some intrinsic relationship which it must bear to the wickedness of the criminal's act, rather than the effect of the punishment on society and on him."[19]

Much of the literature of philosophy on this topic deals with what factors make like cases alike, and once one decides what factors bear upon desert and deterrence, one tends to assume that the equally guilty should be equally punished. As you see, it is a severance I am seeking to make and to suggest that though desert determines the justification of punishment it is only limiting in the distribution of punishments so that equality is only one value in fixing punishment.

How does all this square with the views of John Rawls? It is true, of course, that Rawls was writing in A Theory of Justice[20]

17. I. Kant, The Metaphysical Elements of Justice, pt. 1 of The Metaphysics of Morals, trans. John Ladd, 100 (1965).
18. Supra note 1 at 24.
19. Id. at 163.
20. J. Rawls, A Theory of Justice (1971).

of strict compliance theories of justice and not of the problems of punishment with which we are concerned, but it seems to me that his principles are applicable and in conformity with the argument that I am trying to offer. He writes that "all social values ... are to be distributed equally unless an unequal distribution of any, or all, of these values is to everyone's advantage. Injustice, then, is simply inequalities that are not to the benefit of all."[21] It seems to me that the type of parsimony and inequality in the use of punishment which I suggest works to the benefit of all and does not offend sound principles of justice as Rawls defines them.

Let me put aside the philosophic implications of the argument and turn to some more lighthearted psychological reflections.

"It isn't fair," the prisoner tells me. "Here I am, serving two years for that bank robbery when others who have done just as bad, have ripped off even more, have not been caught or have not been convicted or are serving lesser terms." My usual reply is to wish that they were in there with him, but to ask him if he thinks that for what he actually did, as distinct from that for which he was convicted, he deserved the punishment he has received. The general answer, I find, is an enthusiastic reassurance that he certainly has done enough to deserve this punishment and that his only complaint is that others haven't been treated likewise. Is this a good complaint? In terms of utilitarian analysis it may be. We might well have a much safer society if we were capable of catching, convicting, and rationally sentencing more of our predatory and violent criminals. But in terms of justice, I am not at all sure. I am prepared to allow that he has been treated unfairly, if fairness presupposes equality of punishment, but I always argue to prisoners, and usually without too great animosity on their part, that principles of justice do not require an equality of punishment. You would be surprised how much more sensible prisoners are about matters of punishment than are my colleagues at the University of Chicago Law School.

I used to hear the same argument interminably in my family. "Here you go," said my second son, "imposing these cruel depriva-

21. *Id.* at 62.

tions on me. This brutal temporary denial of use of the car, whereas my elder brother, as usual, gets away with much worse without even detection, and that younger brother, who is discovered in his wickedness, is treated with maudlin, senile sentimentality, and not punished at all." I used to find these confrontations with my second son more difficult than those with the prisoners—I miss them now.

V. The von Hirsch Reply and the Problem of Range

In a vigorous attack on the Report of the American Bar Association's Task Force on Sentencing Alternatives and Procedures (1979), Andrew von Hirsch[22] cites me as the authority on which the task force relied, in his words, for its "floor-ceiling" view of desert which allowed it to reconcile its prediction-oriented scheme of punishment with the constraints of justly deserved punishment.[23] The gravamen of his criticism is that my view and that adopted by the ABA Report "permits the infliction of unequal punishment upon those whose criminal conduct is equally blameworthy."[24] To this one cannot take exception; he is right. He then chides us both for our failure to confront a great philosophic tradition:

> To reduce, as Morris and the ABA's Task Force propose, equal and proportionate treatment to a mere "guiding" principle—to be ignored whenever utilitarian considerations dictate—is to depart strikingly from that tradition. One would expect some attempt at a philosophical justification for this surprising view of equality, but neither Morris nor the Task Force offers one.[25]

Again, *mea culpa*, unless this chapter begins the task of filling the gap.

So far, I confess, I am not moved by these criticisms; they seem to me rather to restate the conflict than to resolve it against my view, but von Hirsch does develop one line of criticism, drawing

22. "Utilitarian Sentencing Resuscitated: The American Bar Association's Second Report on Criminal Sentencing," 33 *Rutgers L. Rev.* 772–89 (1981).
23. *Id.* at 782–83.
24. *Id.* at 784.
25. *Id.* at 785–86.

a distinction between my analysis and the recommendations of the ABA task force which does cause difficulty that I cannot precisely resolve. It is the problem of the proper width of the range of a deserved punishment, if desert be seen as a limiting principle. Professor von Hirsch phrases the problems well, as follows:

> Professor Morris . . . faces the problem squarely. To justify unequal punishment of the equally deserving, he asserts that equality is not one of the essential requirements of justice. It is, he says, only a "guiding" principle: one that will "enjoin equality of punishment unless there are substantial utilitarian reasons to the contrary." . . . What Professor Morris leaves ambiguous is the width of the bounds provided by the requirements of desert as he sees them. Is he speaking of a scheme where desert remains a truly important criterion; where his upper and lower desert limits substantially constrain the sentencer's chance; where the utilitarian "fine tuning" of which he speaks is indeed, merely fine tuning? Or is he speaking of a system where the desert limits have been relegated to the margins, and utilitarian grounds constitute the main basis for selecting penalties? . . . The ABA Report opts for the second interpretation.[26]

There is difficulty here. Professor von Hirsch is right that the ABA Report gives a quite modest role to retribution in defining punishment; it is not our intent "to reject retribution as a sometimes relevant consideration in the allocation of punishment; rather, the recommendation is that the role it is allowed to play be kept modest."[27] He interprets this to mean that the ABA Report argues that "desert should operate as little more than a prohibition against inflicting lengthy imprisonments on car thieves or burglars, or giving probation to those convicted of the worst violent offenses."[28]

There is clearly a difference of emphasis here which is not unimportant. My case for inequality is for mercy and clemency within an ordered system of justly deserved punishments; it aims at avoiding the severity amounting to tyranny that rigidly insists

26. *Id.* at 784–85.
27. *Id.* at 785, citing ABA Task Force on Sentencing Alternatives and Procedures, *Sentencing Alternatives and Procedures* (1979).
28. *Id.* at 785.

on equality and seeks to exorcise discretion and mercy from sentencing. It accepts the long tradition of justice as equality but seeks to moderate it by acceptance of the uncertainties attending our utilitarian purposes in the distribution of punishment and to allow for a slippage of inequality to achieve parsimony in punishment. The ABA Report seems to go further than this and, insofar as it does, von Hirsch's strictures seem to me well founded. But even he is tempted to avoid the rigidities of his own system. Let me quote him further:

> Suppose that, as a member of a sentencing commission, one is writing guidelines for the "in-out" decision of whether or not to imprison. Suppose the commission has already ranked crimes in seriousness, using ratings from "1" for the least serious to "10" for the most serious offense. At what level of seriousness should the in-out line, that is, the cutting line on the penalty scale between the cases that normally warrant imprisonment and the cases that normally do not, be drawn? Here, one should have relatively little difficulty in deciding that the least serious conduct (say, conduct with a seriousness rating from "1" through "4") does not deserve a severe sanction and hence should not be punished by imprisonment. And one should, similarly, be able to decide that the most reprehensible conduct (represented, say, by seriousness levels "8" through "10") certainly deserves imprisonment. The difficulty will be in deciding exactly where between these extremes the imprisonment line should be drawn. Should that line be drawn between seriousness levels "5" and "6"? Or between levels "6" and "7"? Here, the notion of a reasonable proportion between the conduct and its punishment may not be precise enough to furnish an answer: either decision about the location of the cutting line could be consistent with notions of desert. Where this is so, the rule-maker might properly invoke various non-desert considerations to assist in deciding the issue.[29]

Professor von Hirsch would thus allow utilitarian considerations within desert constraints to guide a sentencing commission

29. *Id.* at 788, and see also A. von Hirsch, *supra* note 5, at 93–94.

but would deny them to a judge. I don't see why, except to protect the elegance of his thesis or the robe of the judge.

I am well aware that I have not defined the proper range fixed for all crimes and all criminals by the upper and lower limits of undeserved severity and excessive leniency which exaggerate or depreciate the gravity of the crime. My view is merely that such ranges exist, that they should be defined as punishment categories in some form such as that set forth by the Minnesota Sentencing Commission, and that they must give some play to irrational mercy. And to that difficult issue I now turn.

VI. The Prodigal Son and the Laborers in the Vineyard

I mean no heresy nor even flippancy: the central figure in the Christian tradition saw no difficulty in treating like cases differently and unlike cases the same. I certainly stray beyond my competence, but the issues remain unsettled after thousands of years of discussion and therefore one must not let caution impede.

I shall not restate the parable; Luke 15:11–32 does it admirably. The point emerges inexorably: Christ rejected the complaint of the elder son that unlike cases had been treated alike, that the undeserving had been treated at least as well as the deserving. It is true the parable speaks to distributive justice but its relevance to retributive or rectificatory justice is obvious. Indeed, a recent papal encyclical makes this clear:

> The prodigal son, having wasted the property he received from his father, deserves—after his return—to earn his living by working in his father's house as a hired servant and possibly, little by little, to build up a certain provision of material goods, though perhaps never as much as the amount he had squandered. This would be demanded by the order of justice.[30]

It is a cautious commentary, as cautious as mine about the proper range of deserved punishments, but the adjuration to leave some room for inequality in ordered justice is unequivocal.

30. "Rich in Mercy" (*Dives in Misericordia*), by Pope John Paul II, 2 December 1980.

The same is true of the parable of the Laborer in the Vineyard (Matt. 20:1–16). Again Christ tells the laborer who has worked longer than others that he should not complain that the others are paid equally: he does not complain of his own treatment independently of what others have received; he has no valid complaint if they are advantaged relative to him. In the terms of this chapter: provided he receives what he deserves, that others are differently treated within their just deserts gives him no valid cause of complaint.

It may be objected that these parables of heaven—as they both were—speak to repentance, forgiveness, and divine mercy, so that it is contrived and possibly unseemly to relate them to the squalid secular issues of sentencing convicted criminals. Perhaps, but surely the analogies are helpful. Judges, even in their own eyes, lack the embracing and perceptive charity of the Judeo-Christian ethic; they can hardly dispense both forgiveness and mercy. My point is, however, narrower: sentencing must leave room if not for forgiveness then for mercy. A rigid equality of deserved punishments will reduce discretion; it will also fill our prisons more than they need to be filled for any valid social purpose. No one wants even-handed justice for himself; what he wants is justice tempered by mercy. A "just deserts" system of punishment could be lenient or severe; but it could not provide room for mercy which, I conclude, presupposes some room for treating like cases differently and unlike cases the same.

VII. An Excursus on Selective Enforcement and Isonomy

The view I have advanced here of desert and equality as respectively limiting and guiding principles of punishment offers a useful perspective, I believe, on the operation of the criminal justice system as a whole. Let us assume a continuum of decreasing discretion in the functioning of the criminal justice system ranging from "selective enforcement" at one extreme to punishing the equally morally undeserving equally, "isonomy," at the other. Let us take a few samples along this continuum at different stages of the criminal justice system to test if any pattern emerges.

It is common knowledge among scholars and administrators of the police that, faced with a great deal of crime, the police allocate manpower and exercise both strategic and tactical discretion to enforce the criminal law selectively. We don't want all traffic offenses detected; we want a selective, discretionary enforcement to keep a lid of deterrent control on dangerous driving; we certainly would not aspire to any equality here. Even so, lingering strands of isonomy remain. You are exceeding the speed limit; you are stopped: "But officer, I was just passed by a huge truck." This is an understandable but ineffective plea, unless you think the policeman did not apply equal *procedures* in selecting you; then the complaint against the policeman takes on an independent validity. But if the policeman arrived on the scene after you were passed by the truck, and even if he believes without a hint of doubt your story about the truck, you will still get the ticket and pay the fine!

Selective enforcement is characteristic of all police work even among those police forces in western Europe which deny that this is so. Nevertheless, it is possible to move much of this discretion along to the prosecutor and, for example, West German practice does so in all but minor offenses.

Selective enforcement also varies in police practice in accordance with the gravity of the crime. The police exercise relatively little discretion in relation to homicide, a lot more in relation to burglary.

As one moves from the police level to that of the prosecutor, the exercise of the prosecutorial discretion takes on a perhaps larger visibility and thus possibly initiates larger isonomic constraints. This may not be particularly easy to perceive in the United States, so powerful and uncontrolled a figure is the prosecutor, with much substantial influence over the grand jury, but there is probably a diminution in selective enforcement and the beginnings of a movement toward isonomy as one moves from policeman to prosecutor.

The prosecutor and, to different degrees, the judge (at least as approver of bargains already struck) are both involved in the charge and plea-bargaining process. The constraints of isonomy are weak in both federal and state practice, but they are larger than those applying to the prosecutor's discretion in relation to the *nolle prosequi*, which are clearly less fettered than when he decides to proceed with a charge.

As one moves to judicial sentencing from discretions controlled by the police or by prosecutors, the constraints of isonomy grow increasingly strong and desert-equality becomes a powerful guiding principle. One sees this when one considers the Denver doctors' hypothetical as a judicial sentencing decision as distinct from a prosecutorial decision. Nevertheless, as I believe I have shown, isonomy remains only a guiding principle of morally just judicial sentencing.

Now the pattern reverses: From policeman through prosecutor to judge, selective enforcement declines and isonomy increases; from judge to prison administrator to parole board and to whoever controls the pardon power isonomy declines and selective enforcement increases. Let me try to sketch this inverted parabola.

The selective enforcement–isonomy continuum is greatly influenced by who makes the punishment decision and how visible that decision is. Consideration of the principles that should properly guide this balance falls outside the scope of this chapter (mercifully, since in large part the nature of these principles escapes me).

It merits notice, finally, that occasionally we are willing to accept gross departures from the isonomy principle. A powerful example is that of the anisonomic benefits we allow to a co-conspirator who turns state's evidence, who is not infrequently at least as morally culpable as his partners in crime, and who may gain not only immunity from prosecution but sometimes also immunity from taxation of funds acquired in the criminal enterprise as well as resettlement with a new, validated identity in a new and congenial community. Here, indeed, utilitarian considerations triumph over the desert-equality principle, and the triumph is accepted, though sometimes uneasily, by every functionary of the criminal justice system including the judge. In many cases it is impossible to argue that the co-conspirator by collaboration with the prosecutor manifests repentance and lesser moral guilt since not infrequently all members of a discovered conspiracy are willing to follow that path; but they are not on the road to Damascus, and only one will be chosen—on utilitarian grounds by the prosecutor!

The conclusion: Treating like cases alike is by no means a categorical imperative of justice; it is merely one of several interacting, guiding principles of justice to be accorded respect up to the point that it decreases community protection or increases individual suffering without sufficiently compensating social advantage.

Appendix

Here is a summary of the main case law and legal literature bearing on the issues raised in chapter 3, "The Planter's Dream."

I. Case Law

ATTORNEY GENERAL V. GALLAGHER, 1963 A.C. 349 (1961). Gallagher killed his wife during a drunken rage. There was inconclusive medical evidence that he was an aggressive psychopath. At trial, he sought to prove that he was insane at the time of the crime within the meaning of the McNaughtan rule, or that he was incapable of forming the intent necessary for murder due to his drunkenness. The House of Lords ruled that he was properly convicted of murder following the trial judge's instruction that the jury should apply the McNaughtan test to him at the moment before he began drinking rather than at the time of the crime.

BRATTY V. ATTORNEY GENERAL, 1963 A.C. 386, 408–15 (1961). Bratty, who had strangled a girl, raised as defenses automatism and insanity, presenting evidence that an attack of psychomotor epilepsy had caused him to act unconsciously. The House of Lords affirmed Bratty's murder conviction, holding that the jury's rejection of his claimed epileptic fit as the cause of his "unconscious act" precluded any finding of insanity or automatism.

The decision recognized two types of automatism: insane and non-insane. Accordingly, a court must determine the cause of a defendant's alleged unconscious act and decide whether his condition is a "disease of the mind" under the McNaughtan test of insanity in order to determine whether a defense of automatism separate from insanity may be raised.

Lord Denning defined automatism as involving an involuntary act, including "an act done by a person who is not conscious of what he is doing, such as an act done whilst suffering from concussion or whilst sleepwalking." He stated that epilepsy is a disease of the mind, and that where the cause assigned for the defense of automatism is a disease of the mind, only the defense of insanity is available.

CARTER V. STATE, 376 P.2d 351 (Okla. Crim. App. 1962). Carter was involved in a fatal car accident, allegedly after drinking. He claimed that he was not fully conscious during the period he was allegedly seen drinking, and that he became unconscious due to a previous injury that caused him to experience occasional dizziness and blackouts. Reversing Carter's conviction for first degree manslaughter, the court held that he should have been allowed to introduce evidence to prove his claim, and that the jury should have been instructed that if he was unconscious he would not be guilty of first degree manslaughter, and that if he knew he was subject to blackouts and nevertheless drove, he might be guilty of second degree manslaughter because driving under such circumstances might constitute criminal negligence. The court also distinguished the defense of unconsciousness from one of insanity.

FAIN V. COMMONWEALTH, 78 Ky. 183 (1879). Fain shot a hotel porter who was trying to wake him up after he fell asleep in a public room in the hotel. Reversing his conviction for manslaughter, the court held that he was entitled to introduce evidence proving that he was a somnambulist and had shot the porter in a state of full or partial somnambulism and under the false impression that he was being attacked. The court held that this would be a good defense, even if the defendant knew he was predisposed to somnambulism and therefore should not have gone to sleep in the public room with a deadly weapon on his person. Even in that case, the court stated, because the shooting would not have been voluntary, Fain would not be punishable under any law.

GOVERNMENT OF THE VIRGIN ISLANDS V. SMITH, 278 F.2d 169 (3d Cir. 1960). Smith was involved in a fatal car accident and was convicted of involuntary manslaughter. His defense was that he had suffered an epileptic attack while driving and had become unconscious or quasi-conscious.

Reversing Smith's conviction, the court held that the trial judge erred in requiring him to prove unconsciousness: he had only to present evidence sufficient to raise a reasonable doubt on the question. The court also stated, however, that proof that Smith was unconscious would not necessarily exonerate him, if he was aware that he might suffer such an attack. Under those circumstances, driving a car might be sufficiently negligent to support the charge of involuntary manslaughter.

HILL V. BAXTER, [1958] 1 Q.B. 277 (1957). The Court rejected Baxter's contention that he was in a state of automatism when he collided with a car at an intersection; he had asserted that he was in this condition, but he presented no reliable medical evidence in support of his claim.

PEOPLE V. DECINA, 2 N.Y.2d 133, 138 N.E.2d 799, 157 N.Y.S.2d 558 (1956). Decina, who had a history of epileptic seizures, experienced such a seizure while driving and ran down several children. He was convicted of criminal negligence in the operation of a vehicle, and the Court of Appeals affirmed, citing Decina's knowledge of his condition. One judge, dissenting in part, stated that recklessness in deciding to drive was not sufficient to constitute criminal negligence in operating the vehicle, and that Decina had to be conscious while operating the vehicle in order to commit either element of the offense, i.e., driving voluntarily in a reckless frame of mind.

PEOPLE V. FREEMAN, 61 Cal. App. 2d 110, 142 P.2d 435 (1943). Freeman claimed that his apparently negligent driving, which resulted in a fatal accident, occurred while he was unconscious because of an attack of epilepsy. Reversing his conviction for negligent homicide, the court held that the jury instructions were prejudicial because they did not state clearly that the jury should acquit if it found Freeman was unconscious when the collision occurred, and that such a state had wholly or materially overtaken him before beginning his drive.

PEOPLE V. GRANT, 46 Ill. App.3d 125, 360 N.E.2d 809 (1977), rev'd, 71 Ill. 2d 551, 377 N.E.2d 4 (1978). Grant, who had been drinking, leaped onto a police officer escorting someone else out of a bar and struck him twice. Grant had a history of psychomotor epilepsy. Reversing his conviction for aggravated battery, the appellate court held that even though he had not specifically requested an automatism instruction, the trial court should have given one. It also held that the jury's finding of no insanity was not the equivalent of a finding of no automatism: the insanity defense has three elements, presence of a mental disease, lack of cognition, and lack of volition, and the automatism defense has only one, lack of volition. The appellate court also stated that even if he was unconscious, if Grant knew he was susceptible to violent behavior after drinking or some other conscious casual behavior, he would be criminally responsible for his actions. The Illinois Supreme Court reversed the appellate court and reinstated Grant's conviction, holding that the trial court's failure to instruct the jury on the defense of automatism did not deprive him of a fair consideration of the issues of capacity and control. The supreme court stated that the trial court's insanity instruction and summations drew the jury's attention to the evidence regarding Grant's capacity. By finding him sane, the jury had rejected the evidence that would have supported an automatism instruction.

PEOPLE V. NEWTON, 8 Cal. App.3d 359, 87 Cal. Rptr. 394 (1970). Newton claimed that his shooting of a police officer took place while he was in a state of shock from a gun wound in the abdomen and that he was unconscious at the time. Reversing his conviction for voluntary manslaughter, the court held that the trial court should have given the instruction on its own motion that unconsciousness was a complete defense.

REGINA V. CHARLSON, 39 Crim. App. 37 (Wales 1955). This is the case discussed on pages 103–4. Charlson struck his son with a mallet and was charged with inflicting bodily harm on the boy. The jury acquitted him after an instruction that it should acquit if it was in doubt whether he knew what he was doing or was acting as an automaton.

REGINA V. MINOR, 15 W.W.R. (n.s.) 433 (Sask. 1955). Minor had been hit on the head and suffered a concussion before driving and being involved in a fatal accident. Reversing his conviction for manslaughter, the court held that if he could prove that because he blacked out he was unable to form an intent and therefore did not know what he was doing, he would make out a defense separate from insanity, contrary to the trial judge's instruction to the jury.

REGINA V. QUICK, [1973] 1 Q.B. 910 (C.A.). Quick, a nurse at a mental hospital, had physically attacked a patient without provocation. He presented evidence that he had hypoglycemia, which, as a result of his drinking and taking insulin, might have caused the uncharacteristic conduct. The trial judge rejected a defense of automatism and required Quick to plead guilty to assault. The court of appeal quashed the conviction, holding that the defense of automatism, as distinct from insanity, should have been allowed to go to the jury.

214

STATE V. GOOZE, 14 N.J. Super. 277, 81 A.2d 811 (1951). Gooze, who had a history of Ménière's syndrome, a disease that causes dizziness and blackouts, and who had been warned by his doctor not to drive alone, was involved in a fatal car accident while suffering a blackout. He was convicted of "driving a vehicle carelessly and heedlessly in willful or wanton disregard of the rights or safety of others," and the court affirmed. The court held that, in light of Gooze's knowledge of his condition, his decision to drive was sufficient to satisfy the elements of the crime, and the fact that he was unconscious while driving did not constitute a defense.

II. Statutes

CAL. PENAL CODE §26 (West 1970) ("All persons are capable of committing crimes except those belonging to the following classes: . . . Persons who committed the act charged without being conscious thereof.").

ILL. REV. STAT. ch. 38, §4-1 (1979) ("A material element of every offense is a voluntary act, which includes an omission to perform a duty which the law imposes on the offender and which he is physically capable of performing.").

MODEL PENAL CODE §2.01(2) (Proposed Official Draft, 1962) (A voluntary act does not include "(a) a reflex of convulsion; (b) a bodily movement during unconsciousness or sleep; (c) conduct during hypnosis or resulting from hypnotic suggestion; (d) a bodily movement that otherwise is not a product of the effort or determination of the actor, either conscious or habitual.").

III. Commentaries

W. LaFave & A. Scott, *Handbook on Criminal Law*, §§25, 44 (1972). Section 25 discusses the general requirement of an act, and section 44 addresses the specific issue of automatism.

G. Williams, *Criminal Law: The General Part*, §§156–57 (2d ed. 1961). Section 156 analyzes the first question under the McNaughtan rule, whether an accused knew the nature and quality of his act. Williams specifically investigates those situations that involve insane automatism and mistake or ignorance of fact. Section 157 discusses the defense of non-insane automatism and the problems raised by that defense.

Beck, "Voluntary Conduct: Automatism, Insanity and Drunkenness," 9 *Crim. L. Q.* 315 (1967). Beck discusses problems of the test arising from the Bratty case, which requires the court to identify whether a condition is a "disease of the mind" in order to determine whether a defense of automatism separate from insanity may be raised. He also criticizes a holding that the defense of automatism is not available where the automatism was induced by alcohol, and urges instead that a crime of being drunk and dangerous be legislated.

Cross, "Reflections on Bratty's Case," 78 *Law Q. Rev.* 236 (1962). Cross suggests that rather than dealing with the social problems posed by a complete acquittal in cases of automatism by enlarging the insanity defense, as in *Bratty*, courts should be given more flexible powers than simply choosing between acquittal and insanity. He also criticizes the existence of different burdens of proof for the insanity and automatism defenses. Finally, he urges the creation of a separate offense of causing bodily harm while drunk to handle the problem of drunken automatism.

Edwards, "Automatism and Social Defence," 8 *Crim. L.Q.* 258 (1966). After surveying cases of automatism in Canada, England, Scotland, New Zealand, and Australia, Edwards suggests that the defense should be handled by (1) allowing the prosecution to use the evidence the defense advances to prove automatism in order to argue that the defendant should instead be judged "guilty but insane"; (2) continuing to allow automatism as a complete defense in situations where no moral fault and no mental disease are in evidence; and (3) where the defendant's own negligence led to his being in the condition of automatism, allowing him to be detained or put on probation notwithstanding a verdict of not guilty.

Edwards, "Automatism and Criminal Responsibility," 21 *Mod. L. Rev.* 375 (1958). Edwards reviews the court's treatment of automatism as the defense to a dangerous driving prosecution in *Hill v. Baxter* and argues that the case shows the need for revising the English criminal law of insanity under the McNaughtan rule.

Elliot, "Automatism and Trial by Jury," 6 *Melbourne U.L. Rev.* 53 (1967). Elliot endorses the requirement that a defendant claiming automatism lay the proper foundation for his claim before the case may go to the jury. He also discusses the ramifications for jury charges of the rule in the Bratty case and a number of other procedural issues related to raising the defense of automatism.

Fox, "Physical Disorder, Consciousness, and Criminal Liability," 63 *Colum. L. Rev.* 645 (1963). Fox examines the difficulties of formulating a rational distinction between automatism and insanity, and criticizes the inflexibility of the available categories (criminality, insanity, acquittal). He urges instead a more functional approach, which would take into account three factors: fault, protection of society, and what treatment would most likely be effective in handling a given defendant.

Jennings, "The Growth and Development of Automatism as a Defence in Criminal Law," 2 *Osgoode Hall L.J.* 370 (1962). Jennings examines the extension of the defense of automatism and endorses it as an alternative to the defense of insanity where an accused is not in fact insane.

Leigh, "Automatism and Insanity," 5 *Crim. L.Q.* 160 (1962). Leigh evaluates the Bratty case and discusses the relationship between the insanity and automatism defenses. He concludes that the scope of the automatism defense is limited.

Murphy, "Involuntary Acts and Criminal Liability," 81 *Ethics* 332 (1971). Murphy examines whether there is any philosophical support for the distinction between voluntary acts (caused by the actor's volition) and involuntary ones (caused by something else), or whether the distinction is based on a false mind/body dualism identifying the actor with the mind. He concludes that the distinction remains defensible, because there are some acts one can in fact control and others one cannot (e.g., seizures, strokes, and the like).

Prevezer, "Automatism and Involuntary Conduct," 1958 *Crim. L. Rev.* 361. Focusing on *Hill v. Baxter,* Prevezer discusses automatism and involuntary conduct in English criminal law. He analyzes three types of conscious involuntary action and the law surrounding each: acts involving physical compulsion, acts of one whose will is governed by another, and acts of one whose will is governed by other pressures.

Note, "The Involuntary Actus Reus," 25 *Mod. L. Rev.* 741 (1962). This casenote discusses the New Zealand case of *Kilbride v. Lake*, in which the notion of "voluntary act" played a key role in a non-automatism situation. Kilbride's certificate of inspection was removed from his car by someone during his absence, and he was convicted of operating the car without it. The court held that although the provision in question was a strict liability offense, and thus had no *mens rea* requirement, the defendant still had to be the person responsible for the act or omission involved in the *actus reus*. The author endorses the decision as a way out of a number of potential injustices created by strict liability crimes.

Note, "Automatism and Proper Precautions," 37 *Mod. L. Rev.* 199 (1974). This casenote endorses the *Quick* case's rejection of the equation of the insanity and automatism defenses, but criticizes its holding that if the automatism was induced by the defendant's negligence, it should not be a defense.

Index

Amnesty, as exception to desert-equality principle, 189. *See also* Pardon power

Aristotle: *Nichomachean Ethics*, 180; precept of justice, 181

Attorney General v. Gallagher, 211

Attorney General's Task Force on Violent Crime, 35, 83

Automatism, 211–12, 213, 214, 215–17; burden of proof, 215; insane type, 215; non-insane type, 211, 215; procedural issues, 216; versus special defense of insanity, 211–12, 213, 214, 215, 216, 217. *See also* Fugue states; Involuntary conduct; Somnambulism; Unconscious acts

Baxstrom v. Herold, 135

Bazelon, Judge David A., 56, 58

Blumstein, A., ed., *Deterrence and Incapacitation*, 31

Bishop v. United States, 38

Bolton v. Harris, 80

Brakel, S., and Rock, B., *The Mentally Disabled and the Law*, 136

Bratty v. Attorney General, 211, 215–16, 217

Brawner, United States v., 56, 57, 59

Brown Commission. *See* Dangerous offender laws

Burden of proof: automatism, 215; special defense of insanity, 211; strict liability, 153

Burick, "An Analysis of the Illinois Sexually Dangerous Persons Act," 135

Burt and Morris, "A Proposal for the Abolition of the Incompetency Plea," 36, 45, 46, 47, 50, 146

Butler Committee Report, 36, 49–51, 61, 67; Homicide Act of 1957, 133; reliance on diminished responsibility, 67; sentencing after conviction of "incompetent," 50, 51; special defense of insanity, 58, 67–68; trial of the incompetent, 49–50

Cahn, E., *The Sense of Injustice*, 148

California: capital punishment, 151; diminished capacity, 67, 69, 132; discretion, 146; Lakerman-